Great Britain Parliament

Abridgement of the Minutes of the Evidence

Taken Before a Committee of the Whole House...

Great Britain Parliament

Abridgement of the Minutes of the Evidence
Taken Before a Committee of the Whole House...

ISBN/EAN: 9783744786959

Printed in Europe, USA, Canada, Australia, Japan

Cover: Foto ©Suzi / pixelio.de

More available books at **www.hansebooks.com**

Number I.

A B R I D G M E N T

OF THE

MINUTES OF THE EVIDENCE,

TAKEN BEFORE A

COMMITTEE OF THE WHOLE HOUSE,

TO WHOM IT WAS REFERRED TO CONSIDER OF THE

OF THE

MINUTES OF THE EVIDENCE,

TAKEN BEFORE A

Committee of the Whole House,

TO WHOM IT WAS REFERRED TO CONSIDER OF THE

SLAVE-TRADE, 1789.

Witneſs Examined—John Barnes, Eſq.

Governor of Senegal from 1763 to 1766. Thirteen 1789.
years in Africa, (p. 21). Negro government with
which he was acquainted, in general, a kind of mixed P. 5.
monarchy.

There have been ſlaves in all Africa, as far back P. 6.
as he has heard of; they become ſo by capture in war (not a great proportion, p. 8.), by conviction for theft, murder, adultery, witchcraft; alſo for debt. Has been told of many by gambling. Polygamy univerſally allowed. Witchcraft frequently charged; the trial always full and fair, before the elders of the town. Underſtood principals were put to death, reſt of the family made ſlaves. Does not believe it poſſible, that crimes ſhould have been imputed, from the fairneſs and openneſs of the trial. Perſons convicted generally ſold for the benefit of the party injured.

1789.

P. 8. Never heard of princes going to war, or breaking up villages, to make ſlaves. Make war there as in other countries. If priſoners cannot ranſom themſelves, muſt be ſold.

Never knew of kidnapping by blacks; is confident it would not paſs unpuniſhed.

People in the country poſſeſs ſlaves; ſome an incredible number. Believes they have not any power over their lives, except priſoners of war in the act of capture.

P. 9. Great numbers brought by ſlave-merchants from interiour parts. Much trade in ſlaves to North Barbary and Egypt. Neighbourhood of coaſts and rivers extremely populous. War is very little deſtructive (as he always underſtood from the natives, p. 18.)

Senegal furniſhes from 1000 to 1400 ſlaves.

Believes, but for ſlavery, the laws would be more ſanguinary.

Senegal, beſides ſlaves, produces gum; Gambia a little bees-wax. Windward coaſt a few dying woods; all over the coaſt a little ivory. Trade in theſe articles could not be increaſed; nothing elſe worth mentioning. The country capable of producing all Weſt Indian products; but the inhabitants too indolent to cultivate them. Does not believe it practicable to obtain thoſe products from thence.

P. 10. Not worth while to bring down ivory, but when carried by ſlaves. Very fine cotton grown for home uſe; could never obtain any great quantity.

P. 11. Knows the coaſt to the river Sherbro; no landing heavy goods, except within the rivers; believes no ſafe landing between Sherbro and Benin; all open coaſt for 300 or 400 leagues. Between Benin and Bonny, 40 or 50 leagues; ſome ſmall rivers in which a landing may be made.

P. 12. The prince who can ſell the ſlave, can certainly require labour of him.

Increaſing the number of cultivators of cotton, would proportionably increaſe the produce.

If

If European goods could not be had for ſlaves, 1789.
the princes would be induced to require labour of their people; but is confident could not ſo obtain goods; becauſe cotton only would bear the carriage; and vegetation liable to be deſtroyed by locuſts. All P. 13.
property inſecure, from the imperfection of government. Chiefs averſe to attempt induſtry: does not P. 14.
believe the prince could ſecure the produce of the lands diſtant from the towns.

The people have each their little diſtricts for the year only; the property as ſecure as it can be in a very looſe and imperfect government.

Theft puniſhed generally by fine, as far as the value of the perſon of the thief, (ſometimes 10 or 20 ſlaves, p. 17, or 30, p. 20.)

The mines, he has heard, are conſidered as depoſit P. 15.
of ſacred treaſure, to be had recourſe to only on particular occaſions: ſpeaks particularly of Galam, and believes the ſame of Bambarena.

Between Senegal and Gambia, the women (even of the higheſt ſituations, p.) amuſe themſelves with ſpinning cotton of their own growth. Profeſſed weavers (ſometimes their own ſlaves, p.) weave the cloth for hire. No other mechanicks but ſmiths, P. 16.
who make coarſe hammers, adzes, and gold ear-rings for the ladies. Houſes of reeds, or mud thatched. Nobility and free people ranked between the prince and the labourer. No improvement in civilization during his 13 years reſidence. Obſtructions to it the ſame as among the American ſavages. When in Africa, during the war of 1756, fewer ſhips arrived, ſlaves were conſequently cheaper. Underſtood that thoſe which remained on hand were ſent to North Barbary and Egypt; no attempt was made to ſet P. 17.
them at work. The ſlave-trade always carried on openly between ſhips and the natives.

In 1758 and 1761 (p. 27) very terrible mortality occurred in two King's ſhips (the London, buſs; the Union, hoy; and Goree, ſloop, p. 27) at Senegal, while he was there; inſomuch that they were

1789. forced to man them with hired negroes, of which there are great numbers at Senegal. (p. 20.)

In merchant-men mortality greateſt when up rivers; on open coaſt as healthy as other ſhips between the Tropics.

P. 18. Slaves in Africa pretty well treated; allowed to marry, but with their maſter's conſent; puniſhed for ſlight offences with ſtripes at diſcretion; children well treated. For greater crimes generally ſold as ſlaves, with conſent of their fellow-ſervants; ſpeaks of the practice, not the right of the maſter; believes it a practice of prudence; for were he to treat his ſlaves arbitrarily or cruelly, he would loſe them by deſertion.

Wars very irregular. Buſh-fighting. About 150 leagues inland they uſe fire-arms, furniſhed by the Europeans and Moors; beyond that, bows; and every where the javelin.

P. 19. The people of North Barbary come and buy ſlaves, and carry them back a diſtance of 10 degrees; a great part of that diſtrict an uninhabited deſart, taking proviſions with them, even water. Houſe-ſlaves never ſold but for crimes. Slaves near the coaſt, who ſee Europeans, do not conceive the transfer from African to European ſlavery to be a hardſhip; they know where they are going, and for what purpoſe; the only hardſhip is the being ſeparated from their family. But ſlaves from interior parts are terrified at being put into the hands of people of different colour, not knowing for what purpoſe.—Aſked, if the being ſold to the Europeans, be not conſidered as a hardſhip; has the dread of it any effect in pre-
P. 20. venting crimes?—Replied, only where they have a family; and the ſhame of tranſportation, though they do not dread it, is ſtill a puniſhment. (p. 30.) Does not think domeſtic attachments are ſo ſtrong, as where polygamy is not allowed.

Were the ſlave-trade aboliſhed by the Britiſh, the African princes might no doubt be ſupplied with European

European goods by other Europeans carrying on the trade. 1789.

Believes, that while it is poſſible for thoſe princes to get European goods for ſlaves, through any channel, they would not be induced to acquire them by the improved induſtry of their ſubjects.

His evidence, when he mentions Senegal, relates to that only. In his general evidence, his meaning goes as far as he has been, on the Windward coaſt, as far as Sherbro.

About half the ſlaves exported from Senegal, P. 21. natives of the coaſt; and half from the interior country.

The making ſlaves in the lower country, fell more within his knowledge. He had the mode of making ſlaves in the interior country from hear-ſay, from the moſt reſpectable travellers through thoſe countries (generally prieſts, p. 23.) who gave him no information about their government, materially P. 22. different from that of the ſea coaſt, with which he was acquainted.

Has underſtood, criminals, in interior countries, are tried by the elders openly. Does not undertake to ſay, there are no unjuſt convictions; but believes juſtice is generally fairly adminiſtered. The judge has no advantage in the iſſue of trials.

Conceives the interior countries, of which he ſpeaks, to be the ſame with thoſe which furniſh ſlaves to the reſt of the coaſt, as far as Benin, namely, Bam- P. 23. barena, &c.

Has underſtood, that many ſlaves from thoſe countries, are priſoners of war: they never told him of perſons being kidnapped.

The cauſes he has mentioned, as preventing the exportation of proviſions, apply to the countries between, and bordering on, Senegal and Gambia. A little rice is raiſed by the natives in thoſe countries, but more toward Sherbro. Has always known rice purchaſed by the ſhips; though ſometimes they find it difficult to get enough.

The

1789. The little gold which is bought by the Europeans, is got in the mines; and, upon the Gold Coaſt, he
P. 24. underſtood it was collected by waſhing the ſands in rivulet. The mines belongs to the diſtricts, and are under the controul of the prince and the prieſt. The gold is bought with European goods, but always expended again on the coaſt.

P. 25. During the war, the number of ſhips to Africa was leſſened; but the demand for African produce, gold, wax, ivory, and cam-wood, was always very great; in the pooreſt ſtate of the trade, infinitely greater than the ſupply.

The ſlaves are employed in inland commerce and agriculture.

P. 26. Is confident priſoners of war, and convicts, would not be put to raiſe cotton, if they were not ſold to the Europeans. Does not believe the abolition of the ſlave trade would make any difference in the people's induſtry.

There are no public roads; many horſes between Senegal and Gambia, but they are never uſed for draft or burden. Land-carriage is totally impracticable.

Never heard of any rice ſouthward of the Windward Coaſt.

In Senegal and Gambia, the ſlaves of black maſters are very well fed (except in famines) with corn, fleſh and fiſh. They are not worked for any regular time, nor conſtantly, and never under the whip.

P. 27. There is no landing-place between Sherbro and the Bite of Benin, fit for landing and ſhipping goods, without great danger. A great deal of ſlave trade in that diſtance. At the ſeveral factories there are landing-places, but very unſafe ones. He has heard the anchorage is ſafe on all that coaſt. Has never heard of ſhips being loſt by ſtreſs of weather on the Gold Coaſt; becauſe the wind is always along, or off ſhore. For the ſame reaſon ſhips can put to ſea at pleaſure.

Senegal

Senegal is now in the hands of the French, and 1789.
we have no access to it.

All he says of the Gold Coast, is from informa- P. 28.
tion.

He has not seen an instance of the Tetanus.

For the reasons why fewer females than males are sent out of Africa, he refers to his evidence before the Privy Council.

The punishment for adultery attaches both on the P. 29.
man and the woman.

Men have wives in proportion to their quality and P. 30.
opulence. The first wife bearing a child, is considered as the chief one. Believes the marriage ceremony takes place with every wife.

Knows the Moors on the northern shore of the Senegal do not cross the river to catch the negroes. Asserts this, from his intimate knowledge of the country, and correspondence with the chiefs, page 32.

The African owner holds one description of slaves as merchandize; another, the domestic, he cannot sell but for crimes.

The Africans are fond of European goods, only P. 31.
as far as their necessities require.

In the earlier period of the African trade, beads, &c. were much used, but it is now generally reduced to a demand for necessaries. He is most confident, the natives would rather go without those goods, than raise produce to procure them.

Trials for witchcraft generally secret. He does not know of any fair trial for it.

Does not believe it is the practice to ask those who P. 32.
offer slaves for sale, how they procured them.

Between Senegal and Gambia, the inhabitants wear clothing, chiefly of their own manufacture, and of cotton of their own growth. He never knew them have more cotton than they want. With great pains he never could get more than a few pounds. He might have obtained a few cloths at a very high price. Has known two cloths, 3 yards long, 1½
yard wide, valued at two slaves. They are very sel- P. 33.
dom

1789. dom an article of ſale, hence their dearneſs. The natives manufacture them for themſelves. Believes
their high price ariſes chiefly from the indolence of
the people. The pooreſt female ſlave may have two
coarſe cloths, which may ſerve her for a year. They
never wear more than two at a time; one over the
ſhoulders, and one round the waiſt. The opulent
will have changes; but does not think the conſumption exceeds two for each yearly. Women of the
higheſt condition ſpin, alſo their ſlaves. Profeſſed
weavers, ſometimes their own ſlaves, weave it. Does
P. 34. not believe the ſlaves who, by their maſter's command, manufacture the cloths; would, if ordered,
raiſe cotton. It is the labour of women and children,
except the weaving.

Has never known women do field-work; ſpeaks this of the country between Senegal and Gambia.

Very little wood got from that country. He once imported ſome very bad ebony, and loſt by it; alſo ſome coarſe mahogany, dearer than it would have been here. Knows much ebony could not be got. Believes more mahogany might; but not at a ſaleable price. He has not known wood imported from that part before he did it. Thinks he has heard, that the African company made an unſucceſsful attempt of this kind. The wood he imported was chiefly cut down by the ſeamen, and ſome of it by the ſlaves of a white trader. Does not believe thoſe ſlaves would have obeyed their maſter, had he ordered them to cultivate cotton; becauſe the one is only a ſervice of ſhort duration, to which they would have ſubmitted, to gratify him. Were the cutting of wood conſtant, they would not do that neither.

P. 35. The native ſmiths, free or ſlaves, make a clumſy hoe, axe and knife. There are iron ores in Galam; the high lands of S. Leone, ſeemed entirely iron ore; but the natives know not its uſe.

Is not clear, but believes that the natives, both 1789.
free and ſlaves, raiſe rice. The ſame countries produce rice and cotton. The ſlaves obey their maſters in raiſing both, as far as is neceſſary to the family. Rice (which grows by the water edge, p. 36.) is brought to the ſhips in canoes.

Witneſs examined,—RICHARD MILES, Eſq.

Was eighteen years and a half in the company's P. 37.
ſervice on the Gold Coaſt, from 1765 to 1784. For the firſt ten years commanded at moſt of the ſubordinate poſts. For the laſt ſeven lived at Cape Coaſt Caſtle, and commanded the whole; was abſent about twenty-ſix months of that time.

Gold Coaſt extends from Cape La Hou, to the River Volta, about 400 miles.

Has been at Senegal, Goree, Gambia, and Sierra Leone.

Underſtood the Gold Coaſt language perfectly. P. 38.

His evidence confined to the water-ſide; knows nothing of the interior country; except once, when he was twenty miles inland; does not believe he was ever five miles from the coaſt.

The Gold Coaſt generally petty ſtates; knows but of one deſpotic monarchy there at Apellonia, which may be eight or ten miles of coaſt, (p. 47.)

Believes ſlavery has been practiſed in thoſe countries for centuries.

The Fantees on the water-ſide provide near one- P. 39.
fourth of the ſlaves purchaſed by us on the Gold Coaſt; the other three-fourths from inland (p. 41.) believes the whole from 7 to 8000.

1789. Slaves are ſold by black brokers to Europeans.

They are made ſlaves for theft, debt, adultery, and witchcraft. They have as fair trials, according to the laws, as elſewhere. Trials for witchcraft are generally in the night; but, from generally ſeeing all ſatisfied, except the culprits, concludes the trials fair. Cannot ſay there are no exceptions; believes many; knows ſome. Principals in witchcraft are ſacrificed; the reſt generally ſold. Commonly the whole family ſuffer ſlavery; but here alſo are ſome exceptions.

P. 40. The pynims, judges or elders, in the deſpotic country, are more dependant on the king's will, than on other parts of the coaſt.

Convicts ſold for the benefit of the injured. Has known thouſands of debtors ſold for the benefit of creditors. Does not think crimes imputed to make ſlaves; unleſs witchcraft comes under that deſcription. Judges have a fee at inſtituting ſuits; but believes they have no benefit from convictions.

P. 41. Thinks wars unfrequent; but where they happen, priſoners may be ſold. But he generally found that on ſkirmiſhes (for he admits not wars) between towns, the difference is made up by mediation, and the priſoners exchanged; except that a man or family cauſing a quarrel, is ſold.

Some have gold in conſiderable quantities; but a man, ſpeaking of his property, ſpeaks of his ſlaves; every thing elſe is ſecondary.

Does not know he ever heard the word kidnapping mentioned out of this country. It cannot be practiſed to any extent, without certain detection; for the natives have one general language, and the brokers have daily intercourſe with the ſhipping. Hence a kidnapped ſlave on board would tell his caſe to the brokers, who, from intereſt and regard to the laws, would find out the offender.

P. 42. Has no doubt human ſacrifices are generally practiſed; has had occular proof of it; many thouſands are

are ſacrificed at great mens funerals; (to which ſuch 1789.
ſacrifices are chiefly confined, p. 63.) every one who
knows the language, know this to be general.

Knows of no acts of oppreſſion, but by the king of Apollonia; nor of any committed by the Europeans, unleſs in one or two inſtances; in which he believes the offenders have been puniſhed in this country.

Skirmiſhes, ſo far from increaſing the number of ſlaves, the priſoners are generally exchanged.

Thinks the Gold Coaſt leſs favourable to culture P. 43.
than any other part; except a ſmall part between Accra and the river Volta.

Very ſmall quantities of gold and ivory, he con- P. 44.
ceives, could be procured. A ſhip of 100 tons would carry twice as much ivory as the Gold Coaſt affords in a year (p. 60.) A very ſmall boat would carry all the gold that could be got.

When a broker has ſlaves, he generally endeavours to get ivory for them to bring down.

No navigable river on the Gold Coaſt, except the ſmall one at Chama, a Dutch ſettlement; and he is doubtful, if even its mouth will admit veſſels. What little he has ſeen of the country is an impenetrable wood.

Moſt of the landings at the forts are very dangerous from the ſurf. He knows of no bay or harbour capable of admitting a ſhip of burden; ſhips generally lie two or three miles from ſhore; conceives this would be a great drawback on the value of produce ſhipped.

Should be ſorry to attempt to colonize that country; the natives, and, ſtill more the climate, would oppoſe you.

Never knew the Gold Coaſt produce grain or cotton for exportation, except Indian corn ſold to the ſhips: the quantity depends on that of the proviſions they carry from Europe. The corn to the windward is different.

1789. Never knew of dye-wood on the Gold Coaſt; cannot ſay there is none; but thinks if there had been any ſome of it would have paſſed through his hands. Wood grows there much like wainſcot.

While he was there, the Dutch, Danes, and
P. 45. Portugueze, a few French, and a very conſiderable
number of Americans, traded for ſlaves. The French had then no ſettlement there; underſtands they now have, or are building one; but their trade there is now conſiderable, not with the natives, but with our
P. 46. ſhips. The Americans traded very conſiderably on
that coaſt, on the firſt going, and till the war. Underſtands that they have taken it up again; and that ſeveral of their ſhips are now there, chiefly from Boſton; but he doubts not they will ſoon have ſhips from other ports.

The Slave-Trade might certainly be attempted to be reſumed, if it were given up for a few years; but he thinks it would be very impolitick to relinquiſh it.

The climate is generally very fatal to Europeans; though he enjoyed his health. Believes thoſe on ſhore are more unhealthy than thoſe on board ſhip.

Believes land is generally ſo plenty, that every one takes what he likes, and is not invaded till he reaps his crop.

P. 47. In moſt towns, on the Gold Coaſt, there is a Palaver-houſe, or Court of Juſtice, where the judges or elders (few under the age of 60 or 70) hear the parties, openly, for theft and adultery. But he conceives the trial for witchcraft to be a ſort of ſecret religious buſineſs, which they conceal. Only a very few are ſold for witchcraft.

P. 48. Not one in 100 of the ſlaves exported are natives of Apollonia. The late king took more pleaſure in killing than ſelling his ſlaves; he was a great warrior and monſter; he was many years at war with the Dutch, who attempted to take his country, which he ceded to us in 1765; believes many thouſands were loſt on both ſides.

He

He does not believe affection is very predominant 1789.
in the breaſts of the negroes; but rather otherwiſe;
can give no particular reaſon. He is ſure they do P. 48.
not look upon exile as the greateſt calamity; is
certain that they do not expect to be ſacrificed in P. 49.
the Weſt-Indies.

Thinks they would have the ſame right to oppoſe a ſettlement on their land, as a Weſt-India planter would on his.

Never knew a ſingle inſtance of ſeizing their perſons.

All his live and dead ſtock was bought from the natives.

Rice and millet do not grow on the Gold Coaſt. Thinks the freemen on the water-ſide may be to the ſlaves annually exported from the water-ſide as 100 to one; (p. 51.) ſuppoſes the ſlaves exported from the water-ſide are moſtly domeſtics.

Often a convict's family redeem him with a ſlave; P. 50.
if not, he is ſold. That ſlave is from the inland country; of whom moſt people of conſequence have ſome. A towns-man on the coaſt, to redeem his ſon, &c. if he cannot get a ſlave any other way, will buy one from the Europeans.

The women moſtly cultivate the land, and do the houſe drudgery; the men are chiefly fiſhermen, ſome are huntſmen; but fiſh is the great article of trade.

He knows not of any manufacture on the Gold Coaſt. In moſt villages there is an aukward ſort of a blackſmith, their only tradeſman. In the towns the Europeans have ſhops; the natives none.

Believes a convict's family are not ſold, except P. 51.
for witchcraft.

He conſiders domeſtic ſlaves as freemen, from having all their advantages; but it is difficult to aſcertain who the domeſtic ſlaves in a family are.

Gueſſes there might be more than one, two, or P. 52.
three villages, with 3 or 4000 inhabitants, within five miles of his reſidence.

The

1789. The brokers generally ſell the ſlaves from the inland parts, who make $\frac{3}{4}$ of the whole, as ſoon as they can, to ſave expenſe of feeding and riſk of
P. 53. mortality. They do not employ them. The other $\frac{1}{4}$ are generally ſold juſt after they are made ſlaves, &c. He has known brokers keep ſlaves on hand, to raiſe the price. Convicts are generally confined till ſold.

He who receives a ſlave, in exchange for a convict, may uſe him as he pleaſes; he may ſell him to the Europeans, or incorporate him among his domeſtics; ſuppoſes ſuch are generally ſold to the ſhipping.

For debt and adultery, it is common, and ſometimes for theft, to exchange another ſlave for him
P. 54. condemned. Believes it is ſtipulated, that an adulterer, with the king's, or a great man's wife, ſhall not live in the country.

Convicts for witchcraft are generally put to death, as victims, immediately after the ſentence. There is very little opportunity of knowing what paſſes in thoſe caſes: but he generally underſtood, that they put one, or more to death, to appeaſe the injured. The number ſold or killed for witchcraft is very trifling. Trials for witchcraft being ſecret, in the night, their ſituation can be known only from the ſellers, or the convicts, who, not conſidering it diſgraceful, make no ſecret of what they were ſold for.

P. 55. It is not the practice to aſk the ſeller, or the ſlave, what was his crime; he ſhould not have aſked it, had he known the language. Thoſe of inland ſlaves are different, and wholly unintelligible to Europeans.

Having often miſſed a man or woman out of a town, he has been told by the town's people, they had been condemned for witchcraft. Witchcraft attaching to the whole family, none of that family remain to redeem the convict: but believes it is not unuſual for ſome of the younger children to be ſpared. Perſons ſo condemned, are ſold under expreſs agreement, that they ſhall not be put on ſhore again. Should the European redeem ſuch, he would ſuffer very

very materially. Being conſidered as dangerous, 1789.
they are generally hurried out of the country the
moment after conviction. He has not a doubt, that, P. 57.
in the total abſence of ſhipping, they would all ſuffer death.

Few of the 2000 ſlaves furniſhed by the coaſt are priſoners of war. The Fantees, on the water-ſide, were in peace almoſt all his time. There was a ſerious war between the Fantees and Aſhantees, the two moſt powerful nations we know of, ſhortly after his arrival, for a year or more. It was an inland war, cauſed, he believes, by the Aſhantees wiſhing for part of the coaſt; thinks he can confidently ſay, it was not cauſed or prolonged for making ſlaves; it ſeemed to put a ſtop to the ſale of ſlaves. Believes, in the ſkirmiſhes near his reſidence, the priſoners were redeemed in 19 caſes out of 20.

Conceives that many are ſold for theft, fewer for adultery, and the feweſt for debt.

Three-fourths of the whole are not confined; being from inland, the black broker is not afraid of their deſerting. The men of the other one-fourth have their wriſts faſtened to a log 25 or 30lb. weight.

The natives like European goods very well; but do not like to pay too dear for them, preferring their own gold.

Has generally found ſo little induſtry in them, P. 59.
that he thinks, they would not endeavour to raiſe produce, to procure European goods; but he does not aſſert this as fact. Though the ſhips buy all the corn for ſale, yet many are obliged to make up what they want, at the neighbouring iſlands. This demand is pretty certain; the natives know the number of European ſettlers, and of ſhips expected. If they were diſpoſed to induſtry, he knows of no market for the corn, and the few vegetables they raiſe.

Near the water-ſide it is very rocky; except ſome P. 60.
ſpots. Where he was, (once 20 miles inland) the ſoil is ſo rocky, that it could not produce much elſe

than

1789. than Indian corn. There is no inland water communication, no beasts of burden, (p. 61.) and the shipping of bulky articles, except at one season of the year, would be very dangerous and expensive.

Supposes the inhabitants would not be fond of employing the native slaves and those for sale in agriculture. It would be as dangerous as so employing convicts in England (p. 6 , 65, 68.)

They have all their clothing from Europe; not a yard of cloth is made on the Gold coast. To leeward of the river Volta, he understands, they use indigo; (and bring it to great perfection, p. 70) but not that he remembers on the Gold Coast.

P. 61. Believes he saw 3 or 4 Arabian horses while he was there. He imported horses, but they did not live.

For the last 10 years of his residence, he saw almost every ship sail, (that had finished her business, p. 63.) When a ship happened to sail at night, it was to take the benefit of an early land-wind; but most ships sail from 5 to 11 A. M. (p. 64.)

He is considerably concerned in the Slave-Trade: should have said that at first, had he not been convinced, that it would not influence his evidence.

P. 62. If a cloth 2 yards square is called clothing, they are all clothed.

Families generally plant corn and a few vegetables, which, with fish (a great article of their trade) form the chief of their food.

Most freemen in the towns have 2, 3, or more slaves, who cut fire-wood for the shipping, by their order. If a slave of his disobeyed him, he sold him; and supposes a free native would do the same.

P. 63. The factory slaves and their forefathers have been handed down from time to time; and now are mostly born slaves.

The Gold Coast produces cotton, which might be cultivated; but it would be difficult to get the natives to do it. He planted the only pieces of cotton

ton he ever ſaw there, which might be the ſize of the 1789.
floor of this houſe. The natives would not gather
it, though offered ten times its value. Doubtleſs they
received for ſlaves the ſame articles he offered.

Does not ſuppoſe his having redeemed ſome ſlaves
from ſacrifice, had much effect on the practice; it
leſſened the number in that inſtance.

Has generally heard ſuits for witchcraft have P. 64.
taken place on the ſudden unaccountable death of
the ſlave's maſter or miſtreſs.

Cannot ſuppoſe couples are ſo conſtant there, as
where a man has only one wife. If wives have money
to pay the forfeit, they generally follow their inclinations. Men and women convicted of adultery, redeem themſelves, or forfeit liberty. Says, from much P. 65.
experience, as many females as males could not be
had. He has bought ſome hundreds—ſome thouſands.

He never buried 10 ſlaves, young and old.

Cannot ſay, whether the free natives are ſubject
to Tetanus.

They have no puniſhment that he knows of, but
death and ſlavery, (p. 69.)

No doubt the large canoes which carry off ſlaves,
might carry off produce.

The land may be cultivated; but this removes
not the general inconvenience of the rocks. Does P. 66.
not ſuppoſe 1000th part of the land capable of producing corn, yams, &c. is cultivated. Cotton will
grow there, and does grow wild. Rice has often
been unſucceſsfully tried; it is peculiar to another
part of Africa.

Believes ſlaves generally require maſters at their
heels; and ſo would free men.

Admits his evidence before the Privy Council as
fact (p. 71.) P..67.

It often happens that 1 ſlave in a lot of 8 or 10 is
refuſed, for ſome little defect, though otherwiſe
ſtrong. He has generally found ſuch importunate

1789. to be bought, and endeavouring to ſhow himſelf as capable of labour as the reſt. Generally nine-tenths of all he has bought ſeemed pleaſed at ex-changing Black for White maſters. Believes their
P. 68. joy ariſes from removing from a ſituation, where they think their lives in danger, from being ſubſervient to their maſter's will. Maſters put ſlaves to death in their rites; and probably in caſes unknown to Europeans. He cannot ſpeak to the cauſe ſo well as to the fact.

P. 69. The Europeans are, at all times, ready to buy ſlaves offered to them.

An inland country, between Accra and the river Volta, makes a trifling number of cloths, which being brought to Accra, may have given riſe to the idea that they are made there.

P. 79. Has been told by judges that the wild indigo, between Accra and the river Volta, is very inferiour to that of other parts.

Mr. Baggs's evidence is a mere burleſque of the cultivation of Africa. He admits that from Accra to the river Volta is level and more fertile than the reſt of the Gold Coaſt; the difference between that and other parts of Africa deſcribed by him very ſtriking;
P. 71. but thinks Mr. Baggs paints it in too high colours.

May have ſtated that indigo grew wild about Accra; but remembers not to have ſaid, it was in uſe; nor has he ſeen in the book (viz. The Privy Council Report) that part of his evidence. If there ſtated, as part of his evidence, he does not recollect having ſeen it. Certainly had an opportunity of re-viſing the minutes.

P. 72. Does not know that princes keep women to breed ſlaves for ſale.

Witneſs

Witneſs Examined— KNOX,

Has been between 7 and 8 years commander of 1789.
an African ſhip (firſt as maſter 1782, p. 77.)—not
now—but likely to be again. About an equal time P. 73.
ſurgeon of an African ſhip. Is acquainted with the
Windward Coaſt, more particularly; the Grain
Coaſt, and Angola. Five or ſix voyages on the
Windward Coaſt, the laſt for 33 months.

Governments on the Grain Coaſt are ſmall ſo- P. 74.
cieties very looſely joined, where a few, for ſafety,
find it convenient to aſſemble for buſineſs. Each is
the king and prieſt of his houſe, and is reſpected according to his wealth. Theſe judge of crimes, and
are entitled to reſpect when aſſembled (p. 85.) He
knows of no law binding them to mutual defence.
Hence depredations are general. Such is the looſe
government there.

The Grain Coaſt extends from Sherbro to Cape
Palmas.

As far as he has ſeen, a very ſmall way inland,
it is very populous indeed.

It is very low, and, in the rains, much of it over-
flowed. Apprehends it is unhealthy.

Slavery is univerſal (ſee p. 76.) The ſlaves very
numerous ſometimes. Bought by Europeans from the P. 75.
native brokers between thoſe who bring them from
inland and the ſhips. He apprehends nine-tenths
of the ſlaves come from inland, the other one-tenth
from the ſmall diſtrict on the beach. That one-
tenth made ſlaves for adultery, witchcraft, theft, and
ſometimes debt, and priſoners of war. Believes domeſticks are not ſold but for crimes.

Trials are fair and open, except thoſe for witchcraft, which are ſecret. Other crimes are generally

1789. punished by slavery; but the principals, in witchcraft, are generally strangled and then burnt. The rest of the family are made slaves.

The north of the river Sherbro produces camwood; the south, malaguetta pepper; the whole rice, and some little ivory.

P. 76. Has made 3 voyages to Angola, and always lived on shore.

That part of Angola we trade to, governed by a king, under many severe restrictions.

Slaves sent from Angola, like most other places, generally come from inland; the rest from the kingdom on the beach. They become slaves for the same crimes, as in other parts. Trials fair and open before the princes of the blood, sometimes the king. The party aggrieved has the benefit of con-
P. 77. victs. It is the same on the Grain Coast.

The part of Angola we trade to is very small. In a larger sense, it takes in Loango St. Paul's, and extends about 5 degrees.

It produces red or barwood, and a little ivory: knows of nothing else. A very few ships have been in the barwood trade: believes in nothing else.

In his first voyage as master (of the Fairy of Liverpool, p. 103) in 1782, had 45 men, more than one-half landmen: seamen not then to be got. Out between 6 and 7 months. Lost none. Had
P. 78. 450 negroes on board, of whom he lost 17 or 18. Tons 108, perhaps more. Voyage was to Angola and Tortola (where arrived June 1783, p. 103.) Second voyage in same ship to Angola and Dominica. Out about 14 months, more than 7 on the coast, from the number of Frenchmen then there. Crew 33 or or 34: remembers not going to sea, but that more than one-half (always one-half, p. 79.) were landmen. Lost 4 of fevers. Purchased about 320 negroes, and lost near 40, from the length of the purchase, and the want of their natural food, which that country never affords for negroes exported.
P. 79. Third voyage in the same ship, to C. Mount, on the Grain

Grain Coast, and Dominica. Had 34 men. Sent 1789. the ship off, with 25 of the men he took out, after he had been 17 months on the coast. He was in all 33 months: 3 were officers who staid with him, 3 were lost in craft, and 3 died of fevers. Left the coast, as captain of a ship (Lark of Liverpool, p. 104.) Jan. 1788. Had on board 290 negroes, and lost 1. (Arrived in W. Indies, Feb. 1788, p. 104.)

Believes heavy articles cannot be shipped or land- P. 80. ed, on the Windward Coast, from the heavy, constant, and universal surf. Rice is brought generally in very small baskets, in canoes, and is very generally wet. He often could not get enough of rice.

Knows of no dye-woods near C. Mount. River Sherbro produces much camwood, and no where else, that he knows, in the district. Wax here unknown: the whole produces some ivory, malaguetta pepper in one part, and rice over the whole. Thinks our market overstocked with camwood and barwood. Apprehends it impossible to extend the ivory trade in this place.

On the Wood Coast east of Sherbro there is no P. 81. river where a boat of 4 or 5 feet water could go 12 miles up.

Never knew nor heard of kidnapping.

Slaves on board are, most assuredly, treated humanely. Rice is a principal article of their food on the Windward Coast, also cassada, palm-oil, many glutinous herbs, pepper; on the coast often fish. When rice enough cannot be got, ships carry out beans and stock-fish; and from Africa, palm-oil, pepper, sheep, goats, fowls. The beans are generally split, but has seen them otherwise. Never knew slaves on board without plenty of food. It is almost the sole employment of the officers to serve P. 82. them. The natives of Angola live on cassada, fish, and a little Indian corn. Angola affording no food, ships always carry out beans, and he always called

at

1789. at the Wood Coaſt for rice, when to be got (ſee
p. 93.) Never ſaw the negroes want water on the
paſſage. Ships from the Windward Coaſt ſometimes
water at S. Leone; though all ſhips employ the natives to bring water. They conſtantly take about one gallon per head per day, for two months, but generally 10 weeks, from the Windward Coaſt. The paſſage being more certain from Angola, leſs water is ſuppoſed ſufficient.

The men are generally in irons (a right and left
leg and arm, p. 85) the women never. (This is the
caſe in moſt ſhips, p. 106.) Many take off the irons
only when they reach the W. Indies. Others, of
P. 82. whom he was one, when they leave the coaſt, (ſee
p. 109.)

P. 83. Generally ſhips can only ſail very early in the morning when the land breeze blows. They may ſail along the G. Coaſt; but cannot well get from it any other time. A ſignal for ſailing always flying 3 or weeks before. A few mornings before ſailing, a gun is daily fired. The natives know theſe ſignals.

In good weather, the ſlaves are on deck all day, and the grown ones below at night. Many of the younger ones run where they pleaſe night and day. Never ſuppoſed one died from crowding. Trade-wind, they go from under the gratings to keep from cold.

Every attention is paid to the ſick. For his 6 voyages as ſurgeon he viſited them 3 or 4 times in the night. All ſhips are amply ſupplied with medicines, ſago, wine, &c. Cleanlineſs, fumigations, &c. and above all, freſh air ſupplied.

P. 84. Never knew repellents uſed to make ſlaves up for ſale. (Never uſed them himſelf, nor heard of their being uſed, p. 110.) The whites' health particularly attended to. The greateſt mortality falls on landmen from being unſeaſoned to the country.

Saw no manufactures on Windward Coaſt, but a few ſleeping mats. Some chiefs wear clothes from a country they cannot deſcribe. In Angola they

make

make a ſmall graſs-cloth, the medium of trade, alſo 1789.
a few caps and pipes curiouſly formed. A ſhip load
would not fetch 5l. in England. Apprehends few
of them could be procured.

Has often heard that a very few ſlaves from inland are priſoners of war. On the coaſt war always P. 85.
deſtroys the ſlave-trade. Never heard they were
made or prolonged for making ſlaves.

The firſt voyage one man left him in the Weſt
Indies. The ſecond voyage alſo one, and four died.

In moſt ſhips you may ſtand upright under the
gratings, in others all over the ſhip. In very ſmall
ſhips often not above four feet. His ſhip 5 feet 10
inches, under the gratings 6 feet 10 inches, with
platforms all round nearly in the middle between the P. 86.
decks, about 2 feet 11 inches from each, quite full
of ſlaves.

Slaves who ſpeak the ſame language are chained
together. Recollects not an inſtance to the contrary. (ſee p. 106.)

Never ſaw it neceſſary to force the ſlaves to dance.

Thinks, but for the negroes, no ivory would come P. 87.
down, and that all we receive, and for which we give
every encouragement, would not pay carriage, independent of the negroes.

The natives, no doubt, wiſh for our goods. Near
the beach, making no cloth, they are always clothed
from Europe. Guns, powder, ſpirits, and tobacco,
from habit, may be reckoned neceſſaries.

Ivory is their only article that could be uſeful to
us. Some mats and cloths have been imported, but
never fetched a price. Believes more of them might
be produced, but not ivory. Apprehends rice could
not be greatly cultivated; for the quick vegetation
makes the labour of clearing land almoſt incredible.
No doubt ſome of the ſoil might be applied to many P. 88.
articles of produce. Much is now uncultivated.

Moſt generally the ſlaves in his ſhip had room to
lie on their backs — ſometimes not. In moſt of laſt
war, all the French, and many Engliſh, quitted the

1789. trade. Thoſe that went found plenty of ſlaves, and
cheap, (believes ſomething under 10l. each, p. 104)
hence ſome crowded ſhips. In his laſt voyage, (in
the Tartar, p. 103.) as ſurgeon, to Angola, in 1781
and early in 1782, the ſlaves wanted room. Of his
602 negroes, few, except upon deck, had the breadth
of their backs, and he loſt only nine to Jamaica.
Believes the tonnage from 130 to 150 tons, (old
regiſter, p. 92.) but not poſitive.—In his next voyage, as maſter, they were pretty much in the ſame
ſituation. The veſſel, 106 or 108 tons by regiſter,
the ſlaves 450, the loſs 17 or 18.—45 whites, p. 89.
P. 89. In his laſt voyage, the ſhip might be about 120 tons,
(old regiſter, p. 92.) Seamen ſlept upon ſpars between fore and main-maſt, as in all Guinea-men.
From 50 to 60 ſlaves perhaps ſlept on deck, and 40
to 45 in the cabin, the reſt below; but does not preciſely remember. The cabin, (which would have
held 25 to 30, and with platforms ſuppoſes 15 more,
at leaſt, p. 91.) taken up by a ſick white trader, ſo
that perhaps all the ſlaves had not the breadth of
their backs. (70 boys and 20 men ſlept on deck.
None at all in irons, p. 92.) Had 290 ſlaves, and
loſt but one. In ſix other voyages, as far as he re-
P. 89. members, they might have lain on their backs, had
P. 90. they choſe.—In the ſhip of 108 tons, with 450 ſlaves,
the breadth might be 22 or 23 feet.—Proviſions
abaft in rooms for the purpoſe. Water in hold; and
for 10 days on deck — carried ſeveral puncheons to
the Weſt-Indies. Water took up little of the deck,
and the negroes, not one of whom was in irons, had
P. 91. room enough for amuſement. The two boats ſlung
on the quarters. Two main hatchways, about five
feet ſquare, but not poſitive. A ſmall one forwards
into the fuel-room. Two ſmall ones abaft, into the
proviſion-room.

Guinea ſeamen ſubject to fevers, ſeldom to dyſenteries. Recollects no other general diſeaſe.

Negroes, in Africa, daily rub themſelves with
palm-oil,

palm-oil, when to be got. This is alſo done in the 1789.
Middle Paſſage, from cleanlineſs.

His greateſt mortality was from Angola, where the P. 93.
natives live on caſſada ſoured, which reſiſts the
ſcurvy, of which 9 of 10 that he loſt, died.—Of his
600 ſlaves from Angola, he loſt but 9, from quick
purchaſe. From 50 to 200 were then offered for
ſale in a day.

The trade is made on ſhore, and they are ſeldom P. 94.
heard of till they come into the factory. He made
the trade on ſhore for two voyages. When they
were ſo plenty, 1782, thinks they coſt about one-
third of the price he afterwards paid.

Guinea ſhips obliged to take more men than are P. 95.
neceſſary for navigation. Cannot ſee that their all
remaining on board after arrival in the Weſt Indies
would hurt owners. Never knew maſters of Guinea-
men perſuade or oblige ſeamen to deſert in the Weſt
Indies. In three voyages he left only three men
there. In his paſſage to Africa, he never reſtricted
the men in proviſions. On the coaſt was obliged to
put them to allowance, to prevent embezzlement
with the natives—generally 1 lb. beef and 1 lb. bread
daily. Never knew them ſtinted in water. Flour,
peaſe, and oatmeal generally half a pint daily, or
more, with ſome butter. Different maſters, he believes, give different articles on different days; with
him generally flour twice a week, peaſe as long as
good, oatmeal, if ſound, for breakfaſt, and butter
occaſionally. He had always water abroach for the P. 96.
ſeamen. The continuance of this allowance through
the Middle Paſſage, will depend on the length of
purchaſe. Thinks a ſhip, with two ſlaves to a ton,
and the uſual crew, can take enough of proviſions to
keep up this allowance for the voyage.

Thinks no ſeamen were ever better treated than
his. Wiſhes not to go on hearſay. Never ſold
ſpirits to his crew; but has ſeen it done in one or
two ſhips. His had a dram every morning. They P. 97.
receive half their wages in the Weſt Indies. Knows

1789. of no deductions but one ſhilling per month for the
hoſpitals, and for a few ſlops they may have had,
(ſee p. 100.) There is an invoice-price; but the
ſale-price fixed by the captain, who has no intereſt
in it, (ſee p. 100.) Half-wages paid in the Weſt
Indies, to enable men to lay in things to preſent their
P. 98. friends with on their return. Has known officers in
their agreement prohibited from trading in Africa;
but no reſtriction on the diſpoſal of men's wages in
the Weſt Indies. In ſeamens articles there is one,
that if an officer or man enters himſelf for a ſituation
he cannot fill, the maſter and two officers, named by
him, at ſea, ſhall make a reaſonable deduction from
his wages, which goes to the owner, one ſeaman be-
P. 99. ing ſtipulated to be preſent.—The captain has a diſ-
cretionary power to remove any officer of whoſe
conduct he is not ſatisfied. It is very generally expreſſed in the articles, that if ſeamen enter on board
a king's ſhip they ſhall be paid all their wages in the
currency of the country in which they are paid, but
P. 100. ſuch agreements in the ſlave-trade between maſter and
ſeaman having been ſo often ſet aſide by lawyers and
men of war's officers, a man would be a fool to proſecute him who had nothing to loſe. Means that the
articles would not warrant withholding any of the
ſeaman's pay, however he might have behaved.
Conſiders thoſe articles of very little uſe indeed,
though he never went without them. It is very
P. 101. generally agreed, that half of their wages ſhall be
paid in currency. On that account we generally
give (10s. per month, p. 105.) one-fourth more
monthly-money than in any other trade. Thinks
this rather given as an equivalent for half-wages
currency, than for greater danger of the voyage, (p.
106.) Is very certain they do not conſider their 40s.
per month as ſterling. It is ſeldom neceſſary to ex-
plain the difference between currency and ſterling,
for any of the men can do it, as no Liverpool ſhip
carries all new men. Believes Antigua currency 175,
at Jamaica and Barbadoes always 140. Thus the
wages

wages paid in the Weſt Indies, which is never half, 1789.
may fluctuate from 40 to 75. To ſuch as enter in
king's ſhips, they are often obliged to pay the whole P. 102.
in ſterling, in defiance of the articles, and by the rule of force, by which one delivers his purſe to a highwayman, and which has been exerted in unbending the ſails and diſabling the veſſel from ſailing. This was done in Kendal's ſhip, as he often told him, (p.
107.) Wages paid to repreſentatives of dead ſea- P. 103.
men, in currency and ſterling, as if they had lived.

Of his 450 ſlaves, ſix only were put in the ſecond P. 104.
claſs, upon ſale, and they were ſold in an hour—no refuſe ſlaves.

The ſlaves appeared very indifferent as to their fate.

Never knew an inſtance of locked jaw on the coaſt.

Carried nearly two men ſlaves to one woman, both
at the ſame price. From the number of great men's P. 105.
wives, thinks it impoſſible to procure as many women as men.

Half a pint or more of water ſerved to each ſlave P. 106.
morning and evening; in very hot weather, the ſame at noon. The ſlaves meſs in claſſes of 10, ſo that none can be overlooked. The ſick conſtantly have gruel or rice-water.

The captains, mates, and ſurgeon's profits, all but a trifle, depend on preſerving the ſlaves health.

A ſeaman in the navy has leſs room above his
head than an African negro. He makes no account P. 107.
of the diſtance of the hammock from the floor, but only of the ſpace above their heads.

In every cargo there is a few from near the beach who generally ſpeak Engliſh. Moſt of them know the language of their neighbours, and thoſe of others ſtill farther back, and thus ſurgeons come at the complaints of the negroes, by three or more interpreters.

The leg-iron is nearly a ſemicircle, each end having an eye to receive a bolt which goes through the eyes of the rings on the negroes' legs. The bolt is

1789. ſix or eight inches long. The wriſt-irons the ſame, but more ſlender.

P. 108. All the negroes are upon deck from eight to five daily. It muſt be very bad weather when they are not brought on deck.

Has no doubt but the negroes lie in the night in tolerable comfort.

By every ſymptom, he always underſtood their complaints proceeded from the body. Never heard otherwiſe from the interpreters.

The captain and officers, as well as the meaneſt landman, receive half their wages in currency.

P. 109. The ſlaves, in his ſhip, had no additional chain or irons, by night or day, from their ſailing from the coaſt, in his three voyages as maſter. The ſafety of the ſhip and crew depended on his and his people's good behaviour to the ſlaves.

Never knew any expedients practiſed to ſuppreſs the appearance of diſeaſes previous to the ſale of them.

He never was conſulted by the owners as to the number, but often as to the accommodation, of the ſlaves to be taken on board; that is, whether they had room to lie, whether their food was well dreſſed, whether their little wants were well ſupplied, and whether their food was duly ſerved, and in ſufficient quantity.

Witneſs examined—Capt. WILLIAM MACINTOSH,

Commander of a Ship in the Eaſt-India Company's Service.

P. 112. Was, from early in 1760, to July 1762, as midſhipman and captain's clerk of a king's veſſel, at Senegal, to defend the river's mouth. She was ſta-
P. 113. tioned there in the ſickly ſeaſon, and in the healthier ſhe was generally 20 miles higher, off the fort. The crew was originally 57 men. Were often ſupplied, with a few men at a time, by men of war, and buried

ried many more than their original complement. 1789.
Thinks only two, beſides himſelf, came off the coaſt. The veſſel was at laſt ſunk in the river, for want of men to bring her off, it not being thought an object to ſend men to do it.

Went again to Senegal in 1774, as maſter of a Weſt-Indiaman. Took no ſlaves on board, as he went merely for information.

Went again in 1775, and again in 1776, in the ſame capacity. Bought above 200 ſlaves each voyage. Did not ſtay on the coaſt above two or three P. 114.
weeks each time. Sold at Grenada. (the ſame veſſel each time, about 250 tons, p. 118.) In both voyages, both on the coaſt, and on the paſſage, his ſlaves and crew were in perfect health, till the ſale, which was ſoon; loſt none.

Went again 1778, with government ſtores to the Gold Coaſt. Staid on the coaſt five months. Bought 70 ſlaves at Senegal. Stopped at Gambia and S. Leone, and finiſhed his purchaſe on the Gold Coaſt, after landing his ſtores, cargo when compleated under 400 ſlaves. Crew 48, very healthy. Slaves P. 115.
generally ſo; five or ſix died. Sold at Grenada. (Ship the Symond, about 300 tons, p. 118.)

When in the king's ſloop, he often went into the country ſeveral days at a time, and once walked from Senegal to Goree, and back, (ferried acroſs to Goree, p. 118.) Always heard that on the coaſt of Senegal particularly, ſlaves were made for crimes; but moſt
of them come down the river from inland. Never P. 116.
heard of villages in that country being pillaged to procure ſlaves. Certainly never heard of their being kidnapped by the natives. Has heard of their being kidnapped by Europeans; but no man ever told him he ſaw it. Never knew it happen.

In 1778, he was there a ſingle ſhip, when the war had ſtopped the ſlave trade, and he wiſhed to reduce the price. He reaſoned with them about the folly of keeping it up, when there was likely to be no buyer. Aſked a chief what he would do with his

ſlaves

1789. ſlaves then? obſerving that he muſt let them go again, (meaning priſoners of war.) The chief re-

P. 116. plied, " What them go again, to come to kill me again." In ſhort, he gave me to underſtand, that they would put them to death.

P. 117. Ships, from that coaſt, always ſail in the day, generally in the morning. Signals, perfectly underſtood by the natives, are made ſeveral days before ſailing.

In 1778, found at S. Leone, that the Minerva frigate, inſtead of going to the Gold Coaſt, had gone to the Weſt-Indies with above 80 ſick.

Has not underſtood there is any particular mortality, in ſlave ſhips or others on the coaſt, but only up rivers. He never was up any but Senegal.

P. 118. Senegal produces cotton and corn chiefly. Believes neither is exported.

Has had no connexion with the African trade theſe ten years, nor likely ever to have any.

Attributes this healthineſs to the ſhortneſs of the time on the coaſt, not to the ſmall number of ne-

P. 119. groes on board. He did not carry ſlaves as a common guineaman, had much room; but few in irons, and had plenty of proviſions and water. Thinks a gallon of water a day for a white man, and three quarts for a negro, a great allowance. Includes dreſſing of food. Never ſtinted them.

Made no agreement with ſeamen to pay them one-half wages in currency. Paid them the whole in London. Sold the ſeamen very little ſpirits or tobacco, ſpirits particularly. Recollects not the price; but always treated the men very liberally.

P. 120. Numbers of Guinea ſailors come home from the Weſt Indies, by the run, for which they get more than double the wages they would have received in the ſlave ſhips; this a ſtrong inducement to deſert the African ſhips.

Does not believe the Moors ever croſs the Niger to take the women out of the villages, while the men are at work.

Does

Does not think the natural affections of the negroes by any means ſo ſtrong, as thoſe of the Europeans. 1789. P. 121.

Does not think wars are ſtirred up to get brandy.

Slaves come from very great diſtances inland. Many of the 70 ſlaves he took from Senegal, and who came from Gallam, knew the language of thoſe he got on the Gold Coaſt. Hence he infers, there is an uninterrupted traffick through all the tract from the Gold Coaſt to the head of the Senegal.

His ſhip was not ſo conveniently fitted up as the Liverpool ſlave ſhips then were.

Thinks the ſlaves in the Weſt-Indies appear contented.

Free Africans ſeldom come on board ſlave ſhips to viſit ſlaves.

Thinks not quite half his 400 ſlaves were females. P. 122.
Thinks the men coſt about £16 or £18 the women about £4 leſs. Did not wiſh for an equal number of females; becauſe he thought the men would turn to better account. Certainly an equal number of females might have been procured, when he was there.

Able ſeamen in the Weſt-India trade have from 23*s.* to 30*s.* per month, according to the time of the year in which the ſhips are fitted out. He generally brought home two-thirds of his men at leaſt. There are few voyages (to any place, p. 123.) in which ſeamen do not run away. Of the ſeamen taken out in the Weſt-Indiamen, ſome die, ſome go to America, and ſome to the French iſlands.

Had he taken 500, inſtead of 200, ſlaves, he believes they might have been equally healthy, had he
ſtaid no longer on the coaſt. In general, ſtaying P. 123.
long on the coaſt is more fatal to ſlaves and crew, than length of paſſage or crowding. Thinks the mortality proportioned to the time; for ſhips are twice or thrice as long on the coaſt, as on the paſſage. Thinks the open coaſt, three or four miles from ſhore, as healthy as the Middle Paſſage.

More

1789. More die after the ſhip is full ſlaved, and is gone off the coaſt, unleſs ſhe is long on the coaſt. When
P. 124. there is a greater proportion of mortality on the paſſage than the coaſt, it probably ariſes from crowding or ill fitted ſhip, unleſs diſeaſe gets among them, which all great numbers of people confined in a veſſel are liable to.

Believes, were the trade aboliſhed, it would be impoſſible to prevent our planters from ſupplying themſelves from the neutral or French iſlands. Thinks foreigners would immediately take up the ſlave trade.

The ſlaves are ſold in the Weſt-Indies, in lots of eight or ten. The whole cargo is divided into pretty equal lots. When he ſaid ſlaves coſt £16 or £18 on the coaſt, he meant prime ſlaves. The average price of men, women and children was then about £12 or
P. 125. £13. They were then particularly low. The average in the Weſt-Indies was then from £28 to £40.

Slave ſhips ſeldom bring home any Weſt-India produce, becauſe there are always plenty of ſhips in
P. 125. that trade. When there are not, they ſometimes ſhip produce on board ſlave veſſels, not elſe.

Thinks it would anſwer, as a mercantile concern, to ſend Weſt-Indiamen to take in ſlaves on the coaſt, if ready for them; but it would require only a ſmall proportion of the Weſt-Indiamen, to carry the ſlaves from Africa; and it would be impoſſible to get ſlaves quick enough to diſpatch the ſhips. As far as S. Leone, the delay would not be very great; but if they went below that, it would be a loſing concern.

P. 126. Has heard that a houſe in this town, have agents on the coaſt, to diſpatch their veſſels quicker. Does not believe they have a ſhip ſtationed there for the purpoſe; but they order one to ſtay there for a time, and, when there is no longer occaſion for her, ſhe goes off with ſlaves.

Thinks his being able to get as many females as males,

males, was owing, his being the only ſhip then on 1789.
the coaſt.

Never heard of ſending boats to ſeduce boys and other people, in order to make ſlaves of them.

Witneſs examined,—JEROME BARNARD WEUVES, Eſq.

Was fourteen years in Africa, chiefly as Governor P. 128.
of moſt of the Britiſh forts on the Gold Coaſt. Left it more than five years ago. Underſtood the language as well as moſt Europeans.

That country is divided into petty ſtates. At P. 129.
Anamaboe there is a King. At other parts, Pynims and Elders, and Cabiſhers above them.

From Succundee to Accra is the Fantee country.

Slaves are the greateſt part of their wealth, (ſee p. 147.) There are born ſlaves and purchaſed ſlaves. P. 130.
A born ſlave cannot be ſold but for a crime. They are tried by judges of their own clan, (i. e. ſlaves belonging to, and inherited by, one man, p. 140.) the puniſhment generally ſlavery. They are made ſlaves for theft, adultery, and witchcraft, and from gaming themſelves away. For theſe crimes freemen are alſo made ſlaves.

Criminals ſold for the benefit of the injured. Free- P. 131.
men are tried by the Pynims, who wear a peculiar ſtraw hat, and who meet in the market-place, if there is no palaver-houſe (an open court of juſtice) and try them openly. Believes the Judges, either of a free or ſlave criminal, receive no reward.

Gameſters become ſlaves, by throwing dice. There is no trial. They ſurrender themſelves. But gaming is not frequent on the Gold Coaſt.

Believes there is a trial for witchcraft; but never ſaw one (p. 140.) He once bought a family of nine (neither of the ſuperior nor inferior claſs (p. 148) one of whom only had been accuſed of witchcraft. The whole town came to ſee them fairly off the P. 132.
beach. Hence he infers they had a fair trial. Witch-

1789. craft certainly involves the whole family (who are always extirpated without regard to persons p. 149).

Fancies from 6000 to 8000, perhaps more slaves are yearly exported from the Gold Coast. Dares say above two-thirds by the English, the rest by the Dutch and Danes.

There was no war while he was there. Is certain the natives of the Gold Coast sold in that time were not prisoners of war but merely criminals.

Knows nothing of kidnapping, is sure it would be impracticable. Canoe-men being natives it would be impossible to get off kidnapped slaves, without
P. 133. being known No captain would risk his trade by taking off any person unlawfully.

Ships before they can trade must pay customs. The King sends town-elders on board to receive his customs and their own. Then three, five, or seven guns are fired, and the ensign hoisted, to show that the ship may trade. Scarce a day passes afterwards, but black brokers come and sleep on board, at pleasure, to see the trade properly carried on. Hence a person wrongfully seized would certainly be able to convey his complaints on shore. He hardly knows a trade more fairly carried on. The black broker or slave's owner has the choice of the goods. If they suit him he sells the slave, if not he takes him away.

Never heard of breaking up villages to make slaves. Nothing of the kind existed in the fourteen years he
P. 134. was there. Has heard the natives say, there was a want of slaves during inland wars.

A great many, perhaps one-half or two-thirds of the slaves sent from the Gold Coast, come from far inland (p. 154). The black brokers told him they go three, four, or five days journey to a market inland, to which slaves are brought, by more inland brokers, and so from many more inland brokers. He judges such slaves to be of various tribes (from their different mode of marking their bodies, some filing their teeth, above all their different languages, p. 135). Has had 20, 30, or 40 who did not know each

each other's language. Thinks they are bred inland 1789.
for ſlaves, becauſe ſome of them do not ſeem ſufficiently robuſt and ſpirited for wariors. Slaves are P. 135.
not bred for ſale, on the Gold Coaſt, but ſold for
crimes.

Human ſacrifices prevail on the Gold Coaſt, and he believes, have prevailed from time immemorial. Slaves, he believes, born ſo or purchaſed, are ſacrificed on the death of ſome great man. They think the manes of the dead will be uncomfortable unleſs perſons are ſent to wait upon him. Believes refuſed
ſlaves are generally ſacrificed. But recollects no in- P. 136.
ſtance of it.

The Gold Coaſt people wear no clothes, but a yard or two of cloth round the waiſt.

Thinks our abolition of the trade would not aboliſh it there. It would change its courſe, and the ſlaves be diſperſed from weſt to eaſt and bought by the Moors, Arabs, &c. But this only opinion. The other Europeans engaged in the trade would ſhare the number we did not take off. There would not be one ſlave the leſs on the Gold Coaſt, nor one more
or leſs convicted of crimes on the Gold Coaſt (if the P. 136.
trade was aboliſhed by all the Europeans, p. 141).

There are no manufactures on the Gold Coaſt. P. 137.
They get their clothing from the Europeans, by the ſlave-trade. That coaſt produces no articles for commerce but ſlaves.

The Gold Coaſt extends from Cape La Hou to the River Volta, about 400 miles.

It produces a little Gold and Ivory. Little Gold got on that coaſt. Believes the little Gold and Ivory there is brought from inland. Ivory generally brought on ſlaves ſhoulders. It helps to pay charges of journey. That coaſt produces Grain and Cotton,
but not for exportation. Supplies the ſhips food for P. 138.
the ſlaves. Cotton not cultivated. Has heard that the Dutch attempted to cultivate it; they took great pains, but it came to nothing (p. 151 at Axim). The natives would not take to the cultivation. Sup-

1780. poſes the Dutch now hardly raiſe enough for wicks for the lamps of their ſettlements. (They had many of their own ſlaves on the cotton plantation. Very little ſlave trade near it, p. 147).

Never ſaw any dye-wood there. Knows of no other woods there, except common wood for gun-carriages and other carpenters uſe. From the little induſtry of the natives, even for their own maintenance, he apprehends they would not raiſe produce for exportation. Believes that, though land is very plenty, they would not permit the Europeans to ſettle there. They are obliged to pay rent for their ſettlements. Apprehends they would not ſell the land.

While he was in Africa, many Americans reſorted there, and he believes, they do now. (They traded briſkly till the war, p. 139).

Could the natives be brought to raiſe produce, it
P. 139. muſt be conveyed to the coaſt on their heads. The beſt landings there are indifferent (p. 151) but from May to Auguſt the ſurf makes it dangerous for the natives to go to the ſhips and return. Thinks it impoſſible to ſhip a hogſhead of ſugar, in thoſe months, when the ſhips lie about four miles off, in fine weather, about three miles.

Recollects not ſeeing a ſhip ſail in the night. They generally ſail, in the morning, with the land-wind. They always make ſignals, ſometimes a month before ſailing, which, he underſtood was done to make the natives ſettle their accounts. The ſignal is a gun, looſe fore-top-ſail and enſign hoiſted every
P. 140. morning.

For the ſmalleſt Theft the offender is ſold for the benefit of the injured. Does not recollect ſaying, but might have ſaid, before the Privy Council, that convicts for witchcraft were ſold for the benefit of a town at large, but chiefly for that of the principal people: if he did ſay ſo, he alluded to nine perſons, part of the family of a man condemned for witchcraft, and who were ſold at the requeſt of the whole town, who received their value, and he ſuppoſes, divided it.

Has

Has heard that ſome refuſed ſlaves have been ſold 1789.
to be ſacrificed. Believes they are religious ſacrifices.
Sometimes a great man's favourite girl or boy is ſa- P. 141.
crificed to attend him in the next world. They think
this a duty (p. 152). Doubts not, but if refuſed
ſlaves were not bought for this uſe, thoſe of the deceaſed would ſupply their place.

Believes the Dutch or Danes often buy ſlaves of
inferior quality.

As ſlaves are not bred on the Gold Coaſt for ſale, P. 142.
he thinks the number from inland muſt far exceed
any thing of the kind on the Gold Coaſt. As there
were no wars in Africa while he was there, he preſumes the ſlaves brought down muſt have been bred
ſlaves or convicts. Moſt ſlaves of the coaſt are undoubtedly criminals.

The natives of the Gold Coaſt are vindictive and P. 143.
thieviſh in general.

Convicts are generally allowed to be redeemed,
if they have friends to do it.

Has ſeen, at a diſtance, intended victims dreſſed and P. 144.
dancing chearfully. Has no doubt but this aroſe from
thinking they were about to attend their deceaſed
maſter.

The Gold Coaſt not fertile, being very rocky.
Indian corn is the chief produce. Has ſeen the natives raiſe a few ſugar-canes, by juſt throwing them
into the earth. Cotton alſo grows there. Has ſeen
ſomething called Indigo; but is no judge. Never
ſaw any dying-wood, but what came from other parts
of Africa. P. 145.

The Gold coaſt is very populous. There are a
good many conſiderable towns there, which are ſupplied with proviſions from a good way inland, by
people who bring corn on their heads, or from other
parts of the coaſt by water. Canoes are ſometimes
obliged to go thirty or forty miles along ſhore, to
fetch corn and yams; for though the land behind
the towns is cultivated he ſuppoſes to ſome diſtance,
it was not already productive to maintain the peo- P. 146.
ple.

1789. ple. When he has been obliged to buy provisions from them, they brought corn to him, five, six, or seven miles, on their heads.

They have no idea of cultivation. After cutting the brush-wood, they let it dry, burn it, and throw the corn on the ashes, without digging the ground. This is done by the family where there is no slaves. If a man has slaves, they help him. Famines are

P. 147. frequent. He has known corn very scarce indeed.

The natives do not work in the ships, but when sickness renders it necessary. They are often employed in the boats, to save the seamen.

Where the Dutch attempted to raise cotton, there is very little trade in slaves, but chiefly in gold and ivory, which last is brought down on the slaves shoulders, or by the people brought down to carry back the goods bought with the gold.

The natural indolence of the natives is a total bar to all industry whatever.

Has heard the natives say the Gold Mines are a great way inland. Believes the teeth brought from a good way inland.

There are few iron tools but what are imported from Europe. A kind of noe is made from the bar-iron imported from Europe, and with which they cultivate yams. Does not know if they can make a hatchet there.

He is certain persons convicted of witchcraft and their innocent relations would be sacrificed, were the sale of slaves prevented. An old woman accused of witchcraft, or the wife of an accused man, whom he refused, had her head cut off.

Does not know he ever purchased a prisoner of war.

Is at present concerned in the slave-trade.

P. 150. On the Gold Coast, the considerable men may have from twenty to three dozen of wives. Has not a doubt but these women may entrap the unwary. Dares say it may be as common there as in London; only in Africa is attended with the loss of liberty. Does

Does not believe it is uſual for chiefs to ſend out 1789.
women for this purpoſe.

Has been told wars ſtop the ſlave-trade. There was no ſcarcity of ſlaves while he was on the coaſt.

Three, four, or five black brokers, according to the ſhip's ſize, attend the ſhip daily, while on the coaſt. They are paid for this attendance.

Europeans ſeldom aſk the black brokers how the P. 151.
ſlaves are procured. Being brought on board in canoes, they know they are fairly got, and take no farther trouble.

The largeſt canoes he ever ſaw were two with 21 padlers each. No doubt a caſk of the ſize of a water-caſk might be carried on board full of ſugar as well as water.

Believes they were about a month in landing four P. 152.
or ſix 42 pounders, on a catamaran, at Anamaboe.

The ſlaves belonging to the Company make hinges, &c. in the blackſmith's ſhop, in the Caſtle Yard, at C. Coaſt.

Believes human ſacrifices, on the Gold Coaſt, are
only made on the death of great men. Their num- P. 153.
bers depend on the rank of the deceaſed.

When there were many ſhips on the Gold Coaſt they did not go off ſo quick with cargoes as when there were fewer. Hence he apprehends, if the demand was increaſed, there would be ſtill nearly the ſame number of ſlaves, unleſs they came from other parts.

Thinks, if there was no ſlave-market on the Gold Coaſt, petty thieves would be ſold to inland tribes, who do not now come there for ſlaves; becauſe they cannot afford the price, nor give the goods the natives want.

As Europeans could not cultivate the ſoil them- P. 154.
ſelves, thinks, if they attempt cultivation, they muſt employ ſlaves.

Thinks ſlaves from inland, are both bred ſlaves, and convicts.

The convict for witchcraft whoſe relations he bought, had his head cut off. His father, mother,

1789. two wives, and three children, were ſold to him, on condition they ſhould never return to that country.

Never heard of the locked jaw on the coaſt.

Thinks as many females as males could not be had on the coaſt; becauſe conſiderable men keep as many wives as they pleaſe, who do the drudgery, fetch water and proviſions; but very ſeldom work in the fields.

Has known of an inſurrection where the ſlaves overcame the crew, and got back to ſhore, where he fancies they were all ſeized by the natives and again ſold.

P. 155. Thinks the intercourſe which the Africans on the coaſt have had with the Europeans, has had ſome little effect upon their external appearance, but with reſpect to government and morals, believes them ſtill in the ſame ſtate they were centuries ago.

Has reaſon to belive, from the tradition of the natives, that the mode of trial before deſcribed has exiſted from time immemorial.

There are no cattle of burthen on the Gold Coaſt, and very few bulls and cows; might ſay none, for it is a luxury to poſſeſs any.

The Europeans have gardens or plantations on the Gold Coaſt, to ſupply themſelves with vegetables, theſe they raiſe with great trouble, the exceſſive heat and dryneſs of the ſoil requiring much attention to the plants.

Has ſeen free Africans ſettled on the Gold Coaſt, who had formerly been tranſported to the W. Indies, had been carried from thence to London, from whence they were ſent back to Africa. Theſe for the firſt month ſeemed very proud to ſhew themſelves to their friends in their European dreſs, and got drunk with them as often as they could: they ſoon, however, got tired of this clothing which they found too warm, and betook themſelves to the two yards of cloth wrapt round the middle as worn by the reſt.

Was

Was never present at the trial of any person con- 1789.
victed of offences which subjected them to be sold for slaves.

Has before said, that the whole town participated in the profit arising from the sale of convicts for witchcraft, but applied this only to the family sold to him for that crime, not supposing it in general to be so. A number of people in that town having died from unknown causes, these deaths were charged upon the principal of this family.

This was the only instance of a condemnation for witchcraft, of which he had ocular proof.

Has generally observed that the large canoes are more easily overset by the surf than the small ones. As to the twenty-one-hand canoes, has before observed, that he never saw more than two, and those he never saw overset.

The surf frequently breaks in upon the large ca- P. 157.
noes so as to destroy or damage the goods on board.

Does not think it possible, by the craft used on that coast, to put on shore, or bring off, with safety, sugar, salt, or any other commodity liable to melt, unless the casks were made so tight, as to be impenetrable to water.

Never saw a canoe upon the Gold Coast capable of taking in a hogshead of sugar.

Corn, the chief article of provisions carried from shore on board, is generally put into tight iron bound puncheons. Sugar in such casks might no doubt be brought on board equally safe.

No expense attends the transporting corn from the shore in this manner, the casks so employed, being the water casks belonging to the ship.

Applies this information respecting the danger from the surfs to the whole Gold Coast, upon which he knows no landing place, where the surf is not more or less hazardous.

Commanded the Fort at Dixcove upwards of two P. 158.
years.

1789. Saw once a boat belonging to a king's ſhip on ſhore there.

Does not think ſuch a boat could land on Cape Coaſt.

Sugar, generally loaf ſugar, is uſed on the Coaſt of Guinea, which is uſually landed in tight puncheons.

The coming off ſhore with a loading is more hazardous, than landing, inſomuch, as for one canoe overſet going aſhore, ten are overſet going off, taking the coaſt all along, good, bad, and indifferent.

King's ſhips, wood and water off Cape Coaſt, by canoes from the ſhore, which are frequently overſet.

P. 159. Can ſpecify no particular inſtance of a canoe overſet when ſo employed, becauſe the King's ſhips while he was in Africa, had generally contrived to come there in the fine ſeaſon when the ſea was very ſmooth, and there was very little ſurf, which is not the caſe at other times, from May to the latter end of Auguſt.

Does not believe there is any wood to be got on the Coaſt of Guinea, fit to be ſplit into ſtaves to make tight caſks of.

Has heard, that the Fort of Anamaboe (the beſt built fort in Africa without exception) was built by an engineer, ſent out under the direction of the Board of Ordnance.

Does not know what uſe the Arabs and Moors make of the ſlaves they purchaſe, but believes it is a traffick which they carry on for their own benefit.

Witneſs examined,—JOHN FOUNTAIN, Eſq.

P. 160. Has reſided at Cape Coaſt Caſtle, Tantum, and Accra, from the year 1778, to January 1789.

On his firſt arrival, had the command of the Company's troops. After that a factor for the Company: then

then ſecond of Accra: afterwards ſecond of Tantum: and laſtly Governor of Tantum. 1789.

Did not go into the country, further than in paſſing from one fort to another.

Did not ſpeak the language of the country, but underſtood the greater part of what was ſpoke by the Fantees.

Is of opinion that the natives become ſlaves from three cauſes, principally convicts, others for gaming, witchcraft, alſo debt.

Did not know any ſlaves who had been priſoners P. 161.
of war. Heard of few wars on the coaſt during his reſidence. Has ſeen a kind of war carried on between the natives of different towns, but not of any duration. Between 3 and 4000 men altogether might meet; no ſlaves made priſoners.

Convicts are generally tried openly by the pynims or elders of each diſtrict.

Does not believe the judges derive any advantage from convictions, but that they are ſold for the benefit of the injured.

Does not include witchcraft among the crimes ſo P. 162.
tried; but remembers one ſimilar ſort of trial for witchcraft at Tantum lately, the accuſed being a perſon of ſome conſideration.

Witchcraft generally involves the whole family.

The people are very ſuperſtitious—a belief in witchcraft is general—but thinks that by it is often meant poiſon.

Is not concerned at preſent with the African trade. P. 163.

While reſident there, acquired ſome knowledge of their government.

Thinks, if wars had been frequent, he muſt have P. 164.
heard of them. Very few of the ſlaves ſold off that coaſt, were priſoners of war.

Never knew Europeans foment wars among the Africans. Has known them frequently aſſiſt in ſettling diſputes.

Never knew villages pillaged for making ſlaves; P. 165
which he conſiders as impracticable by the whites.

1789. Never heard kidnapping by Europeans, nor conceives that ſuch a practice ever exiſted; if it did, it could not be concealed; and any European experiencing a loſs of trade in conſequence, would complain to the Governor and Council on the coaſt, as well as to perſons in England.

When a ſlave is brought down for ſale, the owner applies to a broker, who conducts him to a European trader; ſhould they diſagree, they are at liberty to carry him away, and offer him to another.

There are always ſome free natives, uſually called gold takers, on board the ſhip, while the trade is carrying on.

Says, if a ſlave had been kidnapped, he would have had an opportunity of making his complaint; and being himſelf a member of the Council, had any ſuch practice prevailed, he muſt have heard of it.

P. 166. Never heard of kidnapping by the natives, though it poſſibly may have exiſted; apprehends it would be puniſhed; is ſure it would on the Gold Coaſt.

The natives poſſeſs a great number of ſlaves, which are conſidered by them as a common medium of traffick.

Slaves purchaſed by the natives, may be ſold again at their pleaſure; but ſuch as have fallen to them by inheritance, cannot be ſold, but by the general conſent of the other domeſtics, unleſs convicted of crimes.

The puniſhment of a free African, convicted of a crime, depends upon the offence committed.

P. 167. A man's ſlaves may be ſeized and ſold, to make good the fine he has incurred, or debts he may have contracted; but a long proceſs is neceſſary before he can be deprived of his hereditary ſlaves. A creditor often prefers ſeizing one of the family.

A man condemned to ſlavery, may in moſt caſes redeem himſelf by ſubſtituting another, but there are exceptions. If a man ſhould think himſelf bewitched, and can fix upon the guilty perſon, he will

will then sell him under the restriction, that he shall not be redeemed. 1789.

He knew a late instance, in which (Awishee) a man of considerable note, and one of the best traders at Tantum, was said to be bewitched, and a day or two after died. The person accused (himself a pynim) with his family, had a formal trial; the result was, the old pynim was sold, and the family driven out of the town. Another instance occurred, whilst he commanded at Tantum, the Caboshcer, a king, was taken sick in the morning, reported to be bewitched, but died before six in the evening; the deceased not being a man of any connexions, no inquiry was made; the matter fell to the ground. P. 168.

Has been informed, that slaves accused of witchcraft, are tried by their own family, in conjunction with the hereditary slaves. Freemen by the pynims, as above described.

In cases where slaves have been often convicted of ill behaviour, the purchaser is often restrained from redeeming and keeping them in the country. P. 169.

A man of consequence, convicted of adultery, not only forfeits his own liberty, but may have many of his slaves also seized. But should the crime be committed by a slave of a great man, with one of his master's wives, he apprehends he would be put to death.

Human sacrifices are practised in that country; had been informed at Appolonia, by the governor, who was a respectable man, that he had seen persons seized by surprize in the market place, by a rope thrown over their heads, and thus dragged some distance, and executed in various ways. That at the death of old *Baw*, and *Ammoneer*, the two Cabbosheers, he believed near 300 had been put to death.

Remembers at Cape Coast, upon the death of Quamina, the governor sent to the family, threatening to fire upon the house, should they attempt to sacrifice any person; but notwithstanding their promise to the contrary, a boy and girl were knocked on P. 170.

1789. on the head; one of which was buried under, the other above his coffin.

The governor alluded to above, was Dickſon, now dead, but believes many in Europe and in Africa know the circumſtances to be as related.

Believes, that from the repreſentations of the whites, the practice does not now prevail ſo much upon the coaſt as formerly; but inland it is reported ſtill to exiſt in a great degree. Concludes, that ſlaves not ſaleable, are put to death, from an inſtance of an old woman at Cape Coaſt Caſtle, who, on being refuſed to be bought, to ſave her maintenance, was murdered.

P. 171. Is of opinion that the purchaſe of ſlaves by Europeans, preſerves their lives, and adds to their eaſe and comfort. Has for two or three months together, had 60 or 70 in the fort at once, who have appeared infinitely happier and healthier than when firſt purchaſed; nor did he ever loſe one by mortality.

The Dutch, Danes, Portugueſe, French, and Americans, traded on the coaſt while he was there.

The trade of the laſt has much increaſed of late. That from America is chiefly carried on from Boſton and Salem.

The French have lately taken poſſeſſion of a ſpot adjacent to Anamaboe; and though from the unhealthy ſituation they have loſt many people, they ſtill perſevere; ſend many more ſhips than they did.

P. 172. Trade for ſlaves is carried on to the eaſtward of the Gold Coaſt. From Whydah, all along to Old and New Calabar.

Does not know that the Engliſh ſhips have been in the practice of leaving the coaſt ſecretly in the night. The general cuſtom is, to looſe the fore topſail, hoiſt the enſign, and fire a gun, often for three, four, or five weeks, as a ſignal for ſailing, that ſuch of them as have accounts to ſettle with the captain, may come on board; the uſual time for getting under way, is with the land wind, from two in the morning.

The

The ſhips which lie off the coaſt are much more 1789.
healthy than thoſe which go up the rivers, and lie nearer land; the latter being more expoſed to fogs.

There are no navigable rivers on the Gold Coaſt; two rivers, Elmina and Shemar, belonging to the Dutch, might admit boats under 20 tons, but even theſe would ſoon be aground.

There is neither water nor land carriage for bulky goods from within-land to the coaſt, inſomuch, that P. 173.
a tooth of about 170 pounds weight, was cut into three pieces to be made portable.

There are no good landing places on the coaſt; the beſt ſeaſon for landing or ſhipping goods, is about Chriſtmas, January, or February; but has known it bad in thoſe months.

The coaſt he alludes to, as having no navigable rivers, nor any good landing places, extends from Cape la Hou to the Volta, about 420 miles; a heavy ſurf.

It is ſafer landing than ſhipping goods, though P. 174.
even in landing fiſhery canoes (which are much the ſafeſt) has ſeen ten in a day overſet.

Believes he might inſtance certain ſhips deal for ivory and gold, but theſe alſo trade for ſlaves.

Gold is not an article of export, becauſe it bears a greater price there than here. Ivory is likewiſe an uncertain commodity. While ſecond at Tantum, he bought a great deal in a month, whereas, while laſt there, he had not been able to buy five teeth in two years. Thinks it could not be an object of commerce, independent of the ſlave trade; nay, that it could not be had at all in that event, becauſe the black trader who brings it from inland, loads the negroes with it, whom he is conducting to the coaſt for ſale; and ſo ſmall is their profit, it would not alone pay them for their trouble.

The Gold Coaſt produces no articles of commerce P. 175.
beſides gold and ivory; ſome few pieces of cloth, matts, &c. are occaſionally bought, as matters of curioſity, at ſo high a price as two or three ſlaves for

a cloth

1789. a cloth of eight yards by six yards; but such are not the kinds of cloth the natives wear.

P. 176. It does not produce corn equal to the consumption, nor more of cotton than what is used for lamp wicks. A sort of attempt was made to extend its cultivation near Cape Coast, but the blacks destroyed by night the work of the day, alledging it was prejudicial to their provision ground.

P. 177. Nor does it produce rice in any quantity; knows of none to leeward of Apollonia.

It produces no dye woods, nor, so far as he knows, any article besides what has been enumerated.

He resided in that country during the late war, which in some degree interrupted the slave trade; fewer slaves were brought down than formerly; the demand not so great; the prices lower. Did not observe that more corn, rice, or cotton, was produced then, than before; but he was rather out of the way, being confined during the war chiefly to Tantum.

P. 178. Does not think that abolishing the slave-trade would materially alter the cultivation of the country, the natives being so indolent, as seldom to cultivate more than is necessary for their family, from year to year.

Believes the blacks would rather starve than cultivate to any extent.

Is certain it would not extend the manufactures of cloths and matts, nor produce new ones.

Knows of no iron in the country; of that supplied them from Europe, they make only a kind of bill or hoe, for cultivating their land; but so course and ill tempered that they do not last. Supplied with many articles of iron from Europe.

P. 179. Thinks, if the slave-trade were abolished in Great Britain there would not be a slave the less, as other nations, the French nation in particular would take off, what would otherwise have been brought by the English. The French have lately shewn themselves desirous of extending their trade.

In

In time of peace, the demand for ſlaves, has al- 1789.
ways been ſuperiour to the ſupply.

Thinks, that wars among the natives would be- P. 179.
come rather more frequent, ſhould the ſlave-trade be
aboliſhed, becauſe convicts being left in the country,
would create or foment diſſenſions among the natives. So ſure the abolition would be productive
of a ſcene of carnage all along the coaſt, (ſee p.
166.)

A colony could not be eſtabliſhed there but by
conqueſt, the natives (except upon the ſea coaſt) being very hoſtile.

Never obſerved any inſtance of cruelty exerciſed
by the Engliſh upon ſlaves bought by them; but
much humanity, and particular attention when ſick.

Has never ſeen any particular cruelty to ſeamen in
this trade; they may poſſibly experience inconveniences from the climate, to which the crews of veſſels
trading there for other purpoſes would be equally
ſubjected, and which would alſo affect colonies
ſettled there. Remembers at the Daniſh fort at P. 180.
Accra, that the governor, vice-preſident, ſeven or
eight officers, with 100 ſoldiers, died in a month,
and this on the ſea coaſt.

Has been three voyages from England to Africa,
and two from Africa to England by way of the Weſt
Indies, between 1778 and 1785. Obſerved no ill
treatment of the crews. Never ſaw people happier.

His firſt voyage from Africa to the Weſt Indies
was in the Iris, Maſon, tonnage about 220, about
300 ſlaves on board; exceeding well treated; plenty
of proviſions and water. It is the intereſt of the
owner. If not kept in heart and good ſpirits, it is
odds but they ſicken and die. Paſſage to Jamaica P. 181.
ſix weeks and two days. Slaves not confined below
above two days in all. Appeared quite ſatiſfied and
cheerful. Loſt but one. Left the ſhip at Barbadoes,
but informed by the captain that he loſt none going
from thence to Jamaica.

Before the late regulations, captains were benefited by the numbers they landed. Loſt ſix per cent. on ſuch as died.

Made his ſecond voyage from Africa 30th January
laſt to Barbadoes, on board the Friendſhip, Lamb, a
ſtore ſhip; carried a few ſlaves upon freight; though
a large ſhip, worſe calculated for their conveyance
P. 182. than the common ſlave ſhips in many reſpects.
Slaves exceedingly well treated during the voyage
to Barbadoes. No deaths in the ſhip. Knows not
what happened after leaving Barbadoes; were all in
perfect health. Had no intereſt in the ſlaves on
board; nor has he any connection whatſoever with
the concern.

P. 183. Reſided in Hanover pariſh, Jamaica, upwards of four years, from beginning of 1770 to 1774. Knows of no practice of captains or ſurgeons to repel diſorders of the ſlaves. Never knew of any particular mortality take place in a cargo of ſlaves after their arrival, and before their landing. Has been on board two or three ſlave ſhips at the iſland whoſe cargoes were healthy. Believes few ſlaves of theſe ſhips were in a very diſeaſed ſtate when ſold; one, the Warwick Caſtle had nearly 500; has forgot the name of the other.

Is convinced that the abolition of the ſlave-trade would tend to the deſtruction of many lives on the coaſt of Africa, and to the ruin of the Britiſh colonies in the Weſt Indies.

P. 184. The king of Appolonia is deſpotick, and by his ſingle authority daily takes away the lives of many.

The length of that diſtrict is 25 or 30 miles along the coaſt, but cannot ſpeak as to the breadth.

It is probable that the ſlaves whom Quamina put to death, had previouſly the form of a trial.

Being chiefly confined at Tantum during the war,
P. 185. cannot ſay whether more or fewer ſlaves were taken
off the coaſt than in peace; but he himſelf ſhipped
more there ſince, becauſe, the other forts belonging to
the Engliſh and Dutch being in a ſtate of mutual
warfare,

warfare, the traders choſe to bring their ſlaves to Tantum, where they would not be moleſted. 1789.

The natives are induced to make human ſacrifices from various motives—That their friends may reſt quiet in their graves—That the deceaſed ſhould be properly attended: hence they generally ſacrifice his key-bearer or accraw, and his head wench; has beſides ſeen tombs, and burial-places, paved with ſkulls of perſons thus ſacrificed.

Perſons of conſequence poſſeſs a conſiderable num- P. 186.
ber of ſlaves, which are retained in a ſtate of abſolute idleneſs, while their women provide them with water and other neceſſaries. And in ſuch habits of familiarity do maſters there live with their ſlaves, even the king of Cape Coaſt Caſtle himſelf, that unleſs for a very capital fault they would not be ſubjected to puniſhment.

Along the coaſt, to Accra, the natives owing to their indolence, have little or no ſupplies of corn; has offered a great price without ſucceſs. At Accra, a prodigious large diſtrict, they depend upon their neighbours for a ſupply, from Cape Coaſt, Anamaboe, Tantum, &c. During his reſidence at Accra, has ſeen great want among them.

In exchange for corn, when it is in plenty, they P. 187.
will take, from the whites, cloths, liquors, &c. but when it is ſcarce, hardly any thing elſe than gold duſt. The blacks, natives of Accra, give in exchange, cloth, gold, and a fiſh they call Aporge, which is a great article of trade as well as of ſubſiſtence among the Accras. What gold they thus barter for corn, they obtain in exchange for ſlaves and ivory; chiefly the latter, of which there is more ſold in that country than on any other part of the coaſt.

Suppoſes a great part of the proviſions are from inland.

Has not known any other trials for witchcraft than the two mentioned; but believes them ſtill very frequent.

1789. P. 188. From what he has seen, does not apprehend there is any peculiar mode of trial for this crime, though such trials are publick; yet the whites may not have frequent opportunities of seeing them, from its not being customary to introduce themselves into such assemblies; but, in the course of their walks, will often see the Pynims seated in the publick Palaver-place, and may upon inquiry learn the cause. Has heard it said that the trials for witchcraft are conducted in a particular manner, but this must have been from misinformation.

P. 189. The whole family of a person convicted of witchcraft is generally sold; but in the case of Awishee, before noticed, the people of Tantum were contented with selling the old Pynim convicted of having bewitched him, and driving out the rest of the family from among them.

The price obtained for persons so sold, is generally given to the injured family, subject to some deduction for expense of trial. Persons are sold upon conviction of other offences. Knows it to be so in regard to theft of gold, and some other articles. Thefts of liquor and such like things may be compensated for, by paying back something more than the value.

Judges the natives of the country to be a quarrelsome, turbulent, ungrateful people.

P. 190. A captain never asks a broker how a slave was obtained, because the native is aware, that if he is found to have come by a slave illegally, he and his family are liable to be sold for the offence.

Gold-takers, another name for trading men; however, they do take gold, and are employed in the purchase of every slave brought on board, speaking the language in general spoken by the slaves. Would certainly learn from them if they had been captured or kidnapped.

Slaves are frequently redeemed from the ships, and others substituted in their room, by their families, if their offences have not been great. This

most

most common in the case of adultery, if the offence is not committed with the wife of a great man.

It is not customary to sell domestick slaves from one family to another, unless for some heinous offence.

Such not considering themselves altogether as slaves, but rather attendants on those they serve; lead a lazy indolent life; employed in making Custom, *i. e.* performing funeral ceremonies for the dead, or in diversion or gaming. P. 191.

Natives of the Gold Coast, freemen or domesticks, no doubt consider it as a heavy punishment to be sold to the Europeans, especially such as have been resident near the forts, and in the habits of visiting them; but for those brought from the interiour parts of the country, is certain from their own assertion, as well as their general appearance, that they rejoice in their change of masters. They are in general poor in flesh; great eruptions over all their skin; very scrophulous, and frequently have bad ulcers; but when sold again to the captains, they are often fat and sleek. Sometimes they are brought to the forts in a healthier state; has seen them low and dejected when brought to the fort, and become very cheerful in half an hour after they were brought; has been entreated by several to buy them.

Freemen sold for crimes, no doubt lament their situation; consider it as a heavy punishment, but, conscious that they have deserved it, seldom complained. P. 192.

That upon the Gold Coast the smallest thefts are punished with slavery, he knows not to be the case.

That a man who should steal an ear of corn would be sold for a slave does happen, but knew an instance of a man guilty of that very act, who being taken, and a slave demanded of his master for him, the affair was compromised for an ounce of gold and some liquors.

Has no doubt that the man condemned to slavery for stealing an ear of corn would be satisfied with the

1789. the juſtice of his ſentence; becauſe he knows that ſuch is the law of the country, if he from whom it was ſtolen chooſes to be ſevere.

The manner in which ſlaves are confined to be taken on board ſhip, depends upon the nation they belong to. Duncoes are never put in irons, they ſupply a great number of ſlaves. The Fantees always. The Aſhantees and other nations, according
P. 193. to circumſtances. Slaves generally kept in irons while the ſhip is on the coaſt, though he has ſeen many out of irons. The women and boys never in irons.

The two ſhips he ſailed in from Africa for the W. Indies, and ſeveral others he had been aboard of, had no nettings. It is not uſual where the rails are high. Believes where it is uſed, it is to prevent the ſlaves from falling overboard, or to cut off all communication between them and the Anamaboe traders, who, for the purpoſe of reſelling them, might excite them to cut off the veſſel.

The inland ſlaves are confined in irons to keep them from any connection with the people about the forts who are great rogues, and might excite them to run away; in other reſpects they are never locked up, but allowed to amuſe themſelves about the fort, except at night. On board ſhip, they are kept in irons leſt they ſhould be adviſed by the canoe men, &c. to cut off the ſhip or jump overboard, which they would never of themſelves think of.

The natives from the interiour country are paid for the ſlaves and ivory they bring from thence, in cloth, liquor, guns, powder, gold, braſs-pans, and pewter; of pewter and braſs they are fond, and will take a great proportion. Has ſeldom known traders take more than one iron bar; and of late reject it altogether; for theſe two laſt years it has been in no great demand from Cape Coaſt to Tantum; therefore it has been cuſtomary to pay iron for proviſions when the blacks would take it. The commodities received

by

by the natives in exchange for ſlaves, they carry away made up in ſmall bundles, upon their heads. 1789.

Small defects do not render ſlaves unſaleable to Europeans. P. 196.

Is of opinion, that the ſlaves in the Weſt Indies would decreaſe annually without freſh ſupplies.

Slaves, in paſſing from the ſhore to the ſhip, have ſometimes an iron on their legs, or a log on their hands, from which they are releaſed when purchaſed, unleſs Fantees, of infamous characters.

Never heard of ſuch a thing in his life as an African trading ſhip carrying off free negroes againſt their inclination. Knew, however, that a man, of the name of Griffiths, did carry off two people intruſted to his care, from St. Andrews, or ſome part to windward, whom he never brought back. He reported, on his return, that either one or both died of the ſmall pox, with which the natives not being ſatisfied, put P. 197. him to death. The act was ſeverely reprobated by the Governor and Council, and Reſidents, who wrote home about it. This the only inſtance he ever heard of.

Has heard that gold is procured in the interior P. 198. country in two ways, by digging and waſhing. Believes it is very ſcarce, and few allowed to dig for it.

Has known two or three ſlaves refuſed in a year P. 199. for defects.

The people of Accra, when in want of corn, ge- P. 200. nerally ſend their canoes for it all down the coaſt, though it is ſometimes brought to them by the people who have it to diſpoſe of.

When conveyed by land from one country to ano- P. 201. ther, it is carried upon the heads of negroes in ſmall baſkets.

There is no doubt that war among the natives is injurious to trade of every kind; it ſtops the paths, and prevents every thing from coming down, ivory as well as ſlaves. The reſidents do therefore all in their power to make up any breach among them.

Traders

1789. Traders are afraid to paſs through villages when there is war.

Never knew a pound weight of either cotton or indigo, exported from the Gold Coaſt.

Europeans have no influence over the natives, to make them grow any particular articles; nor to change their cuſtoms.

Believes there are five males to one female exported from the Gold Coaſt.

Europeans, if they choſe it, could not obtain a greater proportion of females, becauſe the exerciſe of polygamy muſt render women ſcarcer.

P. 202. Does not think their attachment to their families ſo ſtrong as that of Europeans; nor that they have ſuch fine feelings; a black woman thinking little to pour a ſpoonful of brandy into a child's mouth, of two or three months old, at the breaſt. Seem to have little affection for their children—attributes it to polygamy.

Governor Miles expended conſiderable ſums to keep the natives in peace.

P. 203. Thinks, if there were no market on the coaſt, they would not bring the ſlaves from the interior country.

Witneſs Examined,—Capt. WILLIAM LITTLETON.

P. 204. Went to Gambia as mate 1762. Lived there 11 years, as a merchant.

Has been frequently up the Gambia. Went up about 300 leagues.

P. 205. Knew enough of the language to do his buſineſs.

Governments various on the different parts of the river—none hereditary. Kings for life, in rotation from one tribe to another, ſometimes from one town or diſtrict to another. Line of ſucceſſion ſometimes broken from caprice.

Slavery general. Some freemen keep many ſlaves.

Slaves

Slaves ſold to Europeans obtained various ways: 1789.
a great proportion from black Mahometan traders, who traverſe the interior parts to get ſlaves. Some P. 206.
priſoners of war, many convicts, and more from famines, cauſed by droughts and locuſts. The crimes numerous for which they are ſold. Believes this, from his own knowledge, and from good information.

Knew a famine in 1786, in the South-Weſt of the entrance of Gambia, from failure of rain, and locuſts. The natives ſubſiſted ſome months on roots, and whatever had nouriſhment, till nothing was left. They were then driven to the dreadful neceſſity of ſelling each other to procure ſubſiſtence. The Mandingoes bought them from the Phroops, between C. St. Mary's and C. Roxo, for corn and European goods, ſelling them to the white traders on the river, and he obtained a large proportion of them. Has been told by the Mahometans, who traverſe the inland parts, that famines often occur in Africa, which drive them ſometimes to ſubſiſt on each other, ſometimes by killing and eating them, often by ſelling them. Locuſts make dreadful havock, on the corn particularly: but it is generally partial, often confined to a ſpot of 40 or 50 miles.

Slaves made for adultery, theft, witchcraft, and P. 207.
other crimes, for which they are regularly, and, in general, impartially tried, by the leading men, and are ſeldom without their friends and advocates. An adulterer loſes life or liberty. If he eſcape, ſome of the family is ſeized and detained till he is taken. If he cannot redeem himſelf, he is ſold. Sometimes the whites are enjoined by the ſellers, who are generally the parties injured, not to let them be redeemed, on any terms. For witchcraft they are tried, and on conviction, ſold — after torture, ſometimes even to death. For conſiderable thefts, the puniſhment is loſs of liberty. Sometimes they are fined, and, if unable to pay, ſold.

1789. The injured party has the benefit of the conviction.

Has learnt from the natives, that, on trials for witchcraft, the principal people assemble under the palaver-tree. Sometimes, before trial, the accused are dragged into the woods, and whipped till they acknowledge themselves guilty of witchcraft, and, they are often condemned from confession under
P. 208. torture, though innocent. Sometimes they endeavour to prove their innocence, by undergoing a kind of ordeal by fire or by water, which is an infusion of a malignant root, drunk on those occasions, and which they seldom long survive.

Very few prisoners of war, taken near the river, are sold to the whites. Believes they seldom take many prisoners: if they do, they generally fall victims to the ferocity of the captors, and a few are sacrificed to the manes of the victor's friends. Believes but few females are taken prisoners in war, (repeated p. 223.) Female prisoners are frequently exchanged. Females, convicted of witchcraft, seldom exchanged. Recollects not an instance of their being redeemed.

P. 209. Owners of domesticks can, but very seldom do, dispose of them, unless for some enormous crime, when they have generally the approbation of the other slaves to sell them. Has been told they are generally tried by those other slaves.

Never heard of wars made to get slaves. Wars always arise from their own dissensions. Wars near the ports always injure trade of every kind. Has been told by black merchants, they have gone 3 or 400 miles to avoid seats of war. In his time, there were wars between the nations near the Gambia.

Never heard of a white kidnapping a slave. It would have ruined that man's trade. Can only speak of the River Gambia. Never heard *that* of the natives where he resided. On making any such attempt, they would be sold themselves.

Never heard of parties going out armed at night to take slaves, except against their enemies, with whom

whom they were at open war—nor of breaking up and ſurpriſing villages, to make ſlaves, but in caſes of open war. Such wars not very frequent near the Gambia; but inland wars are perpetually carrying on, in one country or another. 1789. P. 210.

Produce about the Gambia, country-corn, which is a ſpecies of millet, Indian corn, and rice, not in ſufficient quantities for export. Never heard of ſugar-cane growing there. Believes the climate unfit for it, from droughts from October to June. No articles of export, but wax, a little ivory, and a little gold, not worth mentioning. The ivory generally, he believes, about two tons, brought down on the heads of the ſlaves. Moſt of the wax comes from the S. ſide of the Gambia, chiefly about 30 or 40 leagues up; but in ſmaller quantities 2 or 300 leagues up, principally from the Phroops. Moſt of the wax is taken out of hollow trees: believes a little is taken in hives, which are cloſe to their houſes. Never ſaw above two or three hives, which were near the coaſt. Never heard of any inland. P. 211.

Apprehends it would not be worth the traders while to bring down ivory only from any great diſtance. Few elephants near the ports.

Apprehends the wax could not be much increaſed, for lately the whites have given a great price for it, and he has not learnt the quantity has increaſed from it.

They raiſe a little cotton and indigo, not ſufficient for their own uſe. They ſupply the deficiency with our manufactures. They are ſo indolent, that every attempt of the whites to encourage cotton and indigo, has proved abortive. What little indigo they raiſe, they cultivate. They do not reduce it to the ſtate of indigo which comes from other parts. They cut it, pound it in a wooden mortar, and hang it up in the form of ſugar-loves, in their houſes, and then infuſe it in water or lye made of aſhes, and dye their cloth with it. P. 212.

1789. Their cloths are about five or six inches broad, and they sew them together. There are very few manufacturers. These cloths could not be made an article of commerce among the whites.

Has been two voyages to Carolina, and three or four to the West-Indies. In the first voyage to Charlestown, from the commencement of the purchase in Africa, till the end of the sale in Charlestown, he lost about 13 out of about 140. Looks upon that as a very great and uncommon mortality. The last voyage he was upon the coast from the beginning of May to the beginning of November, and lost from the beginning of May to the close of the sale at Jamaica, 38 out of 242. His ship has since made a voyage to Jamaica, and lost 3 out of 216. The same ship went all the voyages, registered at
P. 213. 136 tons. Attributes the mortality of 38 to the slaves being of various nations, and some being very meagre when he received them, from the great scarcity in their country, particularly a number of the Phroops, who had a famine. When he lost 13, his ship was single decked, and he had very bad weather.

We carry hence split and kiln-dried horse-beans, and a great quantity of biscuit and flour. In the country, we buy all the corn and rice we can.

The black traders feed the slaves intended for sale on Guinea corn, chiefly, when they can get it, or any thing else they can procure. They never taste rice, but by stealth.

The ships could seldom get enough of Guinea corn for the slaves in the voyage. The beans are husked in England. They are boiled usually with beef or salt-fish. After eating them once or twice, they become fond of them, so as sometimes to ask for them instead of their country food.

P. 214. Slaves on board, accommodated in the best manner they possibly can. When first brought on board by the black merchants, they have a chain round their necks, generally worn from the place they came from,

from. When the purchaſe of them is completed, 1789.
that chain is taken off, and ſhackles put on their legs, which have a ring, through which a chain paſſes, which ſecures them, while on deck. The men between decks lie cloſe together, juſt allowing room for a perſon to ſtep between them. The men are generally before the main hatch-way, the boys in the main hatch-way, the women, girls, and children, are at liberty abaft, except at night, when they are locked down below. They are on deck all day, except in bad weather.

Believes there are air-ports and gratings in all Guinea-men, and ſometimes ſo much air, that they beg to have part of the tarpaulins laid over them.

From Gambia, the weather is generally fair and pleaſant after they get to windward of the Cape de Verd iſlands, when they fall in with the trade-winds. After this, the ſlaves are very ſeldom prevented by
the weather from being on deck daily. They have P. 215.
ſome heavy but ſhort ſqualls of rain, when they ſpread the awnings over them. But it is a general rule to keep them on deck as much as they can, with prudence.

Cleanlineſs is one of their firſt objects. As ſoon as the ſlaves are on deck, the ſeamen, and generally ſome boys, ſcrape and ſwab the rooms, and generally air them with fire-pans. Twice or thrice a week they are waſhed with vinegar and fumigated.

Soon after day-light they have ſome biſcuit, and a glaſs of inferior ſpirits and water half and half. At their firſt meal, they have generally more than they can eat. About four or five in the evening they have a ſecond meal, of another kind. They ſeldom have the ſame food twice the ſame day. They have a regular allowance of water, as often as neceſſary. This depends on the heat of the weather. To ſupply the ſlaves with enough of food and water, is a chief part of the employment, both of ſailors and officers, at ſea, (ſee p. 216.) The officers are intereſted in
the cargo's health. They have a privilege ſlave or P. 216.
two,

1789. two, according to the agreement. The chief mate and ſurgeon paid on the groſs average at ſale.

Slaves oftener complain of cold than heat in Middle Paſſage. When they think it too cold for them, they put them below; and even then they beg to have part of the tarpaulin laid over them. They often requeſt to go below, when it blows freſh, and they happen to be on the ſhady ſide of the deck.

The ſurgeon every morning viſits them, and often gives them medicines below, as well as on deck.

Sale advertiſed four or five days after arrival in the Weſt-Indies. Never heard of means being uſed to repel diſorders of ſlaves, before ſale. In all his voyages, ſlaves always treated with humanity and tenderneſs.

P. 217. In his voyage to Carolina, loſt 2 out of 16, or 18, (thinks 18) ſeamen. In his laſt voyage, which was to Jamaica, from being detained on the coaſt, loſt 7 ſeamen in the Gambia, and 2 or three in the Middle Paſſage. The crew, with himſelf, originally 21. The ſurgeon died firſt. To his death he attributes the increaſe of his loſs both of ſeamen and ſlaves. The ſeamen's health, as much as poſſible, attended to. It is their intereſt to take care of the ſeamen, the ſucceſs of the voyage depending on it. (The loſs of ſeamen is from England to the Weſt-Indies, p. 220).

The time of day the ſhips leave the Gambia depends on the time of the tide. On entering the Gambia, they have 2 or 3 black linguiſts, a black meſſenger or two, and 6 or 8 people to row the boats, and preſerve the ſeamens health. They do not ſuffer a ſeaman to go into a boat, if they can avoid it. The blacks attend them out of the river, returning in the ſhip's long-boat, (which is generally left behind) or in a canoe. They uſually ſtop a tide at the laſt port of the river, to fill water. The time of ſailing is always known to the natives, ſometimes before the ſhip comes down.

The

The climate in general noxious to European con- 1789.
ſtitutions. He found no difference in it 2 or 300
leagues up the river, and at the entrance.

Rains from about the end of May till the end of P. 218.
October. Dry weather the reſt of the year. Believes the rains unhealthful—but he has generally been as healthy in rains as in dry weather. He avoided expoſing himſelf, which they cannot prevail on the ſeamen to do. Rains the moſt prejudicial to Europeans. They never carried the ſeamen up above 140 leagues, and there they were as healthy as at the river's mouth. The French and ſome Engliſh ſhips go no farther up than James Fort and Albadar. They have as much or more mortality than the ſhips 150 leagues up the river.

One voyage returned to Liverpool, once to Briſtol, the other times to London.

Believes there are people in London who make it their buſineſs to go on board ſhips to obtain litigious
caſes. (Has ſeen this in London, p. 220). The P. 219.
ſeamen who have complaints, bring actions againſt the maſter or mate, as the caſe may be. He never had an action commenced againſt him.

In the ſingle deck ſhip there was a platform, in the other none. In the ſhip where he ſaid there was room to ſtep between the ſlaves, there was no platform.

Computes a gallon of water per day ſufficient for each man, white and black, including what proviſions are boiled in. They have a ſhort paſſage from Gambia, and allow them plenty of water, generally three or four times a day.

The ſlaves have water in the night, if they call for it. They have generally ſomething below to hold water, and it is poured through the gratings, through a funnel.

Poſſibly the extreme heat below, and their being P. 220.
naked, make them ſo ſuſceptible of cold, when they come on deck. They could not keep them clean and

1789. and healthy, if they had clothes. The apartment below is cleared in order to clean it.

More timber than underwood on the coaſt. Mahogany has been brought thence for trial, but has not anſwered.

Corn, rice, and other proviſions might be cultivated where the ſoil is fit for corn. About 30 or 40 leagues up the Gambia, the ſoil is not adapted for corn, and produces but little. The natives cultivate as much land as they can, about the lower parts of the river, but do not raiſe enough of corn for their own uſe; hence they ſend canoes for it up

P. 221. the river. Thinks the land would not be productive without manure. Soil looſe and ſandy at the river's mouth; up the river more loamy. Believes it would receive the plough, if cleared from roots which the natives do not take up. Apprehends the ſoil and climate unadapted for European corn. The natives ſow their corn early in June, after the firſt rains. They cut their early corn, which is Indian, in September. Their greateſt crop is about the end of October. They generally cut and eat the Indian

P. 222. corn before it is ripe, in the early ſeaſon. They depend on the October corn. They have little or no manure, and ſcarce any horſes. They tie their cows on the corn ground, in the dry ſeaſon. The Phoolas have a good many cows.

Seldom above one-third females purchaſed. They buy all that are fit for the market who offer. The number of females varies every year. The trade to Gambia very much reduced. Has heard the ſlaves bought by the Europeans, ſome years ago, on that coaſt, eſtimated at 3000 annually: believes it does not now average 1000. Females are always ſcarce, when ſlaves in general are plenty. Perhaps 1-4th of the 3000 might have been females.

P. 223. A conſiderable part of the women are ſold as convicts for witchcraft—there are beſides ſome brought from the interior parts of the country—of theſe it is not always known for what crime they were ſold.

The

The gratings over the hatch-way are always kept open—when it rains, a tarpaulin is ſpread over the booms, 7 or eight feet from the deck, in form of an awning—has known the ſlaves deſire it to be laid cloſe over the gratings to keep them warm.—Never heard them complain of foul air,—if they think themſelves at any time too warm, a number of them are immediately brought upon deck. 1789. P. 224.

Never heard ſurgeons, officers, or ſailors, when viſiting the ſlaves apartments in the morning, complain particularly of the noiſomeneſs and foulneſs of the air,—they have obſerved at times it was very warm,—or that there was a particular ſmell—but nothing is ſuffered to remain long below to occaſion any offenſive ſmell. A thorough draught of air is kept up between decks, when the weather permits the air-ports to be kept open. A partial air is admitted through the gratings when the ports are ſhut.

Cannot ſay the exact height between decks of the ſlave ſhips ſpoke of above—ſuppoſe the loweſt about 4 feet. Had no platform in his ſhip. Does not recollect having been on board more than two ſhips who had. The height between decks in them, he thinks, was 7 feet. P. 225.

Slaves, on board the ſhips he has been in, might lie on their backs, though perhaps it might be difficult all at the ſame time.

They are ſubject to be ſea-ſick for two or three days. Seldom excoriated by their chains, care being taken upon the firſt appearance of injury to wrap ſomething round the limb to guard it. P. 226.

It was his endeavour to render the ſituation of the ſlaves on board as comfortable as poſſible, by giving them plenty of food and drink, and the beſt lodging he could.

The perſons charged with exerciſing witchcraft are ſuppoſed to diſtribute drugs; in particular ſuch as occaſion abortion.

Is of opinion the abolition of the ſlave-trade, by this country, would encourage the evils which it is P. 227.

 meant

1789. meant to relieve—ſuch as human ſacrifices, and murder of captives and convicts, it being a maxim among the blacks never to give a man an opportunity of revenging an injury.

Does not think the natives could be induced, from any conſideration, to raiſe produce worth the attention of this country. Nor that Europeans could ſtand the climate, in clearing woods, and cultivating the lands.

P. 228. Cotton, of very excellent quality, is produced there, with very little labour.

Has generally found, that ſeamen on board ſlave-ſhips, were as healthy as thoſe belonging to other ſhips, trading on the ſame coaſt. Did not loſe a ſeaman in his laſt voyage. Returned in November.

Attributes the unhealthineſs of ſeamen in a great meaſure to their expoſing themſelves to the night

P. 229. dews, more prejudicial than rains, and not to their food. They will not ſleep under cover, but bring their beds upon deck, that they may be cool.

In the voyage, when he loſt 7 out of 21 ſeamen, the reſt were in a relaxed ſtate. Did not take on board any freſh men, to re-place the 7. Had on board 236 or 238 ſlaves at leaving the coaſt, which

P. 230. were permitted to come upon deck as often, and as many at a time, without additional irons, as if the crew had been full and healthy: ſome of the irons were even taken off after getting to ſea.

Cannot ſay he has been acquainted with any inſtances of notorious cruelty in the captains of ſlave-ſhips. Some are more ſevere than others. Can only ſpeak to the ſhips that have frequented the Gambia.

Witneſs examined,—THOMAS KING, Eſq. a Merchant of London.

P. 232. Went firſt to Africa in 1766, ſecond mate of the Royal Charlotte, of about 300 tons; not a regular ſlave

ſlave ſhip; carried out the African company's ſtores 1789.
to Cape Coaſt; took in 120 ſlaves on the Gold Coaſt. Generally healthy on the voyage. Loſt only two or three, till landed in Jamaica. About fourteen days intervened between arrival and landing of the laſt man. In this interval no means uſed to repel diſorders of the ſlaves. The ſailors, ſeventeen in all, healthy the whole voyage. Loſt not one from P. 232.
leaving London, to return there.

Sailed next to Africa in 1767-8, in ſame capacity, ſame ſhip. Took in 455 ſlaves from Gold Coaſt, for Grenada. In general very healthy. Thinks he loſt ten in the voyage. Believes he loſt none on board at Grenada, which was for about a week. P. 234.

Thinks the crew were eighteen, very healthy, loſt none in the voyage, nor at Grenada, where he left the ſhip.

Sailed a third time to Africa from Grenada, as Captain of the Molly, about 110 tons. Touched at America, there took in the cargo with which ſlaves were to be purchaſed. Proceeded to the Gold Coaſt, where he thinks took on board 105 ſlaves. Had twelve or thirteen ſailors. Was about twelve months on the Gold Coaſt, and near it. The voyage was unfortunate to ſailors and ſlaves. Of the firſt, ſix or ſeven died. Of the latter, about one half. He attributes this to the following circumſtances. Though near twelve months on the coaſt, he loſt few ſlaves or ſeamen; but his ſhip ſailed very badly, and loſt ſome of her maſts, by which he was driven into the Bite of Bonny, a very unhealthy part of the coaſt, and was ſeven months from the Gold Coaſt to Grenada. During which he was ſeveral times obliged to put into different places for proviſions, and could get but ſcanty ſupplies. Hence P. 235.
both whites and negroes were two or three times, during the paſſage, reduced to a very ſhort allowance.

Sailed, latter end of 1770, a fourth time to Africa, in the brig Ferret, about 70 tons, twelve or thirteen

1789. men, from London to the River Cameroon. Bought
105 ſlaves, which he carried to Grenada. About
eight months on the coaſt, and about two months
from thence to the Weſt-Indies. Crew and ſlaves in
general pretty healthy; loſt two or three of the firſt,
four or five of the latter.

Sailed a fifth time to the coaſt of Africa, in De-
P. 235. cember 1771, from London, in the Surrey, of 180
tons, 25 ſailors, to the River Cameroon. Staid
there ſix months. Took in 255 ſlaves. Had a paſſage of eight weeks to Grenada. Crew and ſlaves
in general healthy. Loſt ten ſlaves.

P. 236. In the River Cameroon (more unhealthy to Europeans than the open coaſt) himſelf, officers, and moſt
of his crew were ſick. Loſt there the ſurgeon and
three ſeamen.

His ſixth voyage to Africa, early in 1773, in the Three Friends, 70 tons, himſelf and crew twelve. Remained on the Gold Coaſt three months. Took in 144 ſlaves for St. Vincent's. Loſt two ſailors on the coaſt, and eight ſlaves in all.

Sailed a ſeventh time to Africa, in 1775, from
London, in the Venus of 150 tons. Crew in all 21
or 22. Staid on the Gold Coaſt four months. Took
P. 237. in 321 ſlaves for Jamaica. Loſt in all one or two
ſeamen and ten ſlaves.

His eighth voyage was in 1776, from London, in the Harriet, of 135 tons, eighteen men. Staid on the Gold Coaſt between three and four months. Took in 277 ſlaves, for Jamaica. Loſt ſeven ſlaves in all; none of the crew.

Has all along, in ſpeaking to the mortality of ſlaves, reckoned from the firſt man brought on board, to the laſt man landed in the Weſt-Indies.

Sailed for the ninth and laſt time, in November 1780, from London, in the Cambden, of 335 tons, whole crew 65. Bought on the Gold Coaſt 580 ſlaves. Stay ſix months. Sailed for Jamaica. Loſt four ſailors, two of them by accident. Loſt 50 or 51 ſlaves

ſlaves in all, by a diarrhea on the coaſt. Some it 1789.
was apprehended had brought the diſeaſe on board.

P. 238.

Has ever ſince been ſettled in London as a merchant.

All the veſſels in which he ſailed for Africa (except the two firſt) were regular ſlave ſhips.

In all the ſhips he commanded, or was concerned in, is ſure they never buried one per cent. of the negroes after their arrival in the Weſt Indies, and before ſale.

Never knew any means uſed by ſurgeons or others, to repel the diſorders of ſlaves before their landing.

Had frequent opportunities of being on ſhore in Africa, and by the natives accounts, ſlaves become ſo chiefly for crimes, witchcraft included; and ſome few priſoners of war.

Never heard of wars for the purpoſe of getting ſlaves, nor, that Europeans ever ſtirred up ſuch. Nor ever heard of towns or villages pillaged or deſtroyed for this purpoſe. P. 239.

Never heard of the natives being ſtolen, except from ſlaves from the inland country. Theſe have mentioned a few being ſtolen or taken away; but thinks they preferred telling this ſtory, to giving the real fact. Water-ſide people, had any of them been kidnapped, or improperly detained, would have had opportunities of making complaints, and getting redreſs.

Free natives are daily on board the ſhips, with whom the ſlaves have conſtant opportunities of converſing.

It is uſual for all ſhips, where he has been, to give a week, more commonly a month's notice, of ſailing. Ships generally ſail with the land breeze, which is from early in the morning, until nine or ten o'clock.

In the ſhips in which he ſailed, or has been generally concerned, one half the crew conſiſted of captain, officers and ſeamen; the other half of landmen, P. 240.
and of men, who may have been one or two voyages, and boys.

As

1789. As far as he knows, thinks this the uſual proportion in ſlave ſhips.

A certain proportion of ſlaves proviſions is always carried from England; becauſe the Gold Coaſt does not furniſh enough; ſometimes, though not frequently, none at all is to be got there. Beſides, the ſlaves prefer a change of food; which conſiſts chiefly of ſplit beans, a little rice; has known wheat, but that is now laid aſide. Beans are very wholeſome, and preferred by the Gold Coaſt negroes to Indian corn, their native food. When he went firſt to Africa, inſtead of beans, at leaſt two-thirds white peaſe were carried; the ſurgeons afterwards adviſed an equal quantity of both. But neither did this agree with the negroes ſo well as beans given alone, therefore mer-
P. 241. chants now ſend out only tick beans (a ſpecies of Windſor beans as he is told) kiln dried, ſplit and ſhelled. Never carried or ſent, nor ever ſaw or heard of, horſe beans being ſent to Africa for the negroes. The beans ſent are frequently eaten by the whites.

In a well regulated ſhip, every poſſible attention is paid to the ſlaves on the paſſage, as alſo to the dreſſing and quantity of their diet, which he thinks was more comfortable than in their own country; better ſeaſoned, better dreſſed, and ſerved in cleaner veſſels. Great attention is paid to the health of the ſlaves on board. Early every morning, inquiry is made, if they have any complaints; and again after breakfaſt, it is the duty of the ſurgeon to examine carefully every ſlave on board. It certainly is the intereſt, and duty of the captain and ſurgeon, to take care of the negroes.

P. 242. Has not obſerved in the parts of Africa where he has generally been, any produce, except proviſions, and of theſe, not ſo great a ſurplus as the ſhips wiſh to have. Could ſhips depend on getting a ſupply there, they would not carry ſo much out with them.

There are no other articles of produce worth notice. There is ſome gold duſt, ivory, bees-wax,

gum-copal,

gum-copal, bar-wood and cam-wood, but not in 1789.
quantities, to become a conſiderable object of trade.

The genius of the people on the Gold Coaſt, he thinks, equal to extending commerce in any thing practicable, but from their indolence, thinks that commerce could not be extended among them.

Does not think a colony could be ſettled on the Gold Coaſt, but by force.

Beſides, the coaſt is unfavourable to an extenſive
commerce, in reſpect of rivers, harbours, or landing
places. The rivers have all bars. There are no
harbours, bays, or creeks, where even one of our P. 243.
boats can land with ſafety on, except two, on that
part of the Gold Coaſt frequented by Engliſh ſhips;
and even thoſe two, are very unſafe, except in fine
weather. Believes, that under the Dutch ſettlements,
there are one or two places of the ſame deſcription,
where a boat may land.

Whilſt he frequented the coaſt, the Dutch, French Portugueſe, and by chance a Daniſh ſhip traded there.

The French have exceedingly increaſed their trade to Africa the laſt four years; this he has learnt from Frenchmen, both here and in France, and from his correſpondence with French houſes.

Before the late war, the Americans carried on a conſiderable trade, chiefly from Rhode-Iſland and New-Providence, to Africa, which was totally given up in the war, but is revived ſince the peace, and he believes carried to rather a greater extent than before.

Thinks, if the ſlave trade ſhould be aboliſhed in P. 244.
Great-Britain, the ſame number of ſlaves would be
bought among the other nations.

Is of opinion, that the treatment of ſlaves on board Engliſh ſhips, is preferable to that of any other nation.

Has touched at different parts of the Windward Coaſt, in his way to the Gold Coaſt, and ſo far as he obſerved,

1789. obſerved, ſlaves are procured in the ſame way there, and on the River Cameroon, as on the Gold Coaſt.

The ſoil on the river can produce whatever the climate will admit; but they only cultivate proviſions, and ſome little fruits and vegetables; no grain.

P. 245. It never was his practice, nor that of any ſhips in which he was, or is concerned, or has known, to compel the ſailors to take their diſcharge in the Weſt-Indies. It is not their intereſt ſo to do. Though they have, when they arrive in the Weſt Indies, ſome few men more than abſolutely neceſſary to navigate the ſhips home; yet the additional charge of getting three men in the Weſt Indies, in lieu of nine men diſcharged, would be nearly, if not quite, equal to the expence of bringing the nine men home, (vide the Minutes for his explanation.)

P. 246. It is cuſtomary for ſailors to deſert from African ſhips in the Weſt Indies. Attributes it to their receiving half their pay at the ſelling; their getting on ſhore, and intoxicated; and often getting higher wages for the run home, in other ſhips.

Never knew a captain of an African ſhip, uſe his men ill to make them run away in the Weſt Indies; it was ever his wiſh to preſerve them as much as he could, knowing the additional expence, and ſometimes difficulty, of getting others at any rate. Believes it is not very common for ſailors to go ſeveral voyages in the ſame ſhip, with the ſame captain, in the ſlave trade: at the ſame time his houſe have had the ſame ſeamen go many voyages in their employ.

His opinion of the probable conſequences of aboliſhing the ſlave trade from this country only, is, that as many negroes would be exported from Africa as now. Reſpecting the Weſt India iſlands, concludes, they would be very materially affected by loſing that moſt valuable branch of the trade, the exportation to foreigners, of a large proportion of the negroes imported in Britiſh ſhips, which are paid for generally in ſpecie, or in Weſt India produce.

Formerly,

Formerly, on the Gold Coaſt, more than one-third 1789.
females was procurable. For the laſt two years, believes every poſſible encouragement has been given P. 247.
for females, but now they cannot obtain more than one-fourth generally; and by the laſt accounts, the price given for prime females, exceeded by £5 a head, what is generally given for men. Cannot account ſufficiently for this ſcarcity. Polygamy being tolerated in Africa, believes many prime young females are kept as wives in the countries they paſs through.

On the Gold Coaſt, more has been given by 40s. per head for males than females; but to get more of the latter, they have offered an advanced price.

One houſe in London has ſent goods to the amount of £.100,000 in a year to Africa, including the value of their ſhips. Has been told of houſes in Liverpool that ſend more.

Believes, that the voyages in which he commanded ſlave ſhips, in 1770, 1771, 1773, 1775, 1776, 1780, were all attended with a certain profit.

Has heard of the locked jaw in Africa, but it is P. 28.
not common there. Does not recollect ever having had a ſlave ill of that diſorder on board.

The natives on the Gold Coaſt raiſe a few yams at one or two places; very few ſweet potatoes; no rice; no wheat.

The difference in price between peaſe and ſuch beans as are carried out to feed the ſlaves, is very little. Thinks that the beans may in common be rather cheaper. Should think the peaſe as heavy as the beans per buſhel.

The cuſtomary allowance in quantity to the ſlaves, was exactly the ſame of either.

The land towards the ſea on the Gold Coaſt is P. 249.
generally low and rocky, but riſes as you go inland. Some of it in the back country, within view, is mountainous.

1789. Impoffible to fpeak generally to the depth of water within 100 yards of the beach. At the landing places, 100 yards from the fhore it may be fix to eight feet; in other places it is not deeper near a mile off. At a medium the fea breaks 300 yards from the fhore: there are feafons, and particular days in thofe feafons, when the fea is fmoother, and may not break 20 yards from the fhore. At other feafons the fea breaks in fix fathom water; and in general the fea is worfe near the full and change of the moon.

No tide can be perceived in fhips at anchor. On fhore thinks there may be a rife of at moft three feet.

Such Guinea feamen as have wives and families, or dependents, the owners pay from 10s. to 15s. per
P. 250. month out of their wages to fuch relations; and continue their allowance to their return, death or defertion of the feaman.

Thinks a feaman caufelefsly difcharged, againft his confent in the Weft Indies, may, on his return, profecute the mafter for full wages till the fhip arrives in England; and knows that fuch profecutions have taken place here; when the feaman recover his wages, but does not recollect that he received any thing for his paffage home, though that might have happened and efcaped his knowledge.

Has given the tonnage of the fix laft veffels in which he traded for flaves, according to the old regifter, as near as he could recollect: that of the laft fhip was what fhe afterwards meafured.

He laid upon the table a fample of the faid beans, with a note from the perfon who furnifhed the fample, and who had always fupplied him when in the African trade. The note was read, and is as follows:—

P. 251. "Mr. Stray fays, thefe are the only fort of beans "that are fent to Africa, they are called tick-beans; "they are alfo fent to the Weft Indies for provifion "for

" for the pegroes. If eat when green, they are equal 1789.
" to the garden beans produced at this time of the " year. Horſe-beans are a different ſort, and not " uſed for ſlaves proviſions. Mr. Stray alſo ſays, " he does not know that the tick-beans are uſed " for any other purpoſe than for exportation to " Africa and the Weſt Indies."

Knows that the trade of the French to Africa is conſiderably increaſed in theſe two years, and is now increaſing. They grant conſiderable bounties, to the ſhips fitted from France for that trade; and alſo ſo much a head upon negroes imported into their iſlands. Believes there are only two or three places in St. Domingo where no bounty is given on negroes; in all their other iſlands a bounty is allowed.

The idea of aboliſhing the ſlave-trade in this country has undoubtedly given additional vigour to the French African trade; and many adventurers in the the French trade, anxiouſly watch the buſineſs now before this Houſe.

Does not know the prices of horſe and tick-beans; nor, that when horſe-beans ſell from 21s. to 22s. 6d. tick-beans are from 19s. to 21s. Knows that tick-beans, at leaſt the beans laid on the table, have never P. 252.
been bought here for leſs than 34s. per quarter in the laſt five years; have been at 48s. and bought by his houſe at 52s. in that time; he would be underſtood to ſpeak to the price of theſe beans in the ſtate in which they are put on board What price they may be ſold at before they are kiln-dried, ſplit, and ſhelled, he does not know.

Imagines, that a Weſt India ſhip of 200 tons uſually employs 14 ſeamen. The number for a ſlave ſhip of the ſame burthen muſt depend greatly on the part of Africa ſhe is bound to. To the river Cameroon he thinks 30.

Does not think ſuch a veſſel on her return from the Weſt Indies to London could be coveniently navigated by 14, out of ſuch a crew as an African ſhip carries.

1789. Such a veſſel when light, might be ſafely navigated by eight or ten able ſeamen, and four or five landmen, or leſs.

P. 253. Their houſe had a ſhip which went from England to lie ſome time at Anamaboe, to buy ſlaves; ſome part of which were diſpoſed of in two or three other veſſels. She lay there 15 or 16 months; had, when ſhe went out, a crew of 35 or 36, of which has been told by her commander ſhe loſt four only.

Has known crews of ſlave ſhips cut off while the veſſels lay in rivers by the natives, and at ſea by the ſlaves.

Believes in well regulated ſhips the ſlaves are gene-
P. 254. rally ſatisfied; but there are nations whoſe prieſts induce them to make thoſe attempts, in expecting to get the ſhip to ſome ſhore, where they may form a community of their own. Other nations have an idea, that the whites buy them to kill and eat them. They are ſometimes a good while on board before they are quite reconciled. Slaves ſold for crimes from near the ſhore, are for a time diſcontented at ſeparation from their friends and families; particularly while they lie near the ſhore, and ſometimes attempt to cut off the ſhip's crew, and by chance ſucceed.

Is himſelf now concerned in the ſlave-trade.

Very few ſhips have been run away with by the
P. 255. ſlaves, and thoſe only from Gambia, and its vicinity, they having deſtroyed the whites except one or two, kept to navigate the ſhip to the neareſt land. Thinks, he recollects one inſtance of their having got back to their coaſt; and another, of a ſhip being met with at ſea, and taken poſſeſſion of.

A part of the men ſlaves only are fettered on board. Out of 500 from the Gold Coaſt 120 or 125 may be women and girls; of the males, at leaſt 100 or 125 are from the age of 15 downwards; and are never put in irons; and of the reſt, a certain proportion, from the moſt interiour parts of Africa, who are quiet, are never put in irons; ſo that of 500, he eſtimates,

eſtimates, not above 200, 230, or 250, would be in 1789.
fetters at once; and in the latter part of the paſſage, not near ſo many. They are generally chained two and two together, the right leg of the one to the left leg of the other. Some of the moſt reſolute are chained by the hand alſo; the bolt of the fetters is about 14 or 15 inches long; the ſpace between the two ſhackles about ſix; but they vary in proportion to the ſtrength and ſize of the men. The weight of the leg fetters ſhackle and bolt may be from 2 to 3 lb. Are fettered thus night and day.

The largeſt proportion he ever had on board was P. 256.
rather better than two ſlaves to a ton, who certainly had room to lie on their backs.

On Gold Coaſt he, and he believes others, laid in from 45 to 50 gallons for every white and black on board. From the river Cameroon rather more, the paſſage from thence rather the longeſt and more uncertain. The uſual paſſage is from ſeven to nine weeks, and the calculation is made for 90 days, at half a gallon per day. Proviſions alſo for 90 days; and for ſome time after the ſhip ſails, care is taken not far to exceed that allowance; but, when they get into the S. E. trade-winds, when they can calculate pretty nearly the reſt of the paſſage, they have generally as much water and proviſions as they chooſe.

In ſome ſlave ſhips from London, a ſtill-head and worm is fixed to the ſlave's boiler to procure more water. When he mentions the eſtimate of half a gallon of water, that uſed for boiling, &c. was included.

Witneſs examined—ALEXANDER ANDERSON, Eſq.

Is a merchant in partnerſhip with his brother, four P. 258.
or five years proprietors of Bance Iſland, in S. Leone. They have in that time, ſhipped ſeveral cargoes of ſlaves

1789. slaves for the West Indies and S. Carolina. The average mortality from sailing to arrival at the port of delivery, has been about 1¾ per cent. and about 1¾ per cent. more, between arrival and sale, a space, at
P. 259. an average, about ten days.

They put on board, for the negroes, provisions considered sufficient, with the addition of rice, which the captains might get on the coast. Wine was also supplied for the sick slaves, and plenty of medicine.

They have attempted to buy ivory and camwood, the only produce in that part fit for a European market; and, to encourage their agent to procure these articles, have allowed him a commission about three to one more than for buying slaves; yet not more than 120 tons of camwood in a year, and about three or four tons of ivory has been obtained.

A statement from the books, bills of lading, and letters of the house, of the average mortality of the slaves, was delivered in at the table, and read; and is inserted p. 260 of the Minutes at large. By that statement it appears, that of 1318 slaves shipped, not one three-fourths per cent. died on the passage, and not one 1-fourth per cent. died between arrivals and sales; in all not three per cent. died.

P. 261. The house keeps considerable stores on the island, and factories, with goods on other parts of the coast.

They have an agent and several clerks on the island to buy slaves, camwood, and ivory, loading their ships with those goods; and when their own ships are not on the coast, chartering others. The people on the island are altogether dependant on them.

The house had an intention of settling a cotton plantation in the neighbourhood, but were dissuaded from it by their friends, who knew the impossibility of making the Africans labour, otherwise is certain from the lands and slaves they had, they must have made a good plantation. Has heard, that Mr. R. Oswald, proprietor of the island for 20 or 30 years before they bought it, in 1785, had often regretted that he could not make the people labour; and, in

1783,

1783, he directed one of his captains to offer a pre- 1789.
mium to the natives for indigo and cotton, and that the ſlaves reſiding at Bance Iſland (Mr. Oſwald's order produced, ſee p. 283) might be employed in raiſing rice, but without effect.

A letter produced concerning a ſettlement at the mouth of the river S. Leone, of free negroes from this country. Their conduct, and a great mortality among them (ſee p. 271 to 278) Minutes at large.

A ſecond letter produced (ſee p. 279) Minutes at large.

The three voyages by the ſnow Mary in 1785, P. 279.
1786, 1787, and the two of the ſhip Concord in 1787 and 1788, referred to in the ſtatement given in, he conſidered as profitable.

Has no other account of voyages for ſlaves, be- P. 281.
ſides thoſe delivered in.

The ſlaves are brought to the factories of the P. 282.
houſe, and a valuable conſideration paid for them by their agent.

The ſlaves on Bance Iſland, called Grumettas, are generally good ſervants, though there are ſometimes complaints againſt them.

Witneſs examined—Captain JACOB LORAN.

Has been 20 years maſter in the Weſt India trade. P. 263.
Made 50 voyages in that time, reckoning out and home as two.

In St. Kitts, there is an act againſt leaving ſailors on ſhore. The maſter, with one ſecurity, enters into a bond of £2000 currency, that he will carry off the ſailors he brought with him. This law extends to ſhips coming from other places, as well as Great Britain. Yet he could not prevent his ſailors from deſerting in the Weſt Indies. Has been often obliged to hire others to bring his ſhip home. Did not P. 264.
know from what veſſels they came. Some from merchantmen,

1789. merchantmen, some from Guineamen. Has had
four, five, or six from Guineamen at a time. The
sailors in the African trade look on the West Indies
as a second port of delivery, where many of them in-
sist on their discharge. They go into West India
ships which want hands, where they generally get
more for the run home, than they would get by their
months wages in the ship, African or other, they
were in. Greater wages for the run home, is most
certainly the reason, why sailors belonging to African
ships, wish to go into West India ships.

Has known, in war, from 25 to 30 guineas, and as
many gallons of rum, per man, given for the run
home. In peace, from 7 to 10 guineas, according
P. 265. to circumstances; and generally they agree for a gallon of rum for every guinea. In 1775, at Dominica,
in the ship Amherst, he engaged four by the run, and
gave 8 guineas and 8 gallons of rum; but though
he still commands a ship, he knows of no such thing
in the present peace. That in every trade he has
been in, seamen are engaged for the voyage out and
home; but, upon getting to the West Indies, they
generally go on shore, get drunk, and the first captain who wants men, if he advance them a little
money to pay their debt, will get them to go by the
P. 266. run. Those in the West India trade are not paid
half wages there, nor are entitled to any, until a
month after their return to the Thames. Seamen
desert in the West Indies, both from African and
West India ships; can make no distinction. Has
known the security, in such a bond as he has mentioned, threatened; and has seen a security pay for
a master £40 for a man left. Seamen deserting from
West India ships, in the West Indies, by the articles
they sign, forfeit all their wages

Seamen happened to be scarce when he was at Dominica, and shipped those people, though it was not wholly owing to that, that he paid so much; for when he sees a good hearty fellow that he can trust in a gale of wind, he always gives him a guinea

or

or two more, than to a man he could not trust. Be- 1789.
lieves one or two of his sailors came out of a Guinea
ship Has employed men out of the King's ships. P. 267.

Never sold spirits, tobacco, or cloths to the seamen in his life.

Sailors often leave their ships in the West Indies. Knew an instance about four months ago, where all the sailors but one deserted; not know the cause. Was never prosecuted on his bond for sailors left behind, but has an account of a negro unintentionally carried off, whose value, £98 he was afterwards obliged to pay.

He never knew the owner or captain get a farth- P. 268.
ing by desertion, though the articles stipulate that the wages shall go to them. When a seaman runs away, he generally applies to a lawyer, and the act is over-ruled generally. What is given to a sailor for the run home, is generally a good deal more than the amount of wages due to him who deserts; hence it is a heavy charge upon the ship to have their men run away. Does not know what becomes of the forfeited wages.

West India ships desire in general to come home P. 269.
stronger handed than they go out.

The crew of a West India ship have their river pay, and in general a month's advance, on leaving Gravesend; and notes left with several of their wives, for so much a month till the ship's return. All which, in general, amounts to more than the wages due to the seaman at his desertion; hence it is certainly for the owner's interest, that the same people who go out in his ship, should return.

Ships of equal tonnage, by register, very much differ in real tonnage. Suppose two ships of 300 tons each, carpenter's or register tonnage, one nine feet depth of hold, the other twelve, the latter would certainly carry most.

Does not well know the construction of African P. 270.
ships. Has sometimes been on board them. Never

1789. was in the trade. Believes they are in general ſharp built, for ſailing. The Weſt India ſhips are built for burthen, full.

Witneſs examined—Captain JOHN MAN.

P. 284. Captain of the Grenville Bay, Weſt Indiaman. Has been nearly 20 years in the trade. About 16 years to Grenada, and 4 to Jamaica.

Is not, nor ever was, at all concerned in the African trade.

It is the law or practice, in Grenada and Jamaica, to compel the captains of Weſt India ſhips, to carry back all the ſailors they carried out.

It is in general very much an object to the ſailors, to get diſcharged from their ſhips in the Weſt Indies, that they may get home by the run.

Has always underſtood, but not from his own knowledge, that the Weſt Indies was conſidered as
P. 285. the ſecond port of delivery in the African trade.

It is common for ſailors to demand their diſcharge at the ſecond port of delivery.

In war, the pay they get for the run home, is more than their wages would have been, had they continued with the ſhip they came out in; but in peace it ſeldom is ſo much.

Has known them paid for the run home, in war, from 10 to 18 guineas, and ſometimes from 25 to 30 guineas; and generally a gallon of rum for every guinea.

Has ſhipped ſailors in the Weſt Indies, which have deſired, againſt the maſter's wiſh, to be diſcharged from African ſhips.

When the ſhip is entered at the Cuſtom Houſe, Grenada, the maſter muſt enter his muſter-roll, and
P. 286. with a ſurety, ſign a bond, each a £1000 penalty, that a ſingle man ſhall not be diſcharged. Yet ſailors very often get away in war; the temptation of going by the run in the Weſt Indies, may make them deſert; but believes this has little or no effect in peace.

End of Number I.

Number II.

ABRIDGMENT

OF THE

MINUTES OF THE EVIDENCE,

TAKEN BEFORE A

COMMITTEE OF THE WHOLE HOUSE,

TO WHOM IT WAS REFERRED TO CONSIDER OF THE

SLAVE-TRADE,

1790.

ABRIDGMENT

OF THE

MINUTES OF THE EVIDENCE,

TAKEN BEFORE A

COMMITTEE OF THE WHOLE HOUSE.

TO WHOM IT WAS REFERRED TO CONSIDER OF THE

SLAVE-TRADE, 1790.

Witneſs Examined—JAMES FRAZER,

1790. Part II.

Has been 20 years in the African ſlave trade—went out firſt as ſecond mate, afterwards as chief mate, till 1772, when he became commander. P. 3.

Has made (from Briſtol) 4 voyages to the coaſt of Angola, 1 to New Calabar, 5 to Bonny, 1 to the windward and gold coaſt—a part of a voyage to the windward coaſt, where he was captured—another voyage to the windward coaſt, drove from thence by a man of war—went to Angola, where, having purchaſed half her cargo, returned and completed it upon the windward coaſt. P. 4.

In his firſt and ſecond voyages as maſter, to Angola, he reſided on ſhore on Melimba hill—3 months the firſt, and in the ſecond voyage 7 months.

The government is monarchical at Melimba, Cabenda, Loango, and at different other places he has heard—each of which are governed by diſtinct monarchs—whoſe authority, however, is frequently oppoſed by the principal officers.

1790. Part II. These officers have the power of life and death—they punish sometimes by mutilation, but commonly adjudge the convict to be sold. (P. 6.) When sentence is passed, the person in whose favour it is given is generally obliged to put it in execution; and when he cannot, he has often no other redress. In some cases the convict is fined—the fine going to the judge.

Vassals flying from one district, to put themselves under the protection of a master in another, often occasion petty wars—private feuds between particular families, continued from father to son, are another source of war. Many other causes provoke war between the principal men of the country, which the king has not power always to controul.

The number of freemen in the country is proportionally small—many find it unsafe to be free—and for protection, become voluntary vassals, or slaves, to a great man.

There are a certain description of slaves, who, by the laws of the country, cannot be sent out of it; but may be transferred from one master to another, within the country.

P. 6. The crimes cognizable by these judges are:—Blood drawn in any quarrel—abuse of men in power, by cursing in a mode peculiarly offensive in that country—adultery—poisoning and witchcraft; in the latter case, after a summary examination—the accused sometimes farther tried by ordeal, taking pills and a drink, administered by the Feticke doctor—The doctor, it is supposed, according as he is paid, so composing those pills, as to have a favourable or unfavourable effect—if the accused is found guilty, the magistrate pronounces sentence—to be sold, or put to death, if the convict is of the lower or middling rank; and a heavy fine upon such as they cannot compel to undergo the trial personally, but who do it by deputy, and who are too powerful to be reduced to slavery. Having acquired their language in a

great

great measure, he has sometimes attended one of 1790.
these trials for 12 hours. Part II.

The families of the persons sold become the slaves
of the accuser. The fines are paid, either in slaves, a P. 7.
common medium of payment in purchases of large value, or in goods, or in the proper money of the country (which is a grass cloth).

Has understood, that debts of long standing have, P. 8.
by order of the magistrate, been adjudged to be paid seven fold, agreeable to custom.

Debtors unable to pay are liable first to have their slaves seized—then their children—their women next—and lastly themselves, if the debt still remains unsatisfied.

Cannot speak to his own knowledge of any human sacrifices in this part of Africa.

The national productions of Angola are, cassada, calavances, plantanes, bananas, a few yams, a few sweet potatoes, pumpkins, water melons, Indian corn, tobacco, and, though he never saw any, there must be some cotton, as they make a sort of cloths like what are made in the Portuguese islands, but of no value in trade—having been long absent from that country, cannot particularize any other articles.

A little tobacco is produced on the banks of the river Ambris (after being fertilized by the inundation in the rainy seasons) with very little labour.

Has heard of partial famines in that country, and felt the effects of them sometimes—in not being able to purchase sufficient country provisions for the slaves
—these may be occasioned by a failure in the rainy P. 9.
seasons, but oftener by the indolence of the natives; and, perhaps, by the impossibility of preventing their crops from being stolen. The people are professed thieves.

Every article of cultivation in that country has been by the women.

Europeans, trading on the coast of Angola for slaves, have factories on shore at Melimba, Cabenda, and Loango—to which the people from the interior

1790. parts bring down ſlaves, a journey of one, two, and
Part II. ſometimes three months—thoſe they barter for goods,
and ſometimes return with freſh ſlaves in a month or
ſix weeks.

Thoſe brought for ſale to thoſe factories are commonly of three nations—the Majumbas, ſuppoſed to come from a tract of land ſituated from the equinoxial line, to the latitude of 3 or 4 degrees ſouth —the Congoes, from the kingdom of Congo, ſuppoſed to extend from 5½ to 7 degrees ſouth—the Madungoes, from the interior part of the country, and are a long time in coming down to the coaſt; they are ſuppoſed to be Canibals, and, when the queſtion has been put to them, if they eat one another in their country, they owned it, ſaying it was the ſweeteſt fleſh they knew—Of the the Madungoes, few are brought for ſale.

As to the Congoes and Majumbas, he generally
underſtood that the black traders bought them in the
country; and ſometimes they were brought down for
P. 10. ſale by the original proprietors. The number from
thoſe two countries are nearly equal, with this difference, that when a war ſubſiſts in either country, there are ſeldom any ſlaves brought from the country at war. Either from the attention of the natives being by that means diverted from every other object, or that the merchants find it dangerous to travel through the country at the time, war is carried on by
ambuſh and ſurpriſe, rather than by pitched battle
P. 11. in the open field.

The captives thus made, are ſold, and he has had their friends come and redeem ſuch as he had bought ſome weeks after. Numbers of ſlaves are obtained in this way, though but few ſold to him; and the proportion of ſuch ſold to Europeans, ſmall upon the whole, compared to what there may be, upon ſome other parts of the coaſt.

Thinks the greater part ſold at Angola were born ſlaves, becauſe they appear generally cheerful and contented, and ſeldom expreſs any reſentment againſt thoſe

those who sold them. Some Congo princes sold him 1790.
some of their own slaves—and one of them in particular sold him one of his wives (p. 10.)—People of Angola have as many wives as they can afford.— Part II.
There may be a greater proportion of convicts among the slaves sold there than can possibly be known, as they all say they were honest, and knew not for what they were sold. Does not know of any slaves obtained by Europeans, by force or fraud. He has been applied to by some principal men of the country to assist in seizing as a slave, a person who, they said, was condemned for crimes, and had armed himself in defence—but he had always refused. Believes (though he has not known any) that cases have happened among the natives of kidnapping each other—the offender, in such case, if discovered, would be severely punished, as well by the friends of the person stolen, as by the sovereign of the country, (p. 9.) The black traders come to the forts attended by some of the people on the coast as brokers. They examine minutely the goods that are offered them, and if satisfied with the quantity and quality, the bargain is completed. In cases where the assortment of goods has not pleased them, or where the slaves have been refused by the Europeans—has known them sell a few to the people on the coast, at very low prices, and carry the rest back—has seen them sometimes beat and threaten the refuse slaves, who appeared always anxious to be sold with the rest. Those of them who were young did not seem to be under the same apprehensions as the old; from whence he concluded the latter to be criminals, under fear of some sort of punishment. P. 12. P. 13.

Ships usually give long notice on the coast of their intention to sail—the notice given, is loosing the foretops sail at sun rising, and firing a gun.—Supposes this notice is understood even by the slaves on board, as well as by the natives—the slaves appear generally impatient to leave the coast.—The hour of sailing, is indifferently in the day or night, as the wind serves.

Thinks

1790. Thinks there is a trade in ſlaves carried on be-
Part II. tween Angola and the eaſtern parts of Africa.

Conſiders the practice of taking Pawns as a very
P. 14. bad one—it prevails at Angola, the windward coaſt, and believes at other places—but ſeldom at Bonny. People will pawn their ſlaves, children, or other relations, to procure goods—ſome of the great men, will, perhaps, in a fit of paſſion, order ſome of their friends to be ſold—thoſe who are obliged to put this order in
P. 15. execution, will ſometimes deliver the perſon as a pawn, taking his value in return—putting it thus in the power of the maſter to redeem the pawn. Captains of ſhips are ſometimes detained 2 or 3 days after they are ready to ſail, waiting for the redemption of the pawns left with them—which, when the friends are unable to do, they will borrow ſlaves for that purpoſe from another veſſel that is to remain a longer time upon the coaſt, and pawn them anew—has known epidemical diſtempers conveyed by this means from ſhip to ſhip, to the deſtruction of many ſlaves. Pawns are always conſidered as ſlaves until redeemed, and when their friends refuſe or are unable to redeem them, they are carried off and ſold—has ſometimes been deſired by pawns to carry them away, rather than they ſhould be ſhifted from ſhip to ſhip upon the coaſt.

P. 16. Uſed to be dayly on ſhore for 2 or 3 months at a time, in each of his 5 voyages to Bonny, has acquired a general knowledge of the government of the country—has heard there are 17 towns dependent on Bonny, ſome of which he knows—there are at Bonny a certain number of people who are ſuppoſed to have an equal right to be at the head of the government.—As it derives its conſequence from commerce, maſters of ſhips have upon the death of a king, a great influence in appointing his ſucceſſor.

P. 17. There are 9 parliament men, who with the king and a number of principal people of the towns make laws for the time—but at preſent the king, influenced by the prieſts, directs every thing. The greater

part

part of the inhabitants of Bonny are ſlaves—but as 1790.
the ſafety of the town depends upon the exertions of Part II.
the whole—many of the ſlaves ſcarce know themſelves ſuch, until by committing ſome offences they ſubject themſelves to puniſhment—or to be ſold.

A certain number of the inhabitants are univerſally acknowledged to be free—there are alſo a number of ſlaves, who themſelves poſſeſs 40, 50, or more ſlaves, and are allowed by their maſters to carry on trade as freemen. Slaves purchaſed from the interior part of the country may be ſold at the will of their maſter—but thoſe born in the town cannot be ſold out of it, but unleſs found guilty of certain crimes. It is generally ſuppoſed the maſter, from his own intereſt, will not falſely accuſe his ſlaves.

Freemen charged with crimes, are brought before P. 18.
a tribunal of freemen, parliament men, and prieſts; if convicted, he undergoes puniſhment, which is generally arbitrary; cannot ſpeak particularly to the crimes thus tried; ſome of them are, poiſoning, formerly much practiſed at Bonny, but rarely now; a freeman convicted of this was to be put to death, and buried under ground—a ſlave thrown alive to the ſharks—adultery and witchcraft are alſo tried before this tribunal—knows not if theft is—believes it is puniſhed, in a freeman, by fine—in a ſlave, at the will of his maſter. For ſome crimes the convict is adjudged to be ſold; but not out of the country, except in particular caſes.

Slaves at Bonny generally procured by people that live in the Up Country. If there are wars, they go in their war canoes to the places in the Up Country where the fairs are held. The old or unſaleable are ſent back by the Bonny canoes, together with the goods received for ſuch as had been ſold.

Has known no inſtances of white traders poſſeſſing themſelves of Slaves by fraud or force; detection in ſuch an attempt would be attended perhaps with deſtruction, if not with a heavy fine—the black

1790. Part II. traders do ſometimes arreſt men for debts real or pretended, and obtain a judgment allowing them to ſell ſuch perſons for ſlaves.

At Bonny there are generally two prices current for ſlaves—the ſhips preparing to ſail paying higher than thoſe newly arrived. The price is ſettled by the king, the factors, and a captain —, When the king breaks, or opens trade with the ſhip, the aſſortment of the cargo is ſufficiently known to all the traders—the captain uſually goes on ſhore to view the ſlaves in the traders' houſes—at night—if any then taken on board are found faulty, they are returned early next morning. The trader comes on board when he thinks proper, for payment—and then, not before, he and his people examine the goods very minutely.

Never knew an inſtance of ſhips leaving the river Bonny, without giving previous notice, although not neceſſary there.

P. 21. There are many circumſtances by which all the people in Bonny are ſufficiently warned of the ſhips being ready to depart.

The mode of carrying on trade at Calabar, does not differ eſſentially from that at Bonny.

P. 22. The government there is ſimilar to that of Bonny—the town has been for ſeveral years paſt governed by a man whoſe condition is that of a ſlave—his name Amachree—he was obliged to ſupport his maſter for ſeveral years, though his own wealth gave him power over him, and he often flogged him when diſpleaſed.

There is generally a weekly fair at Calabar for ſlaves—they can ſell their canoe boys, which the people of Bonny are not permitted to do, even though they may have been brought from the interior country, as they are deemed uſeful to the country in general.

Believes there are no natural productions in the countries of Bonny and Calabar, which might become ſubjects of exportation—there is a little ivory—and a few cotton cloths brought thither from other places; but theſe are too dear, or of too coarſe a quality—the kings at both places are obliged to keep a

certain

certain number of teeth, 2 or 3 for each ſhip— 1790.
ſometimes they make their ſcarcity a pretence for Part II.
non payment—the cloths come from Benin, the Braſs-pan country, &c.—a little palm oil is alſo ſometimes bought at Calabar and Bonny—but ſeldom more than is wanted for the Slaves proviſions.

Has been often on the windward coaſt—not in every P. 23.
part.

The country in general produces rice, Guinea corn, caſſada, plantains, bananas, limes, pine apples, oranges, and ſuch other fruits as are to be found in the Weſt Indies—has bought ivory at moſt parts of the coaſt he frequented, and camwood at one place.

Ships accuſtomed to ſlave there ſend their boats along ſhore and up rivers; they alſo eſtabliſh factories on ſhore.

Knows moſt part of the coaſt of Africa from Cape P. 24.
de Verd to Cape Negro. The ſoundings are for the moſt part very regular, and the ground favourable for anchorage. Reſpecting harbours, ſays there are ſeveral places where he conceives ſhips may lye with ſafety, viz. Gambia and Sierra Leon, and, perhaps, ſome other rivers on the windward coaſt. There are others at Bonny and Calabar, and believes at Old Calabar. The current of the Congo is ſo rapid that ſhips cannot at all times get in. At Mount Negro, lat. 10 deg. ſouth, there is a very deep bay, open, he thinks, from ſouth weſt to north weſt. The anchorage good—a good rivulet of freſh water—the country, as far as the eye can reach, an arid ſand, deſtitute of all vegetation. There is ſome riſque from the bars and ſhoals at the entrance of Rivers—but believes that experienced perſons may at all times, when the wind permits, go into the river Gambia and Sierra Leon.

On the windward coaſt, between the ſhoals of St. Anne and Cape Palmar, and from thence down to the Gold Coaſt, knows no place where, in the rainy ſeaſon, ſhips boats can land with ſafety. The aſſiſtance of canoes is at that time neceſſary, which are

1790. Part II. alſo often overſet and the goods deſtroyed—it is much the ſame at Bonny in the bad ſeaſon; with this difference, that the Tornado blows from the ſhore on the windward coaſt, but towards the ſhore at Bonny; there are ſome places ſheltered by rocks, where a landing may be effected, and boats, acquainted with the bars, can go into the rivers, but no veſſels that draw much water. The currents are ſo ſtrong and the ſea ſo rough, that no ſeamen are equal to the labour of rowing to and from ſhore. The ſea beats more violently on the ſhores than he ever ſaw in any other part of the world, at the full and change of the moon.

P. 25. It is ſeldom that a ſufficiency of proviſions can be got any where on the coaſt, either for the middle paſſage or while the ſhip is trading; believes moſt Engliſh ſhips buy what country proviſions they can get, though generally furniſhed from England with a ſufficiency for the whole voyage; that intended for the negroes conſiſting of beans, rice, ſome ſtock fiſh, flour, bread, and beef.

The ſlaves while in the hands of the black traders for ſale, are fed on corn or plantains; failing theſe, on the root of the caſſada.

The ſlaves who are natives of the ſea coaſt, ſhew a reluctance at leaving it and their relations, but the number of thoſe is very inconſiderable.

P. 26. With reſpect to the arrangement on board for the accommodation of the ſlaves, and their treatment while lying on the coaſt and on the middle paſſage—Says, on the coaſt of Angola, they are ſo long in purchaſing the cargo, that the ſhip is fit for ſea ſeveral days before the purchaſe is completed. The ſpace between decks is uſually divided into 3 apartments—the ſexes are ſeparated, and the boys have a room by themſelves. The Angola ſlaves being very peaceable, are ſeldom confined in irons—and they are allowed to keep below or upon deck, as they pleaſe—it is deſirable to have them all day upon deck, and engaged in ſome exerciſe—thoſe who ſleep

ſleep in the day, diſturb others in the night, and if permitted to talk then, it adds conſiderably to the heat below. Particular attention is paid to keeping the ſhips clean between decks, and ſome think, (though he is not of the number) that frequent waſhing the floors is pernicious, from the difficulty of thoroughly drying them. 1790. Part II. P. 30.

So ſoon as the ſlaves are brought up, a canvas hoſe, or pipe, is fixed to the head pumps, and conveys the water down between decks, which are ſcrubbed uſually with bricks and ſand, then waſhed clean, and ſwabbed as dry as poſſible. Pans with ſtrong fires, are placed in different parts, which generally dry between decks perfectly in an hour—but the fires are generally kept an hour or two longer—if the weather and time of day permit—tobacco, brimſtone, &c. are frequently burnt below to ſweeten the rooms. Every ſhip has gratings, and moſt have air ports, others have different contrivances to admit air. P. 31.

In rainy weather, though not cold, it is thought unſafe to admit them upon deck, when they deſire it. There are alſo cold fogs and dews which make it neceſſary ſometimes to keep them below; but they are commonly ſo ſenſible of cold, that no reſtraint is then neceſſary—they ſeldom complain of heat while the air is ſweet—they complain often of cold between decks—they will often ſleep expoſed to the heat of the ſun—a proof they can bear heat better than Europeans—they are accuſtomed in Africa to have fire in their huts, at once to keep them warm, and drive away the Muskitoes—they lye P. 32. cloſe together, the face of one to the back of another—this is alſo a common cuſtom among the ſlaves on board—care is likewiſe taken to keep them clean in their perſons, by waſhing and furniſhing them with palm oil, when it is to be had. Particular care is taken as to their proviſions, conforming them as near as may be to what they had been uſed to in Africa. Plantains, bananas, &c., will not keep at ſea; but in every voyage he has made to Angola or to any other country, he had always as much proviſions

1796. Part II. ſions as they could eat, and ſufficient wine and ſpirituous liquors for the uſe of the negroes and ſhip's company — when ailing, the ſurgeon's orders were, and he had free leave, to give them any thing in the ſhip. As good a ſtock of freſh proviſions were laid in on the coaſt as could conveniently be kept on board. It is deſirable, and is their own wiſh, to make their meals upon deck; and, though their food is boiled to a conſiſtency to be eat without, a ſpoon is given to each, which, however, they will ſeldom uſe—they are generally 10 in a meſs—when done eating, they are allowed to drink as much uſually as they chuſe —they have regularly 2 meals a day, and almoſt always a middle meal, of bread, and beef, pork, or ſtock-fiſh, &c.; ſometimes calavances, of which they are in general fond. This middle meal not being cuſtomary in their own country, they conſider as an indulgence. The moſt humane of the ſhip's company are generally appointed to attend the ſlaves and ſerve their proviſions. The chief officers have their reſpective ſtations to attend them. Their ge-
P. 28. neral cheerful diſpoſition is encouraged — they have frequent amuſements peculiar to their country—little games with ſtones or ſhells, dancing, jumping, and wreſtling—they are nevertheleſs apt to quarrel; and it is the character of an African to be implacable.

P. 29. A ſum of money is allotted to the ſurgeon, that he may ſupply himſelf with the neceſſary medicines for the voyage: it is his duty, of which he is often reminded, to inquire every morning into the ſtate of health of the ſlaves. For the ſick ſlaves ſome apartment is allotted where they are leaſt likely to be moleſted. The maſter and officers are intereſted in the health and ſafety of the ſlaves. Should any die, the ſurgeon loſes his head money, which is a fee of a ſhilling for each ſlave ſold, paid out of the proceeds of the cargo; and the captain his commiſſion of ſo much per cent. upon the groſs or nett produce of the cargo, according to agreement with his owner.

Should

Should the ſlaves be brought to market in a ſickly 1790.
ſtate, the officers, 1ſt and 2d mates and ſurgeon, will Part II.
loſe upon their privilege ſlaves, for which they are paid at the average rate of the cargo. The captain alſo had formerly privilege ſlaves and coaſt commiſ- P. 30.
ſions; but the mode of paying him by a commiſſion on the proceeds of the cargo in the Weſt Indies is now moſt general, and deemed the moſt equitable, as making the owner's and maſter's intereſts reciprocal.

The climate of the coaſt of Angola generally conſidered healthy; but the change of the ſeaſons P. 31.
have a ſimilar effect upon the conſtitution as in this country, and affects natives as well as ſtrangers—frequently had ſevere illneſſes himſelf, but never P. 32.
loſt any of his crew or ſlaves there.

The weather to be met with from thence to the Weſt Indies depends upon the ſeaſon at leaving the coaſt, but in general the paſſages from Angola are ſafe and ſure.

In the ſhips which he has ſailed in from Angola the mortality has been very moderate, either among the ſlaves or the crew.

Made two voyages as ſecond and chief mate from Angola; one in the Amelia of Briſtol, the other in P. 33.
the Polly, both commanded by Capt. Thomas Duncan. In the Polly (cannot ſpeak to her tonnage) they purchaſed nearly 500 ſlaves; the mortality believes was very ſmall; average price very high—this voyage concluded in 1772.

Commanded the ſhip Catherine in 1772; made 2 voyages from Angola to South Carolina; her tonnage about 140 by regiſter; purchaſed upwards of 80 ſlaves; loſt about 8 on the coaſt; on the middle paſſage, as far as he recollects, the loſs very moderate; loſt one ſeaman on the middle paſſage, and a boy at Charleſtown.

In ſecond voyage purchaſed upwards of 300 ſlaves; was not permitted to ſell them in Carolina; obliged to return to the Weſt Indies; ſhip in a diſ-

1790. Part II. treſſed condition, nearly foundered at ſea; loſt, if he recollects right, 2 or 3 ſlaves upon the coaſt; mortality at ſea very trifling till the ſhip became leaky; cannot ſpeak to the exact number who died; loſt 3 or 4 ſeamen on the coaſt and middle paſſage.

P. 34. Ships bound for Bonny and Calabar carry generally from England beans, ſometimes rice, flour, bread, and beef, but never in ſo large quantities as to Angola, as the ſlaves have commonly one or more meals a day of yams; except in this reſpect they are meſſed exactly as on the trade from Angola—generally eat the beans and rice with reluctance, always preferring yams, the uſual food of their country.

Being more vicious than the Angola ſlaves, they are kept under ſtricter confinement; ſhew alſo more reluctance at leaving the coaſt; of opinion that white men intend to eat them; ſuppoſed to ariſe from their being themſelves canibals.

Many of them appear half ſtarved when brought down for ſale; likewiſe complain of want of proviſions and other hard treatment in their own country; but as officers are not permitted to go up the rivers, little can be known of the inland country.

P. 35. Ships trading at Bonny generally take in their water there; they can water at 3 or 4 different places beſides—at Calabar there are 2 watering places, both frequented.

Some veſſels call at St. Thomas's for refreſhments; he never did.

Does not recollect the mortality on board the Alexander, which he commanded in a voyage from Calabar in 1776, but it was very moderate.

The mortality next year on board the Valiant, commanded by him, was conſiderable—of about 500 ſlaves, loſt above 100, occaſioned by the meaſles.

On board the Tartar, which he commanded in a voyage from the windward and gold coaſt, of from 270 to 280 ſlaves, the loſs did not exceed 3; the crew 60, of which 2 that were foreigners died on the

gold

gold coaſt, and 1 drowned on the windward coaſt, the remainder he believes he carried in good health to Jamaica; thinks the burthen of the Tartar was 140 to 160 tons; in this veſſel he was taken, and loſt all his papers, of courſe has no documents to refer to reſpecting this or former voyages. 1790. Part II. P. 36.

Commanded the Emilia in a voyage in 1783, begun on the windward coaſt; drove from thence by a French ſhip of war; ſailed to the river Ambris, purchaſed there 140 to 150 ſlaves; returned to the windward coaſt and completed his cargo; had nearly an equal quantity he thinks of Angola and Windward-coaſt ſlaves; mortality on the paſſage very ſmall; reaſon why he does ſpeak with certainty, came to town on private buſineſs, and not expecting to be called upon to ſpeak in this buſineſs, brought no papers with him; was on the coaſt on this voyage he thinks 8 or 9 months.

He made 4 voyages in the ſame ſhip from Bonny: in the firſt, of 490 ſlaves, loſt 50, ſold the remainder at Dominica; the mortality in part occaſioned by the ſhip getting aground on the bar in going out, which obliged the air ports to be ſhut; this was acknowledged by the underwriters, who, upon application, were willing to pay a part of the loſs, but P. 37. there being no precedent to go by, the owners dropt their claim; mortality of the crew on this voyage inconſiderable; they were ſeldom employed from the ſhip, and ſheltered there from the rains and dews by an awning of mats.

In the 2d voyage purchaſed 420 ſlaves; loſt on the coaſt and in the paſſage to Jamaica upwards of 30—the crew 40 to 44, of which he thinks loſt 4 on the coaſt and paſſage.

Purchaſed in the 3d voyage upwards of 400; loſt in the paſſage to Grenada about 40—crew upwards of 40, loſt about 4.

In the 4th voyage purchaſed about 570; ſent off 150 of theſe in a tender to St. Thomas's; of theſe has been informed 5 died, and one of the crew was

1790. Part II. lost by accident. He carried the remainder of his purchase to St. Kitt's; lost upwards of 20 on the coast and in the passage; lost near 20 more while lying in Basseterre road by an epidemical disorder which then prevailed over all the island: of the crew (44 or 45 in number) 3 or 4 died, but cannot speak positively.

P. 38. In his last voyage to Jamaica the mortality on the coast, middle passage, Kingston harbour, and on shore, previous to sale, exceeded 100; the hurricane came on before the day of sale, and drove most of the ships on shore; the slaves suffered much during the bad weather; there was a scarcity of water, and a total want of country provisions; the stock of yams brought from Africa was expended; they were indifferently fed, and very badly lodged on shore, the places appropriated for their shelter being destroyed by the hurricane; had been advertised for sale at two different times, but no purchasers appeared; the disorder which they are usually subject to in their own country, together with the fever that then raged in Kingston, broke out amongst them; mortality, after the ship's arrival, 60 to 70, but cannot speak precisely.

With respect to the additional extraordinary precautions taken with the slaves from Bonny, they (the Brass-pan men excepted) are secured as the windward and gold-coast slaves; the full-grown men are chained two and two with leg-irons and handcuffs; when their number is large, and any of the sailors sick or absent, or the captain on shore, it is necessary to confine them below; so soon as the ship was out of sight of land, he usually took off their handcuffs, and soon after their leg-irons; never had the slaves, even from the gold and windward coast, in irons during the middle passage, except a few who were mutinous.

On board the ships he commanded there was always plenty of provisions and water, but not always the sort they liked best.

He

He once arrived in the Weſt Indies rather ſhort of proviſions, but neither the ſlaves nor ſhip's crew were put to ſhort allowance. 1790. Part II.

As to the crews of Guinea ſhips, there was a greater proportion of landmen before the laſt war than ſince—never knew any exact proportion obſerved; but, ſince the laſt peace, there are many half ſeamen that are ſeldom received into any other trade than that to Guinea. In the Alexander, his crew of 39 was thus made up; 10 officers, 6 able ſeamen, about 15 half ſeamen—the remaining 8 landmen. P. 39.

One voyage with the Catharine he had 14 able ſeamen, both theſe in time of peace; aboard the Tartar, during the war, had 16 or 18 able ſeamen.

It was his wiſh and orders, that the ſeamen ſhould be treated with tenderneſs; he paid every neceſſary attention to the health and ſafety of every individual aboard his ſhip The ſurgeon was conſtantly provided with a medicine cheſt, and had liberty to give the ſick wine, freſh proviſions, and every refreſhment on board—their reſpective meſs-mates had orders likewiſe to give every neceſſary attendance and aſſiſtance. P. 40.

Landmen leſs fit, when grown up, to bear the change of climate than ſeamen and young lads; cannot ſay preciſely whether young lads or ſeamen ſuffer moſt, as too many of the latter come diſeaſed on board the Guinea ſhips.

With reſpect to wages, it has been the cuſtom at Briſtol, to pay from 1 to 3 mos. advance ſterling before ſailing; in the W. Indies, the wages for half the time that has elapſed ſince ſailing from Briſtol, is paid in currency. P. 39.

No part of the crew can be diſcharged in the Weſt Indies, but by the authority of a chief magiſtrate, who muſt indemnify the maſter of the ſhip, who has previouſly given bond of 1500l. and the factor another for ſame ſum at the Secretary's office, that none of the crew ſhall be left to diſtreſs the country.

1790. Part II. Some of the crew frequently apply to attornies at law to obtain their discharge; and the Vice-President of the Admiralty, on the request, usually issues an order to the Captain to comply; the men so discharged, are often a burthen to the country, contracting sickness from idleness and intemperance; no seaman or landman can be forced to receive their discharge before the conclusion of the voyage.

P. 41. Thinks it is neither for the interest of the owners, nor the crew, that the Commander should be allowed to discharge a man in the West Indies; because, in discharging one man, he always conceived that every other man in the ship had a right to the same if he desired it; he understood this to be the custom in merchant ships, and that sailors generally avail themselves of it; for which reason if any offender, seaman or landman, wished for his discharge, to remain in the country, he first made him obtain the concurrence of the whole ship's company in writing.

P. 41. In his last voyage to Jamaica, the sailors became very quarrelsome among themselves, and I discharged from 12 to 14 healthy people, upon condition that in case they were not shipped on board other vessels he would take them again, changing their names, a custom very common among sailors.

Has not generally discharged any of his crew in other voyages, unless compelled by the authority of a magistrate, or an officer of the navy.

Some seamen who have made a voyage with him—have waited till he was ready to go on another, refusing the offer of other employment in the interval. Some, both able and ordinary seamen, have gone 3 voyages, and a few 4.

P. 42. Mr. Alexander Falconbridge sailed two voyages with him, one to the windward coast and Angola, and another to Bonny, and part of a third to the windward coast, when the ship was taken—Mr. F. had always declared that he understood little of the language of the country. In one of the voyages, in which

which Mr. F. was with him, recollects the circum- 1790.
ſtance of a man being brought a-long ſide the ſhip, Part II.
and delivered on board, who he believes, did not
know that he was going to be ſold—but from not
underſtanding the language of the country, cannot
ſay whether the man had been invited off to look at
the ſhip or not. (Says he had no buſineſs to queſtion
the right of that perſon who ſold him this man, as
that might have ſtopped further trade between them.
The fact was known to a number of traders, and the
man was put on board publicly in the forenoon; ne- P. 43.
ver was applied to to deliver him up again.)

In that voyage to Bonny, when Mr. F. was with him, a few of the ſlaves there purchaſed, informed him, that they were taken forcibly or by ſurpriſe; (he means in the manner in which he has deſcribed the Angola wars) many of them owned they were ſlaves in their own country, but the little knowledge he had of the language did not enable him to diſtinguiſh thoſe that were born ſlaves, or made ſuch; does not believe the practice of kidnapping by ſmall parties from 5 to 10, and bringing ſlaves to the black people's houſes, can exiſt at Bonny.

Recollects, that while trading at the river Ambris, a ſignal was made one afternoon from the land, for him to come on ſhore with his boat, when a perſon was ſold and delivered to him, who, being a fiſherman, was accuſed of having aſked a greater price for his fiſh than he ought; he was himſelf the only perſon in the ſhip that underſtood a word of the language of the natives; they told him the man was a great rogue; the principal officers, and the King's people were preſent when the goods were paid for him; theſe officers, as their titles implied, he conſidered as the Miniſter of Finance and of the war department; knows nothing at all of this man's guilt, obſerved that he behaved very inſolently, and heard him accuſed of aſking more for his fiſh than cuſtomary—does not know of any other crime beſides ex-

1790. Part II. tortion charged againſt the fiſherman—they were not obliged to tell if there was.

From his own knowledge while in health, and the report of his officers while ſick, he judged that twice as many ſlaves were returned to the country as he bought—for the reaſons before given—that if they had been kidnapped, a trader would probably have ſold them at any price, rather than carry them back, at the hazard of a diſcovery.

When arrived at the river Ambris in that voyage, Mr. F. was with him—he was told by the natives, P. 44. that his was the firſt ſhip that had been ſlaving on that coaſt for ſeveral years—of which he acquainted his officers. His ſhip was ſeveral weeks upon the coaſt at that time, before any ſlaves were offered for ſale—cannot ſay the exact time—he purchaſed at different times a few ſlaves from the towns on the ſea coaſt—the ſlaves, when no ſhips lye there, are ſent to St. Paul de Loando or Cabenda—Every time he has traded at the river Ambris, if there was no veſſel there before him, it was ſome time before the ſlaves from the interior part of the country were brought down—does not recollect any inſtance at this place, of a ſlave being reclaimed by the government of the country, as having been improperly ſold—but has known inſtances at Melimba—in ſuch caſes, he was always offered and accepted a ſlave in exchange.

Believes the Captains ſeldom or never enquire concerning the right which thoſe perſons who offer negroes for ſale have to diſpoſe of them—believes every Captain would be conſidered as a fool by any trading man, to whom he put ſuch a queſtion.

The ſlaves in general have not a great averſion to horſe-beans—thoſe purchaſed at Cabenda and Melimba always eat beans when mixed with rice, with much ſatisfaction The country about the Ambris produces a great deal of calavances.—The ſlaves he purchaſed there, were fonder of calavances, Indian corn and caſſada, than of any other food—they are not very

very fond of beans, but like them well enough when mixed with rice and ſtock fiſh. 1790. Part. II.

When negroes have refuſed their food, he has always uſed perſuaſion—force is always ineffectual.

Never did hold hot coals to a negro, threatening to make him ſwallow them, if he perſiſted in refuſing to eat—and defies any perſon to prove that he has done ſo. P. 45.

Being at one time ſick in his cabin, the chief mate and ſurgeon once and again came to inform him, that there was a man upon the main deck, that would neither eat, drink, or ſpeak—he deſired them to uſe every means in their power to perſuade him to ſpeak, and aſſign reaſons for his ſilence—deſired that ſome of the other ſlaves ſhould be employed to endeavour to make him ſpeak;—when informed, that he ſtill remained obſtinate, and not knowing whether it was ſulkineſs or inſanity, he ordered the chief mate, or ſurgeon, or both, to preſent him with a piece of fire in one hand, and a piece of yam in the other, and to report what effect that had upon him—he was told that the man took the yam and eat it, and threw the fire overboard—this man was afterwards ſhewn to him, dreſt in a frock and trowſers, which had been given him by the ſailors, for waſhing and mending their clothes—and he ſold for upwards of 40l. at Grenada.

He has ſometimes threatened them, when they were ſulky, and would not eat their proviſions, telling them they ſhould have no yams if they did not eat their beans—has ſometimes found it neceſſary to puniſh, or cauſe to be puniſhed ſlightly, ſome of the ſlaves for different offences—Mr. F. was frequently employed to do this with his own hands—who never ſaid he thought what was ordered unreaſonable, or did it in a manner that ſhewed he thought the puniſhment undeſerved—the reaſon for ordering Mr. F. to do this, was, that he judged him a properer perſon than any other; becauſe in general, he was attentive

1790. Part II. attentive to the flaves.—Says that himfelf, Mr. F. and the chief mate have often been provoked to punifh flaves flightly without any great caufe—their peevifhnefs, perverfenefs, and obftinacy, counteracting moft of his endeavours to keep them comfortable, and relieve them in their fea-ficknefs and other complaints—has with his own hands punifhed failors for mal-treating negroes.

P. 46. Recollects, that when lying in the river Ambris, very fick in his cabin, a number of women, by neglect of locking the gun-port gratings, got out and attempted to fwim on fhore. There were 3 among the number from the King's town at Ambris. Believes they were all taken up again, and brought on board. The fhip was then about a mile from fhore. One of the black traders, who had come on board on fome pretended bufinefs, late at night, contrary to the cuftom of the country, was fufpected of having induced thefe women to leave the fhip.

In the river Bonny, and elfewhere, precautions are ufed to prevent flaves from going overboard;—on the coaft of Angola never knew any precautions taken. Women and boys are never confined.

It was his cuftom, in the river Bonny, to fend the ailing flaves on fhore, when there were but few; and if their diforder required the aid of a furgeon, he always fent the furgeon to vifit them; when recovered, they were brought on board; if they died, they were alfo brought along fide, to be fatisfied that they were not ftolen away. The female which he fuppofes alluded to in the queftion, after fuffering much from fea-ficknefs, and feeming to pine and wafte, was fent on fhore, and left in charge of one of her own countrywomen; was informed fhe hanged herfelf;—all he knows is, that fhe was brought alongfide when dead. She was an Ebo flave from the interior country.

Never underftood that it was frequent with the flaves of that country to hang themfelves.

Never

Never knew any one claim a right to diſpute the right of the great men of the country of Angola to ſell their friends, relations, or families. 1790. Part II.

As he always paid the price of a ſlave for every pawn he received, he muſt have underſtood that the perſon who delivered ſuch pawn, had a right to pawn or to ſell him; and ſuch pawn not being redeemed, it was conſidered as a purchaſe;—but is not ſufficiently acquainted with the laws of the country, to anſwer preciſely to the queſtion, Whether no perſons are put on board ſhips as pawns, but ſuch as are liable to be ſold by the cuſtom of the country. The laws being often made for the occaſion, it is impoſſible to tell for what deſcription of crimes perſons may be ſold to the Europeans. P. 47.

On the windward coaſt, where he has mentioned canoes being often overſet, and goods loſt, ſuch accidents happen more frequently in going on ſhore than in coming off. The ſlaves in general are brought off in canoes, the people on ſhore aſſiſting to puſh them clear beyond the ſurf, when they are taken into the ſhips boats.

Never knew an inſtance of ſlaves confined in thoſe canoes.

He has ſometimes allotted a part of the cabin for the ſick; at other times, part of the boys room.

It is often neceſſary on the middle paſſage, but never knew an inſtance of the gratings being covered and the air ports ſhut at the ſame time. P. 48.

Does not believe it a general practice for ſailors to deſert from Guinea ſhips to ſhips of war in the Weſt Indies; it happened twice to himſelf.

It is common for ſailors to deſert from Guinea ſhips in the Weſt Indies, when ſeamen are ſcarce, and a high price given for the run home;—has heard them often declare, before they left England, that this was one of the reaſons for which they endeavoured to have a higher advance of wages before they embarked.

Is

1790. Part II. Is at present unemployed in the slave trade, but shall be soon.

P. 49. The fines imposed on convicts, go, first, to the relations of the persons poisoned. The doctor is paid by both parties, and shares in the fines, and the King and chief officers have also part of them.

Respecting the treatment of slaves in that country—has seen them at meals sitting round their master.

Never saw an instance of a vessel lost on the coast of Africa; has heard of some, but few.

He used to lay in, for a passage from Angola, Bonny, or the windward coast, from 60 to 80 gallons of water per man, and had generally a fourth of his stock left at the end of his voyage.

P. 51. Does not recollect any instance of Captains being convicted of leaving sailors in the West Indies, and paying the penalty;—never had any law dispute himself with any of his people.

Grass cloth passes for money in Africa as brass money or small change does with us;—has seldom seen a sufficient quantity of it to purchase a slave.—Much of it is destroyed in wrapping up the dead;—has also seen it worn by the natives.

P. 52. Believes persons supposed accessary to witchcraft, are liable to be burnt.

Believes a number of the aged slaves are criminals, or considered as such. A circumstance at the river Ambris, related to him on his second voyage with Capt. Duncombe, makes him think that a number of them are put to death. A Cabenda boy, whom he had with him as a linguist, informed him that a slave whom he had refused to purchase, was put to death in the following manner: The owner, (who was from the inland country) calling the traders and fishers together under a tree, accused him of dishonesty; said that he had run off thrice, and thereby cost him more than he was worth, in the customary rewards for apprehending him; that he gained nothing by his labour; and that the white man having refused

refuſed him, he would put him to death, to ſave 1790.
further expence, and as an example to his other Part II.
ſlaves. This he inſtantly executed, with circumſtances of moſt horrid cruelty.

From what befel this ſlave, who he did not ſuppoſe P. 53.
to be very criminal, they have a right, it would appear, to put their own ſlaves to death; and of courſe any uſeleſs criminal, or old ſlave, may be ſuppoſed liable to like treatment; in which he is confirmed by another circumſtance. Having gone on ſhore in the evening, for the benefit of the air, accompanied by his linguiſt, he was led by him to a ſpot where ſome of the countrymen were going to kill a ſucking child. Upon being aſked the reaſon, they ſaid it was of no value: having requeſted, in that caſe, that it might be given to him, he was anſwered, that if he had any uſe for the child, it was worth money; he finally bought it for a jug of brandy, and it happened to belong to a young female whom Captain Lawſon had bought that very day. Capt. Lawſon thanked him, and carried it on board. On its being preſented to the mother, ſhe fell on her knees, and kiſſed his feet.

The laſt time he was at Melimba, there were ſome Romiſh miſſionaries ſettled at Chelango, but it produced no effect on the manners of the natives.

Did not mean to ſay that the domeſtic ſlaves, or followers, were well fed; they might be ſo, if induſtrious; moſt parts of the country which he has ſeen being tolerably fertile—but never ſaw any man working in the grounds, that being the women's province. Seldom any of them came to his factory, who were not hungry, and glad of the worſt proviſions he had to ſpare. No large tracts that might be ploughed or planted, but here and there very fertile ſpots.

Has been witneſs to a mode of carrying on war
at Melimba between the great men of the country, P. 55.
but no captives were made in it.

1790. Part II. In every voyage he has made, there was always more than room enough for the ſlaves, except in the firſt voyage to Bonny in the Emilia.

The diſorders incident to ſeamen aboard Guinea ſhips, are ſcurvy and fevers.

The ſeamen got at Briſtol for the Guinea trade, being inferior to thoſe of other ports, it is ſeldom neceſſary to give more wages than in the W. India trade; but in general they have had 5s. per month more.

Was a priſoner of war in Niort of Poictiers, France, for 8 months.

Has been ſince 10 months in France, at Bourdeaux, Nantz, St. Maloes, Havre de Grace, Harfleur, and Rouen.—Returned in Auguſt;—made every inquiry he could reſpecting the African trade.

Several French merchants, having all their own veſſels and officers employed, propoſed to him to fit out from this country, to purchaſe ſlaves, under
P. 56. French colours, and carry them to St. Domingo.—Good ſlaves ſell in general, at St. Domingo, for 60l. to 70l. ſterl.—has ſeen the account ſales of ſlaves.—Such friends as he formerly knew on the coaſt of Africa, and are now eſtabliſhed at Nantz, St. Maloes, and Rochelle, have offered him employment for himſelf, and as many of his officers and friends as he would recommend.

Has been credibly informed, that the African ſlave trade has been conſiderably extended in France, ſince the idea of abolition was taken up in England; has been told in France, and in this country, that the merchants of Bourdeaux and others concerned in that trade, pay from 8 to 10 per cent. for money to carry it on. There were 360 ſail of veſſels, whoſe tonnage, on an average, was 352 ts. employed in the African and Weſt-India trade from Bourdeaux;—their cargoes in general are much richer than ours, having more cotton, indigo, and coffee.

Thinks it more than probable, if the ſlave trade were

were aboliſhed here, that the French would carry it on more extenſively than now. 1790. Part II.

Believes, from the number of ſhips laid up in this country, from the late regulating act, the idea of abolition, and encouragements held out by the French, ſeveral perſons have been employed in ſhips ſold from hence, and fitted out from France. P. 57.

Believes it unneceſſary for the Portugueſe to extend their trade, poſſeſſing great part already, and moſt of that excluſively. The Danes, ſupported by Government, have (to his knowledge) tried to extend their trade from the windward and gold coaſt; believes they already have the means of carrying it on to more advantage than the Britiſh, if their officers and men were equally acquainted with it;—thinks there is no reaſon to ſuppoſe the Dutch will ever forego any commercial advantage which they can lay hold of. The people of Oſtend have ſhewn a diſpoſition to carry on every kind of trade that Africa and the Eaſt Indies preſent to them:—The Daniſh W. Indies are in part ſupplied with ſlaves by American veſſels, bought on the gold and windward coaſt, and perhaps elſewhere.—The Spaniſh Government have opened ſome of their ports for African ſhips of all nations, and it is ſaid that the Philippines have attempted, or are trying to commence a trade to Africa, to ſupply S. America;—has been told, that they wiſh to get their officers employed in the Engliſh or other African ſhips, to gain experience.

Is certain, the French have deprived the Britiſh of the trade on a conſiderable tract of the African coaſt, although he cannot prove it formally, from the diſguiſe neceſſary in conducting ſuch buſineſs.

Never made any calculation between the number of ſlaves he carried and the tonnage; there is no geometrical proportion between the tonnage and the places allotted for the ſlaves to lie in, that depending upon the form and conſtruction of the ſhip, few of them being exactly alike;—believes no ſuch idea P. 58.

1790. Part II. ever entered the head of a ſeaman, as apportioning the number of ſlaves to the tonnage.

Has known (to the beſt of his recollection) two inſtances, in which nine-tenths of the ſlaves made no complaint of ſickneſs; has known ſlaves recovered by the care of the doctor, and other officers, without medicine;—every experienced ſurgeon knowing how averſe the Africans are to taking medicine, does all he can to recover them, without giving what to them is ſo diſguſting.

Witneſs Examined.—MR. FRANCKLYN.

P. 78. Gilbert Franklyn, Eſq. a native of England, went to the W. Indies in 1766, where he principally reſided in Antigua till the latter end of 1787. He chiefly ſuperintended a number of negroes let by
P. 79. contract to government by himſelf, and the late Mr. Ant. Bacon, (his partner) in order to attend the ſurveyors marking out the lands to be ſold in the ceded iſlands, and the troops, &c. employed in the ſervice of the commiſſioners, which led him much among the iſlands, from Barbadoes to St. Kitt's incluſive. He lived from 1766 to the latter end of 1767, and from 1768 to 1770, in Antigua; from 1774 to 1776, and from 1779 to 1789, in Tobago. He was about 7 or 8 months, in 1788, in Jamaica.

Was particularly attentive to the negroes belonging to himſelf and his partner, which were about 400. The firſt negroes he knew were in Antigua. The firſt of which he became owner, were bought by his agent, and by contract ought to have been either ſeaſoned, or uſed to the climate. A knowledge of the Engliſh language was alſo required, to enable them to take directions. This obliged them to give high prices for negroes no otherwiſe qualified, as good-ſeaſoned negroes were ſeldom found on ſale, except

except from diſtreſs of maſters; in conſequence of 1790.
which, when a few ſeaſoned negroes were obtained Part II.
for the moſt neceſſary employments, the commiſſioners and others in the ſervice preferred new and active negroes.

Theſe negroes were found, and, in caſe of death P. 80.
or deſertion, replaced at contractors' riſk. The iſlands in which they were being in a very uncultivated ſtate, they were obliged to ſupply them with the ſame proviſions, as the troops, flour, peas, beef, and pork. The quantity was directed by the king's officers. They had rum alſo given them when thought conducive to health. There was an agent appointed to take care of them; and the ſame ſurgeon who attended the troops, attended them at the expence of the contractors.

Except carrying the chain to the woods, which may be an unwholeſome taſk, he believes this work was neither heavy nor laborious. The moſt of them were employed in attending the officers and ſoldiers, drawing this wood and water, and aſſiſting to cook their proviſions.

There was rather more mortality among them than on ſettled plantations. They had ſores in their legs and feet, diſabling them for ſervice, and frequently incurable. They were particularly well clothed; and in order to ſave their feet, ſhoes were provided, till it appeared evidently they would not wear them. Some of them, he fears, were ill uſed by the ſoldiers; and as he had occaſion to complain, and had the ſoldiers puniſhed: he knew of none neglected in illneſs.
He does not aſcribe their mortality to this ill uſage, of P. 81.
which not more than ten inſtances had come to his knowledge.

He bought largely in the ceded iſlands, particularly in Tobago, where, till lately, he had 2,000 acres. He purpoſed cultivating, and by the only practicable mode, the labour of the negroes. He believes there is no other mode by which land in the W. Indies is cultivated, to whatever nation it belongs;

thoſe

1790. those negroes he expected to receive from the coast
Part II. of Africa. If he had understood the importation of negroes was to be prohibited, he would not have bought lands he could make no use of. Believes a great part of the lands he purchased is still uncultivated. There is a great deal of land in Grenada uncultivated—he is well convinced in St. Vincent, the Grenadines, and Dominica—there are not negroes enow to cultivate ½ the land—but cannot say so of
P. 82. his own knowledge. Many of his friends bought land in Grenada under faith of H. M.'s proclamation. He believes in Dominica and St. Vincent's, much the greatest parts of the land sold by the crown under commission is not yet brought into cultivation; but he has never been in either of these islands since 1776. He found the settlement of lands in the ceded islands difficult and expensive—he laid out 40,000 l. in Tobago.

The negroes being much the most valuable part of a man's property, whose welfare are intimately connected with his own interests, it can scarcely be doubted that he will pay every attention to them.

Every prudent proprietor endeavours to study the temper and disposition of slaves; they are therefore treated with kindness and attention. There are some negroes that neither chastisement will correct, nor good treatment reform; such are sometimes treated with severity: but for crimes which most civilized nations would punish capitally, the generality of well-disposed negroes are seldom or never chastised. A prudent master is cautious how he offends a negro of good character; for if dissatisfied, they shew their resentment either by working unwillingly, or frequent desertions. When negroes, therefore, are
P. 83. treated with severity (which certainly is sometimes the case) the master suffers, both in reputation and fortune. In general, therefore, it may be said, that negroes are well treated, well lodged, well clothed, and well fed; well attended in sickness, and supplied with medicines, and even the incurable with every neces-

necessary. This the interest of the owner requires, 1790.
even if not possessed of humanity. Neglect of such Part II.
negroes would dispirit a gang, and particularly affect any relations and friends they might have on the estate.

In the ceded islands, and where land is plenty, P. 83.
they cultivate large tracts for their own benefit, and in such cases neither require nor receive a large allowance of what is called pound provisions. To those who will receive it, the proportion is from 6 to 10 quarts of Indian corn, flour, and guinea corn, or a very ample allowance of yams, potatoes, and edoes. In Grenada, meal of cassada from 6 to 10 quarts, from 6 to 10 herrings, or from 2 to 3 pounds of salt fish, and in some plantations, of beef or pork, are given for a week's subsistence—A sufficient allowance for a hearty man—Plantanes also make a chief part of their provisions, and (when received) they are allowed of these from 50 to 70 per week—they are of P. 84.
a less size than the plantanes of Jamaica. The allotment of land is such that an industrious negro will be enabled not only to supply himself, but to dispose of such a quantity of poultry, pork, and goats flesh, as to enable him to clothe himself, his wives, and his children, very handsomely. If his master opposed his disposition of that property, it would probably occasion an insurrection on the plantation. Thinks he has known where provisions have been scarce, that a master has objected to a negro's carrying his from the estate to sell; but those instances are very rare, and the gang has been shown the impropriety of it. The master does not, in such cases, take the provisions from the negro, or oblige him to sell it against his will; he only forbids his going off the plantation to dispose of it in time of scarcity. If the negro wishes to sell, the master buys from him as any indifferent person; but the negro will seldom sell to his master as he would to a stranger. 3-4ths of all the poultry or pork used by the planter, are bought from his own or other people's slaves.

1790. The crimes, for which puniſhment of any degree
Part II. of ſeverity is inflicted, are generally deſertion, break-
ing open ſtores, and ſtealing rum, ſugar, or ſalt pro-
P. 85. viſions; breaking open negro houſes, or houſes of people in the town, robbing negro grounds, &c. The puniſhments then conſiſt from 20 to 40 laſhes on the poſteriors, ſeldom more. He ſpeaks in general. Exceptions to the rule prove the generality of it. There are cruel, ſevere, and inhuman people, to be met with every where. With regard to the capital puniſhment of negroes, each colony has its own laws. He has himſelf ſcarcely known death awarded, except in the caſe of premeditated murder. Repeated burglaries have incurred no other puniſhment than a whipping leſs ſevere than a ſoldier ſuffers for ſmall offences. A ſingle laſh every morning for ſix weeks, reformed for a time, a negro of his own, who had broke open at leaſt fifty houſes. In two years he returned to his practices, and died a natural death on the plantation.

He does not ſuppoſe a labouring man in Europe could gain his bread if working no harder than a negro. Conceives the labour of a negro ſlight compared with any field labour in Europe. They are leſs affected by the heat of the climate than Europeans; in general they like heat ſo as to ſleep with fire in their houſes. Rain injures them moſt. When rains are heavy in the ceded iſlands, which is frequently the caſe, they are ſent out of the field into their houſes.

P. 86. In the plantations their puniſhment is a ſlight whipping, or confinement in the ſtocks at noon, or after work: they uſually prefer the former. For ſlight offences, ſuch as not coming in time to their work, they are generally ſtruck over their clothes.

As no man chuſes to buy a negro of notoriouſly bad character, the owners of ſuch uſually ſend them to foreign iſlands, or to N. America, at the riſk of receiving but a very ſmall price for them. The time of harveſt is in the Weſt Indies, as in all other countries

tries the time of greateſt labour; but it is alſo that of conviviality and happineſs. The negroes are generally more healthy and ſatisfied at crop than at any other time of the year. 1790. Part II.

However a maſter may wiſh to diſpoſe of a ſlave, it may not always be in his power; the ſlave being mortgaged or under jointure. Mortgages and marriage ſettlements covenant, he believes, in every well-drawn deed to keep up the preciſe No. of negroes ſo mortgaged or ſettled. To keep up that number without importation, is certainly poſſible, for it has been done; but in general otherwiſe. The puniſhments already deſcribed are plantation puniſhments. P. 87.

It frequently happens in offences of a public nature, the perſons offended remit the negroes to the maſter for that puniſhment which he would otherwiſe receive from public juſtice.

One negroe, at leaſt, he conceives requiſite for every cultivated acre in a ſugar eſtate, and the No. on cotton plantations muſt depend on the ſoil and ſeaſon; in favourable caſes one negro is ſufficient for 3 acres—he ſuppoſes the gang not to have a great No. of old people or children, for otherwiſe more would be required.

He cannot from his experience conclude that a ſufficient ſupply of negroes for the cultivation of the iſlands could be had without importation of Africans.

As ſo many reaſons why the practice of keeping up the ſtock of negroes is not general, while ſome few plantations have maintained theirs, he ſtates the unhealthineſs of ſome ſituations; the diſpoſition of males to females; the diſeaſes the ſex is particularly ſubject to; for the length of time a breeding woman ſuckles a child, ſhe has ſeldom two children till an interval of two years; the promiſcuous amours of many; and a cuſtom with the gang women who are diſſolute, and think themſelves handſome, of procuring abortion. P. 88.

1790. Part II. Where the females exceed the males, it ſeldom happens on a plantation that the negroes do not increaſe; he gives, in proof, a companion of two eſtates ſettled in Antigua, about the ſame time, one by Mr. Carliſle, the other by Mr. Mackennin: the former purchaſed chiefly new negro gang women, the latter chiefly young male negroes, with a view to immediate returns from their labour. The reſult was, that at the end of 50 years, when Mr. Mackennie died, he is ſaid to have purchaſed the gang twice over, and to have left it in ſuch a ſtate that a large ſum of money was then requiſite to purchaſe new negroes; whereas on the Carliſle eſtate (then Sir Ralph Payne's) there were very few negroes who had not been born upon it; and ſuch was his ſurplus, that he was able to obtain large ſums of money by letting them out to work on other eſtates. He ſays, the reaſon why Mr. Carliſle's example is not followed, is, that the breeding women imported are not on an average 1-4th of the cargo. Inſtances of plantations that keep up their ſtock, he believes, are very few.

The diſorders of children, particularly that called the jaw-fall, which carries them off within nine days, is another impediment to population; they die early
P. 29. in great numbers, but not from want of care. He found their deaths ſo frequent, and thought breeding ſo eſſential to the well-being of a plantation, that he built an hoſpital cloſe to his houſe, for more eaſy inſpection; here he obſerved their cuſtoms of refuſing their own breaſt to the child, as not good, for three or four days, and getting a friend to ſuckle it; of waſhing the new-born infants in warm water with rum in it; of leaving the children to ſleep in wet clothes, and frequently admitting cold air to them in their hot rooms; theſe he overcame with ſome difficulty, and from that time to his leaving Tobago, had four or five children born, of which he did not loſe one.

The labour of pregnant women is too light in general, from the time they are 5 months gone; they complain of a ſlight labour, and injure both themſelves and their infants by a ſedentary life. Thoſe who work hardeſt and longeſt, have uſually the ſtouteſt children and eaſieſt births; when pregnant women complain they are generally put into the ſecond gang. They are not out ſo early in the morning. They are employed in weeding, planting proviſions, and ſuch light labour. As they encreaſe they are put to ſhelling peas, or collecting proviſions for the pot-gang. He never knew them treated with any want of tenderneſs, even by thoſe who thought a child born on an eſtate coſt as much, or more than a new negro. This opinion, he believes, is not entertained by many. It is now the pride of a manager to ſhew a number of young children in good order.

1790. Part II.

P. 90.

A pot-gang conſiſts of negroes, unable, or unwilling, from idleneſs, to procure and dreſs proviſions for themſelves; it is diſgraceful, except in ſickneſs, to be fed in this gang, as having plenty is a mark of a good negro.

On every plantation of any magnitude there is a ſick-houſe or hoſpital, with proper attendance for the ſick, of whom care is taken; in proof of this, he relates, that previous to the capture of Tobago, part of the ſoldiers from an unhealthy ſituation, became ſickly, and ulcerated in their legs. That, in conſequence, as freſh meat-proviſions were difficult to procure, the gentlemen of the iſland ſubſcribed money to purchaſe and ſupply them, and that ſeveral took the ſoldiers into the negro hoſpitals, where they received the ſame care and attention as the negroes did, they found the benefit from it they expected.

Midwives attend the lying-in women: medical advice and aſſiſtance is given other negroes when ſick; perſons of medical ſkill are annually retained to take care of the negroes, if they fail in their attendance ſeveral times in a week, or to attend when ſent for, they are diſcharged.

P. 91.

The negroes in general have very comfortable houſes,

1790. Part II. Managers kind behaviour to his negroes, so as to gain their affections, while he makes them do their business, is to him, and believes to most people, a higher recommendation than his skill as a planter. One of the first things enquired into is his character in that respect; no person would employ a manager of a cruel character, believing him to be such; such treatment is scarcely possible to be practised in secrecy.

He does not believe the poor of any country live happier than the negroes on the plantations in the W. Indies;—in many cases they have an evident superiority, their labour is slight; good care is taken of them in sickness and in health, and they have no occasion to fear the distresses of their children from inability to labour, but then they certainly have not those means of bettering their condition, which many English poor of industry and genius may avail themselves: perhaps, therefore, a proper comparison cannot be drawn. He thinks their lot in general to be envied by the poor of all the countries he has seen.

P. 92.

There are several epidemical diseases which contribute to the depopulation of negroes. These are frequent in all countries between the tropics; the negroes bring some contagious disorders from Africa; the yaws in particular which none know how to cure; it kills many, and makes others miserable objects during life, yet they are still nourished and protected by their masters. Ulcerated legs is another disorder in the new settled islands; the loss by that complaint has been very considerable.

A child till 10 years old has ½ the allowance of a grown person; after that age full allowance.

P. 93. A negro, properly speaking, considering the distinction of master and slave, cannot be said to have property. Opinion, however, and the conduct of masters secures them whatever they possess in the W. Indies, in a manner more secure than perhaps in any other part of the world. No master dares

dares violate their perſonal property, without being exposed to deteſtation and contempt. Even when the maſter is ruined, and the negroes with his other effects, ſold to ſatisfy his creditors, their property (though very conſiderable) is inviolably perſerved to them; they carry their money and goods to the plantation of them who buys him. Their plantation-ground is not exchanged without making them a compenſation for the crop on it; when they die they diſtribute their effects among their relations and friends without control. Negroes generally conceal their money, and do not chuſe to be thought rich. He had himſelf a negro, who bought out the freedom of his wife from a lady at Monſerrat, at the price of near 80l. and in her name poſſeſſed two houſes at Tobago; he believes he was worth 6 or 700l. he aſked for his freedom, and on his alledging that his property might be loſt to him in caſe of his wife's death, obtained it from the witneſs, who had before endeavoured to diſſuade him from his requeſt. There is reaſon to believe he has ſince loſt above ½ of what he was worth. Many of the negroes are poſſeſſed of a great deal of property. He cannot tell the amount, but almoſt all the ſmall current money of the iſlands is in the poſſeſſion of the negroes. A ſlave he had at Tobago took with him thence to Grenada about 100l. ſter. He gave 20l. of it to a ſiſter at Grenada, to help to purchaſe her freedom, and ſent forty guineas to Tobago, to buy a negroe. He believes it is not common for ſlaves to be themſelves maſters of ſlaves, few owners would allow it; he knows only the inſtance he has named.

1790. Part II.

P. 21.

P. 94.

When he firſt knew the W. Indies, he bought ſome negroes at 26l. or 27l. a head: In 1788 he paid 41l. for the ſame negroes at Grenada, and has ſince heard of a cargo of 402 ſold at Jamaica, on an average of 49l. per head (ſterling). He ſhould imagine the report of the abolition of the ſlave trade has increaſed the price; it had reached the W. Indies before he left it, but few gave credit to it. In Jamaica

1790. Part II. maica he found the alarm great. The idea of emancipation, and the abolition of ſlavery and the ſlave trade, and other reports induſtriouſly circulated from England, made them apprehend a general inſurrection among the negroes might be the conſequence.

P. 95. If Great Britain were to try to prohibit the ſlave trade, ' it would certainly be very difficult to prevent the Britiſh plantations from purchaſing them. If planters, however, could not procure new ſupplies, the labour of thoſe they have muſt be encreaſed, or the produce of their eſtates leſſened; but the encreaſe of labour would effect a decreaſe of the labourers: they would, therefore, run all riſks to ſupply themſelves, while credit or fortune would enable them; and it is probable they would be ſupplied at a cheaper rate than at preſent, from nations which would then be unrivalled on our leaving the trade. To ſupport this conjecture he ſtates that Mr. Hartman, of Santa Cruz told him lately that the Gold Coaſt cargo, in that iſland averaged only 40l.

If the negro trade was ſo effectually aboliſhed that the Britiſh planters could procure no ſupply of Africans, the conſequence to the W. Indies would be a very rapid decline of produce, its extent he cannot conjecture—He believes an annual ſupply of Africans in to be abſoultely neceſſary to preſerve the colonies even their preſent ſtate, without cultivating a ſingle new acre.

He does not know how a proprietor is to ſupply his

P. 96. male negroes with wives, if no Africans are to be brought.

He conceives it not improbable, that the negroes now in the W. Indies, would be very unhappy if they underſtood that no more new negroes were to be brought among them. Thoſe under his care, on the arrival of a cargo, always ſolicited more help; the young men particularly deſire to have wives bought for them.

An abolition of the trade on the part of Great Britain would only operate partially, and not prevent other nations from carrying it on. The public proclamations and encouragements of France and Spain to their ſubjects,

jects, sufficiently prove their desire to extend their 1790. slave trade; it follows also from their opening ports in Part II. the W. Indies and S. America, to slaves imported in foreign vessels, and particularly from the contracts of the French with British merchants, to supply their ships with negroes, on the coast of Africa. P. 128.

The proportion of old, infant, and able negroes in a stock, varies with circumstances. On an old estate, where the breeding women are as many as he thinks they ought to be, the able negroes will be fewer than on a new estate, for which the owner would only purchase such as were fit for immediate labour. He judges, from his experience, that in a gang of two hundred, there cannot be more than 60 or 70 able slaves, with about 20 or 30 capable of lighter work: it will be thought a fine gang, and in good condition, that, exclusive of house servants, tradesmen, &c. can turn from 70 to 80 able negroes into the field.

In explanation of his former answer, which declared one negro at the least requisite to every acre of a sugar plantation, he says, that he does not mean that 70 negroes, the able part of a gang of 200, are sufficient to cultivate 200 acres to be cut for sugar; but to a plantation of 200 acres which are under sugar and provision, and in which only half part of the sugar land may be annually planted. No portion of the 200 acres are appropriated to provisions, which are occasionally planted in all. In cane land, corn is often planted in the rows, and gathered when the canes are young, and preparatory to canes, yams P. 129. and eddoes are often planted. The planters are satisfied in the ceded islands, if 200 negroes cultivate as much land as yields them from 180 to 200 casks of sugar of about 1200 cwt.

In general, there are not rooms for the accommodation of lying-in women in the W. Indies; the women prefer their own houses; when he had once persuaded them to try the provision he made for them of this sort, and experienced the advantage to

them-

1790. themſelves and children, they afterwards were well
Part II. pleaſed to come to the rooms.

For a conſiderable time, the negroes born on an eſtate of Sir William Young's, exceeded thoſe purchaſed, but then fell off, and he believes they have decreaſed. An eſtate of Mr. Blizzard, who followed Mr. Carliſle's plan, increaſed in Antigua; in following this, the witneſs failed of ſucceſs himſelf.—Several eſtates on the increaſe have, from epidemical diſorders, been reduced to the want of ſupplies to keep up this number.

P. 130. Where the number is kept up by births, if five able negroes die, the birth of ten children does not ſupply their room within ten or eleven years, to which add near 25 per cent. for the diminiſhed labour of pregnant women and mothers, and it will be neceſſary to replace the five able negroes by purchaſing others in their room. (The work of the young is not the ſame with that of the adult able negroes, though equivalent to it, p. 132.)

In the ceded iſlands, the negroes were forced to clear the ground for themſelves; they prefer new ground, and when ſome years cultivated, requeſt to have it changed. He helped them uſually with the gang in clearing.

Scarcity is much more decidedly known in the colonies than in any kingdom in Europe; the maſter is the ſole judge when to prohibit the exportation of proviſions from his eſtate.

Runaway negroes are in general ſeverely puniſhed.

P. 131. On his own eſtates, and thoſe under his care, he thinks himſelf particularly ſucceſsful in preventing the loſs of children by the locked jaw. His neighbours are equally ſucceſsful in other inſtances, making the happineſs and comfort of their negroes their principal care.

The negroes had no prejudices in this reſpect which could not yield to the reaſoning and entreaties of thoſe they have a good opinion of, and think ſolicitous for their welfare.

Some

Some land rattoons longer than other; frequent replanting is preferable. 1790. Part. II.

The ceded islands will therefore require an additional number of slaves to continue the cultivation of land already cultivated, without cultivating any new lands.

The negroes prefer carrying burdens on their heads; they would not use wheelbarrows, which were imported for them; they even put them on their heads. P. 132.

Between 1779 and the capture of Tobago, he believes but few slaves were imported into that island, and none thenceforward till after the peace, but cannot speak with precision. During the war, he believes there was a considerable diminution.

The age at which a negro, born on the plantation, should be put to holing, depends on constitution.—Young men, as soon as able, desire to be put into the holing gang; from 16 to 18 he thinks the time when they are willing and desirous of being employed in the hardest work of the plantation. It will take 16 years to acquire strength to undergo the harder degrees of field labour, as holing, turning dung, &c. which please the able negroes more than lighter works; they generally perform these singing, peculiar to negroes, and a proof of their not considering even that labour as severe. P. 133.

Witness examined — Sir ASHTON WARNER BYAM, His Majesty's Attorney General for Grenada and its dependencies.

Lived in Antigua from 1765 to 1770, when he went to St. Vincent, bought an estate, and lived till 1774, when he went and resided as Solicitor General at Grenada till its capture in 1779; lived the rest of P. 97.

1790. Part II. the war in St. Vincent, Tobago, and Antigua. From 1783 till June 1789 refided, as Attorney General, at Grenada.

Owns no land now in the W. Indies but an uncleared tract in Dominica; never intends to fettle. The land he firft bought was French leafehold, the other lands contiguous, from the Crown.

P. 98. He found, to his coft, a continual importation of flaves to keep up the ftock, abfolutely neceffary; and he fhould conceive it to be fo, from 24 years' experience. Every increafed quantity of land, new or old, will require an addition of negroes. Could he have forefeen that the flave trade would be abolifhed, he would not have bought land either in the old or new iflands. Much land is uncleared in the ceded iflands.

Slaves being property, are fettled on marriages, and are the objects of mortgage. In fuch writings he has known covenants to keep up the precife number of flaves, but they are not uniformly inferted; but in leafes fuch a covenant is almoft always inferted. Is fatisfied fuch covenant could not be fulfilled, without buying flaves, beyond what the population would give. This, as far as it goes, would be ruinous to the families concerned.

P. 99. He believes the trials of flaves vary in the iflands. In Grenada, a flave is triable before one magiftrate for fmall offences; for capital crimes, before two or more, one being of the quorum. Since he left the ifland, he underftands a law has paffed, taken from the Antigua practice, by which 3 or more freeholders are to be called in by the magiftrates as jurors or affeffors.

Compared with the punifhments in England on the fame offences, he thinks the criminal flave laws far from fevere.

Whipping and confinement are the only punifhments, by the mafter or manager, which are confidered as legal. The quantity of punifhment will undoubtedly vary with the mafter's difpofition; but any

any abuſe of the maſter's power was always conſidered puniſhable by indictment or information, (ſee p. 118.) If ſuch abuſe was frequent, he never knew it; and, conſidering the nature of the maſter's power, and the variety of perſons who may acquire it, he has always thought abuſes of it not more frequent than ſimilar abuſes of power in England. (The ſlave's comfort, in this reſpect, depends as much on his owner's temper, as that of the Engliſh apprentice does on his maſter's temper, p. 119.) Thinks the comfort of the apprentice and the ſlave depends on the temper of their reſpective maſters, not exactly in the ſame proportion, p. 125.) In the few caſes where he has had occaſion to proſecute for ſuch abuſes in their Court of King's Bench, Court and Juries always appeared deſirous of ſeeing the offenders brought to exemplary puniſhment.

1790. Part II. P. 100.

In general, thinks the W. India laws ſufficient to protect ſlaves in life and limb; though he has no doubt ſome may eſcape who have abuſed their power over their ſlaves. When he was Solicitor General, in 1775 or 1776, a white man was executed for murdering a ſlave, either his, or in his ſervice. A motion in arreſt of judgment was made, on the ground that the culprit ought not to ſuffer death for killing a ſlave; and a contrary practice having ſubſiſted in ſome of the old iſlands, the priſoner had counſel, and the point was ſolemnly argued; after which the Court decided, he thinks, unanimouſly, that it was no ground for arreſt of judgment, and ſentence was paſſed. Lawyers hardly had any doubt about it; and he conſidered the Court's having it argued as a tenderneſs to the priſoner, and to remove any ſuch doubt. Believes, ſince then, no one has doubted that a criminal would ſuffer for the murder of a ſlave exactly as for that of a free perſon.

P. 101.

On his eſtate, and all others he ſaw, ſlaves were at their field work by daybreak; but nurſing women had always an hour or 1½ hour beyond that time. With ½ hour for breakfaſt, and 2 hours reſt in their

1790. Part II. houses at noon, they wrought till the close of day. They then threw grass to the stock, and went home for the night. In crop they work later; and, on some estates, the work then goes on all night and all day, by spells, both of white servants and slaves. As far as interruption of rest, and number of working hours, are concerned, the crop is doubtless the season of severest labour. Negro boilers and firemen bear a heat, without suffering, which to white
P. 102. men would be intolerable. It is universally remarked, that the negroes are most healthy and cheerful in crop.

The only mode he knows of preparing cane-land is by holing, which is certainly harder than most other works; but it is only done by the ablest negroes, and is but a small part of the yearly labour. To an able negro he thinks it cannot be called severe. He has often seen negro women boast of holing quicker than men. When holing, the men have grog, and the women sugar and water, and work not only without repining, but singing cheerfully. On other estates, holers may have extra food; but does not think his had, or desired it. (Thinks holing and dunging, if constant, would be harder work than he should wish to put negroes to, p. 124.)

Labour is most certainly proportioned to the age and strength of negroes; but he thinks the sex makes no difference in field-work. General practice for invalids, and women some months gone with child, to be put to slight work, as weeding, &c., as much for their health as for the work.

P. 103. Conjectures that some works in England must be severer than any done by the slaves.

In the first settlement of St. Vincent the slaves were fed, at a heavy expence, with grain in large quantities; but, after his slaves had completed their provision grounds, they voluntarily offered to give up all their provisions, except salt ones, for Saturday afternoon, out of crop; afterwards grain was only given to invalids and nursing women. In St.

Vincent and Grenada the slaves' grounds are such as 1790.
not to require much imported food, except in Part II.
droughts, when they have weekly 8 to 10 measures (knows not whether pints or quarts) of grain, with 8, 10, or 12 herrings, according to the size, or an equivalent in salt meat, and beef, pork, and flour, at Christmas. The allowance is ample for any slave that will work even a few hours in his ground. If a slave fall off, it is usual to view his grounds. If indolent and incorrigible, he is fed by the master.

He gave children no fixed allowance of grain, but directed the mothers, when they asked help, to be amply supplied, according to their families. His, and he thinks the general custom, was, to give the mothers ½ allowance of salt food for children under the age of 8 or 10. He had no pot-gang; but has heard of them, and that they consisted of negroes inattentive to the providing and dressing of their food. He usually gave such in charge to some trusty negro to see him fed. He thinks this is the uniform practice where there is no pot-gang, unless among the French, in our islands, who, he believes, often take improvident slaves into their kitchens, or feed them from their tables. But, without some such regulations, many slaves would undoubtedly perish.

By the late Grenada act, proprietors are obliged to allot land to their slaves, and guardians are appointed to inspect each estate's provision grounds.

Saturday afternoon, out of crop, and all Sunday, P. 105.
the whole year, were very generally allowed for working such grounds; and he thinks the said act has fixed it from 12 o'clock on Saturday. This time is sufficient not only for raising the necessary food, but also for the slave's carrying to market his surplus provisions and his poultry, &c. Negroes have usually surplus produce, except perhaps a very few idle ones, probably in all gangs. He recollects no instance of a master interfering with the property his slave has acquired by selling such surplus. Cannot remember particular instances and sums; but from the

1790. the Sunday cloathing of induſtrious ſlaves, and their
Part II. comfortable furniture, has no doubt many acquire and ſpend yearly at leaſt from 10l. to 20l. ſterling,
P. 106. which they lay out openly on luxuries and comforts. He knows of no reſtraint, except in rum. (He ſpeaks of field negroes, for he has no doubt that many tradeſmen acquire and diſpoſe of double that ſum, p. 120.)

He has known many ſuch ſlaves buy their freedom, and generally for higher prices than he ſhould have valued them at. (Can't certainly ſay if they were field ſlaves; but is ſure that 1 or 2 who applied to him on the ſubject had been, or were field negroes, when their maſters allowed them to provide for their freedom, p. 120.)

Slaves near the towns ſell graſs every evening, and vegetables on Sundays, for their own benefit; but on other days it is purchaſed of ſlaves ſent in by the proprietors of gardens to be ſold for their maſter's benefit.

Believes King's ſhips and merchantmen are chiefly ſupplied with vegetables, poultry, &c., by negroes, on their own account.

Negroes' cloathing varies, in quantity and kind, with the maſter's diſpoſition; but lately, in Grenada, the minimum has been fixed by law. This, he dares ſay, is ſufficient; but recollects not what it is. But moſt negroes have much more cloaths than the maſter allows. (Field negroes' cloathing is generally ſent from hence ready made; but their finer cloaths are bought ready made in the iſland, or made by themſelves or perſons they employ, p. 127.)

P. 107. Negroes' houſes are wattled and daubed, and covered with cane-tops. But tradeſmen and other chief negroes uſually contrive to get wooden houſes. The negro houſes are quite wind and water tight; but uſually made much hotter than whites could bear. Slaves generally bear a heat that ſurpriſes Europeans. Cold affects them ſeverely. Has often known them baſk in the ſun when hotter than he could

could bear for a few minutes. It is uſual to allow a 1790.
negro, with 2 or 3 others, time to build his houſe. Part. II.
He uſually brought home the materials for him.

Every eſtate has a hoſpital. A ſurgeon viſits the
ſlaves twice a week, or oftener if required. One or
more nurſes attend the ſick. The owner provides
wine and other comforts recommended by the ſurgeon. It is uſual to keep convaleſcents about the
houſe or kitchen, to be better fed than uſual. Negroes generally diſlike going into the hoſpital; but
the practice of allowing the ſick to ſtay in their own
houſes is attended with ſome danger. Never allow- P. 108.
ed any to do ſo but truſty negroes, or lying-in women. His ſurgeon, beſides the yearly ſum of 10s.
for each ſlave, was paid for fractures, &c., and had
20s. for each inoculation.

He remembers no ill effect from allowing the women to lye-in in their houſes. He was more fortunate than moſt people in rearing negro children.
Some months before his women expected to lye-in
they were put to light work; but this period varies
with appearances; ſo that ſometimes a negro woman
is not delivered till 2 or 3 months after ſhe has pretended to expect it. Inſtances may have occurred of P. 109.
pregnant women being puniſhed; but he ſhould
think very early in their pregnancy, or perhaps before it was known. Confinement would be ſubſtituted where ſhe was evidently pregnant.

Thinks there are local laws providing for old, diſabled negroes; but he ſhould think that ſuffering them to beg about would be cognizable, as a miſdemeanor, independent of any poſitive law. Thinks they are, in general, properly taken care of.

The women, on all the eſtates he knew, were allowed to lye-in in their own houſes, and ſuch negro women as they wiſhed were uſually allowed to ſtay with them the firſt 5 or 6 days. She had candles, flour, wine, and any other things recommended. With him, and many others, they were not expected

to

1790. to work till a month after delivery. A ſufficiency
Part II. of old linen is provided for the infants. It is gene-
rally remarked that ½ the children die under 2 years,
P. 110. and moſt of that ½ the firſt 9 days, from the jaw-fall. If they ſurvive that, they ſeem pretty healthy while ſucking. Some time after weaning they very often have worms, which he has known very fatal. Children, as well as adults, have alſo yaws, which immediately, or in their effects, are very fatal. Fluxes, though not very peculiar to negroes, are a great cauſe of mortality, and baffle the ableſt phyſicians, as they have often told him. Epidemics are frequent in the W. Indies; but he does not know they are peculiar to adults. Venereals are common, and he thinks tend to leſſen population. Small-pox, meaſles, chicken-pox, dyſenteries, and lately the liver complaint, affect young and old, and very often are fatal to many, eſpecially the putrid flux, of which he has known ſeveral examples.

Few hurricanes happen without the loſs of ſeveral lives. Their effects are fatal, by deſtroying the negroes' houſes and proviſion grounds.

The annual loſs of negroes varies greatly. Of 100 and odd ſlaves of his own, he has more than once not loſt one adult in a year. In other years he has loſt 5, 6, and 7. He ſhould ſuppoſe from 3 to 4 per cent. might be about the average loſs, even on a ſettled eſtate. In the 18 years that he owned ſlaves, though he had what was thought a very good proportion of births for his number of breeding women, and reared more children than his neighbours, (and mothers and children had every indulgence and attention, p. 112) he was obliged, every 2 or 3 years, to buy new negroes, or ſeaſoned ones, from the other iſlands.

Ventures to ſay, that on his eſtate diſeaſes were leſſened, as far as poſſible, by human ſkill; he concludes that, from humanity and intereſt, all other proprietors purſued the ſame conduct.

He

He always thought promiſcuous intercourſe, the early proſtitution of females, and the abuſe of rum, as the chief obſtructions to population; he adds the too long ſuckling of children, which he knows the negro women are fond of, though againſt the opinion of medical men. Hence, they ſeldom have a ſecond child in leſs than two years. 1790. Part II. P. 112.

He never had an idea that the treatment or labour of ſlaves was ſuch as to interfere at all with population.

It is moſt clearly impoſſible for Europeans to cultivate W. India lands; and a free negro never was known to hire himſelf for any kind of field-work.—Europeans may do carpenter's or other work, under cover.

Thinks cattle are now uſed as much as they can be in W. Indian cultivation; and that the preſent implements are perfectly fit for the work, and adroitly uſed by the negroes. The plough has been much talked of: he knew 2 or 3 very zealous for it, who tried it in Antigua and St. Vincent, but were ſoon obliged to abandon it. (Even if the plough could be more generally uſed, as he thinks it could not to advantage, ſo many ſlaves are requiſite in crop, that he thinks its uſe would not make fewer hands neceſſary on an eſtate, p. 127.) P. 113.

He hardly remembers any importation of negroes into St. Vincent, Tobago, Grenada, and Antigua, in the war. Hence, in Grenada, inſtead of 30 or 31,000, the number of ſlaves before the capture, the firſt return, after the reſtitution, in about 5 years, he thinks exceeded not 27 or 28,000; but cannot be accurate. He believes, the negroes then decreaſed in the other iſlands named.

It depends on the ſoil, whether it is advantageous to rattoon, or re-plant, canes. In Grenada, where the ſoil is ſtronger, there is much more rattooning than in St. Vincent; but generally, in both, they now rattoon to a 2d or 3d year. Formerly, in Grenada there were rattoon-canes above 20 years old.— P. 114.

1790. Part II. The number of ſlaves neceſſary for an eſtate, varies with the ſoil, poſition, &c. Rattooning leſſens the land to be holed, but increaſes the acres to be cut in crop. Many eſtates have moſt of their holing done by taſk-gangs; ſo that he thinks rattooning does not unavoidably leſſen the number of negroes neceſſary.

It is certainly the planter's intereſt to keep up the ſlaves by breeding, if poſſible. Has known people think differently on the value of new negroes and creoles. A ſeaſoned ſlave, though more ſenſible, is thought more apt to be ill-diſpoſed, and a young, healthy, new negro, near as valuable as a ſeaſoned one not brought up by themſelves. But for a ſlave which, if new, he would give 50l. ſterl. he would, if ſeaſoned, and not of bad character, give 70l. ſterl. Probably, moſt of the negro tradeſmen are creoles, and are the moſt valuable. He looks on an African, bought young, and ſeaſoned by 7 or 8 years work in the W. Indies, full as valuable for field-work as a creole; but others think differently. P. 117.

Were it poſſible to keep up the ſlaves by breeding, 15 or 20 years muſt elapſe before thoſe born could be
P. 115. fit for field-work. In that period, the working negroes muſt, in the courſe of things, be diminiſhed near ½.

He heard of a Frenchman who lived long ago in Grenada, pretending that it was his intereſt to exhauſt his ſlaves by labour in a few years; but it was always mentioned as a ſingular abſurdity, and he is ſure no planter acts on a maxim ſo horrid.

He always heard ſeverity deemed a reproach to a manager, and as likely to preclude him from employment.

Induſtrious ſlaves are happily ſituated, and they appear perfectly contented.

He was well informed of a ſlave who accidentally loſt ½ his foot, and was ſent by his maſter to the part of Africa whence he came, and found many relations; but the ſlave refuſed to ſtay, returned to Grenada, and continued, as a ſlave, with his maſter.

Can

Can now ftate all the circumftances with certainty; 1790.
thinks it muft have been before 1779. Part II.

He fcruples not to give his opinion, that flaves, in general, have fewer wants unfatisfied, enjoy more P. 116. comforts, and are freer from fear of want, than the Englifh labourers, and not having thofe ideas which would make their ftate intolerable to Britons, do not feel the pain people are apt to think, from their degradation in fociety.

Befides leffening their comfort, by increafing their labour, he concludes, from obfervation, that as nothing pleafes flaves more than new negroes coming to an eftate, fo, if the fupply was long ftopped, they would grow difcontented, probably mutinous. The report of the abolition had reached the iflands before he left them, and gave great uneafinefs to all perfons there, and, he fuppofes, raifed the price of flaves. The fear of the effects likely to follow the abolition, was one caufe of his felling his flaves when he fold his land.

As many eftates are cultivated by money borrowed P. 117. on the credit derived from the flaves, he thinks fuch credit will be hurt by the abolition, and, of courfe, the means of cultivating fuch eftates deftroyed.

Thinks, while new flaves can be had, at almoft any price, they will be fmuggled into the iflands, in fpite of every regulation likely to be adopted.

He knows of no other inftance than the one he has mentioned, of a freeman having been executed for flave-murder; nor has he heard, in Grenada, where he has lived almoft entirely fince it happened, (in 1775 or 6) of any other murder of a flave by a free perfon. The man fo executed was an underling in P. 118. the Marfhal's office, an obfcure, illiterate man.— Remembers nothing of this character; but that Mr. Porteous, the Marfhal, handfomely feed one or more counfel to argue in arreft of the judgement.— Thinks that the flave murdered was a woman hired by the prifoner, who, having difobeyed him, he re-

 proved

1790. proved her; that ſhe gave him ſome abuſe; that, in
Part II. his paſſion, he ſtabbed her, as was ſtated, he thinks, partly by the deceaſed and by the priſoner's confeſſion; but he cannot ſpeak with certainty.

P. 119. Slaves are hired by the day, month, year, or years. The price varies accordingly, and as the renter is bound, or not, to make good the ſlave's value. Thinks about 1s. 9½d. the prevailing daily hire. He has known ſlaves hired by year, at 10l. per cent. on their value, (the hirer maintaining them, p. 126) but much more has been given, according to the party's neceſſities, and the difficulty of getting ſlaves.

Thinks the maintenance of his ſlaves in St. Vincent, excluſive of proviſion-grounds, was 7l. or 8l. ſterl. for each man, woman, or child above 12; and perhaps ½ as much for a child under that age.

P. 120. Certainly, far more domeſtics are kept in a Weſt Indian than a Britiſh family of the ſame rank; and this prevails much more among the French in our iſlands than among Engliſh planters. He doubts not that an Engliſh family is better ſerved by 2 or 3, than they by 8 or 10 ſervants.

Thinks he had 40 and odd men, 30 and odd women, and 30 and odd children, when he ſold his ſlaves at St. Vincent.

P. 121. The only efforts to inſtruct the ſlaves, worth mention, as far as he ſaw, were thoſe of the Moravians in Antigua, but he did not live there, and only learnt from thoſe who did, that they thought the Moravians had conſiderably improved the ſlaves.

A free negro's comfort depends on his ability to provide for himſelf and family. Many, in Grenada, live well; others, he thinks, have only a bare
P. 122. ſubſiſtence; but thinks, in general, their ſituation may be full as comfortable as that of ſlaves.

Droughts are more frequent and longer in the old, than the ceded iſlands; hence the planters in the latter can feed their ſlaves better than thoſe in the former, ſo far as relates to proviſion grounds. Were not the trade

trade with N. America reſtricted, no doubt more negro proviſions would be imported into the iſlands. 1790. Part II.

The number of domeſtics varies with the planter's family and diſpoſition. Recollects no caſe where he thought extra domeſtics were kept as a mark of ſuperior ſtate. But the thing is much lamented by all. Yet, on conſidering his own caſe, and ſome others, he never found he could well ſpare any one ſlave he employed. Thinks the true cauſe of more domeſtics being kept in the W. Indies is, becauſe it is not eaſy to get a negro ſervant ſo handy as a good Engliſh one. Believes no planter would buy, for the field, a negro who had been long a domeſtic. When a man happens to ſell a houſe negro, it is uſual to let him chuſe a maſter who will not put him into the field; and this from humanity, leſt he might be put to harder labour than he had been uſed to. He believes planters would rather buy new negroes, than domeſtics, for field-work. (Houſe-ſlaves, though numerous for the uſe, would be ſo ſmall an addition to working gangs, and are ſo unwilling and unfit for field-work, that he ſhould think that reſource almoſt nothing. P. 127.) P. 123.

The weight of baſkets of dung varies probably on eſtates, and muſt vary with the ſtate of the dung; but it is ſo eaſy to the ſlaves, who carry that and all burdens on the head, that he has pretty generally ſeen them run or go quickly with it. He does not mean that the ſlaves would voluntarily and conſtantly uſe that pace; but thinks the drivers would not practiſe it, if found unreaſonable. He never heard ſlaves complain of dunging; though he has no doubt they would prefer any lighter work. (Dung-baſkets may be 2 or $2\frac{1}{2}$ feet over the top, ſhelving to the bottom, and 7 or 8 inches deep, p. 126.) P. 124.

In the ceded iſlands, crop laſts from the 1ſt of Jan. to about the end of May; after which the rains uſually fall, that would interfere with ſugar-making. In Antigua, crop may laſt 2 months longer.

1790. In the ceded iſlands, the land is holed and dunged
Part II. from Sept. to Jan. according to the ſtate of other
work. In eſtates that rattoon long, the land to be
P. 125. opened is a ſmall proportion of the whole. Knows
few eſtates well enough handed to do all their holing
themſelves. Thinks, generally ſpeaking, negroes
are ſeldom holing above 5 or 6 weeks, and, perhaps, as long dunging.

Whites, in the W. Indies, work as plumbers, maſons, &c. and many negroes work under their direction. On the whole, he thinks the labour of ſuch whites not ſo ſevere as that of field negroes. The great difference is, that the former are not ſo conſtantly in the ſun as the latter. They do not ſo conſtantly work, but leave it occaſionally to the negroes under them.

Thinks planters would be indifferent whether perſons hired were ſlaves or free, if the hire were reaſonable; but he never knew free negroes ſo hired. Unleſs it were to be frequent, he thinks he foreſees
inconveniences from mixing many free hired perſons
P. 126. among ſlaves. Thinks planters would prefer having
work done by free negroes, if it could be done, to maintaining many women, children, old men, and invalids; and that it would be much cheaper, unleſs the price of free negroes' work were very exorbitant.

Taxes are raiſed differently in the iſlands. He remembers one or more inſtances of a poll-tax on ſlaves of all ages, though a contrary practice had prevailed during the French Government. A poll-tax ſtill exiſts in Grenada on negro ſailors and others not employed on eſtates, to make their owners contribute, as well as planters, whoſe produce is taxed.—It has varied from 18s. to 12 or 14s. cur. per head; and, he thinks, laſt year, ſlaves, under 10 or 12 years old, were excepted.

Witneſs examined.—Alexander Campbell, Eſq. 1790. Part II.

He reſided in the W. Indies, from 1754 to 1763. P. 134.
Has ſince ſpent about half his time there. Left the
W. Indies June 1788. In 1763, he, on the faith of P. 135.
Royal Proclamations, bought 2 ſugar eſtates, not
then ½ cleared, in Grenada, with above 300 negroes,
which coſt him upwards of £40000 ſter. Has ſince
bought 14 properties, in the new Iſlands, with 350
ſlaves on them, ſome ſettled in part, others uncleared,
but ſince partly cleared and ſettled by him. Can't be
exact, but believes, he has bought, ſince 1763, above
1200 new negroes, to put on his properties; and,
ſince then, has ſold 5 or 6 of his purchaſes, with
about 450 ſlaves. While in the W. Indies, he yearly
viſited the other (many Engliſh and ſome French)
Iſlands. From 1766, till now, has had from 500 to
near 1000 ſlaves: Has now above 900 (more than
180 of them children, p. 180) Has cultivated ſugar,
coffee, cocoa and cotton. Journals of deaths, births
and work have all along been kept on his eſtates, and
ſent him.

Thoſe who know the W. India climate muſt think the P. 136.
lands can't poſſibly be cultivated by whites, and that
the manual labour neceſſary can only be done by negroes. It is impoſſible to keep up the ſtock of ſlaves
by births. Would not have bought lands in the Ceded
Iſlands, had he conceived the ſla. trade would be
aboliſhed.

Grenada is thought to contain upwards of 80000
acres, ſome of which has been in ſugar, and abandoned for want of negroes, beſides as much granted,
but never cleared, fit for coffee, &c. (Much land in
the Ceded Iſlands is yet uncleared, p. 178.) He knows
not how much land has been ſold in St. Vincent;
but believes ½ of that ſold is not cultivated; and that
¼ of the land ſold in Dominique is not cultivated.
Both theſe iſlands are very mountainous: but, in ge- P. 137.
neral, all that is ſold is fit for ſome W. India produce.

Has

1790. Part II. Has an eſtate in Grenada, near the ſea, of 320 acres, 173 ſlaves, has long made 250 to 300 hhds. It is ſtrong land and rattoons; ſo that only from 24 to 30 acres is to be holed yearly. On the adjoining eſtate, farther from the ſea, of 450 acres and 180 negroes, more canes are cut yearly, yet he makes not above 180 or 200 hhds. On the next adjoining eſtate, of 460 acres and 206 negroes, he makes not above 180 or 200 hhds. A foot of cane on the lower eſtate yields as much as 1½ foot on the upper; and he makes 3 hhds on the former with leſs work, fewel and carriage, than 2 on the latter. Theſe facts ſhew the impoſſibility of accurately ſtating the proportion of negroes to acres, or hhds.

P. 138. Is certain, not 3 eſtates in Grenada are fully ſlaved, and that at leaſt 15000 more ſlaves would be neceſſary fully to ſlave the lands cleared, and fit for cultivation. Does not think St. Vincent, to cultivate all the cultivable land, above ½ ſlaved, nor Diminique ¼ ſlaved. Believes Grenada and its iſlands contain 33000 or 34000 ſlaves, St. Vincent 12000, and Dominique 17000.

A gang of negroes conſiſts of tradeſmen, boilers, field-negroes, &c. The crop is from January or February, to June or July, according as the eſtate is ſlaved; if underhanded they begin ſoon. Then ſome tradeſmen work at their trades, others help to take off the crop. In 180 or 200 negroes, there are commonly 50 cutters and tiers, 20 or 25 carters and mule boys, about the works and mill from 30 to 40; about the works from 15 to 20, watchmen, &c. about 15. Theſe, from 12 to 15 years old, weed canes, children from 10 to 12 pick graſs. The reſt are ſuperannuated, ſick, or infants. When crop is over,
P. 139. in Grenada, they have 2 or 3 days to clear and put in order their gardens. After that they all weed rattoons and plants till the middle of Auguſt, when many of the ſtrongeſt (40, more or leſs) go to holing, the reſt ſtill weeding. When the land is holed, and the dung carted out by mules they, carry it to the holes

holes, then they plant the land. This, with making 1790.
dung, repairing roads, and clearing the eſtates' pro- Part II.
viſion-grounds, employed the field-negroes, out of crop.

They are commonly in the field from ſun-riſe, never earlier, till ſun-ſet, which never differs ½ hour from 6 o'clock. In Grenada, and, he believes, the other Ceded Iſlands, they have from ¾ to 1 hour for breakfaſt, and, from 12 to 2, for dinner.

A field-negro works the ſame time in, as out of crop. But in Grenada, and the other Ceded Iſlands, they boil ſugar all night, and commonly have 3 ſpells of boilers, mill people, &c. which are changed at midnight; ſo that only every 3d night, they loſe their 6 hours reſt. On fully ſlaved eſtates, there are often 4 ſpells.

The cutting of canes is not very hard, tying them eaſy; the feeding the mills and fires are the moſt laborious. The reſt of the work is very eaſy. On the P. 140.
whole, thinks the negroes are moſt healthy in, and like the crop beſt. Never knew them complain of work then. The mill-gang commonly ſing all night. Certainly labour in crop is the hardeſt, as ½ their time, out of crop, is weeding. Holing is the moſt ſevere work out of crop.

A baſket of dung for the ſtrong, holds about 30lb. for the weak about 15lb. Theſe gangs go in a row, the drivers with them. Some put more, others leſs into the baſkets. It is impoſſible for any healthy grown ſlave to think this laborious. Dung, in Grenada and other iſlands, where carts and mules with P. 141.
baſkets can go, is carried out by them, univerſally, and the negroes ſeldom have above 200 yards to carry it to the holes.

In Grenada, they gave no proviſion to the healthy (except herrings or ſalt fiſh) unleſs their grounds fail them, and if ſo, they give no more food at one time than another. They often give holers weak grog twice a-day. Holing does not occaſion ſickneſs. Negroes ſeem fond of it, and commonly ſing at it. He

1790. Part II. knows ſeveral taſk-gangs who hole, all the year, by taſk-work, equally healthy with thoſe employed in other works. Nor does he think holing ſo hard as mowing, and other works here. The work of field-negroes much eaſier than the common labour here.

Negroes are fed differently in different Iſlands. In Grenada, where eſtates are large, and have much
P. 142. new ground, they have as much land as they can work, to maintain themſelves and ſell the ſurplus, as it has been univerſally conſidered the greateſt benefit to a planter, that his ſlaves ſhould have plenty, and the more money they got, the more attached they were. They have an afternoon weekly, to work their grounds, and the manager or overſeer calls over the liſt, twice a day, to ſee who were in their grounds, and always on Sunday morning, 9 o'clock, when the negroes were ordered into their grounds, except ſuch as had paſſports, to go to market, or church, or to ſee their countrymen, which he never knew refuſed, when there was occaſion. The manager ſometimes, and the overſeers twice, weekly, viewed the negro-gardens, and always gave an allowance, and often further time, to ſuch whoſe gardens were neglected, or when there was not ſufficient food in them. If negroes had not ſufficient grounds, they would rob their neighbours, and might revolt; and it is of the greateſt conſequence that all the negroes be properly fed. As ſome were not ſo attentive to their intereſt as others, the Grenada legiſlature paſſed a law for inſpecting negro grounds, in 1766, and another in 1788, inſerted in the P. Coun-
P. 143. cil's Report. Negroes may raiſe poultry and hogs, and ſell them for the beſt price they can get. (They are forced to labour at their own ground, p. 179).

They raiſe, for their own uſe, or for ſale, in Grenada and the Ceded Iſlands, plantanes and fig-bananas, caſſada, yams, &c. &c. alſo cabbages, ſhallots, &c. likewiſe pine-apples, water-melons, &c. Every one of theſe the negroes have in their grounds, at ſome time or other of the year. Very little labour

bour in planting them, and they only require 2 or 3 weedings, which can be done by the children. Plantanes are very fruitful, 3 or 4 weedings the only cultivation required. The negroes need not work half their allowed time in their gardens, and that only out of crop, as the rains ſet not in till May or June, before which they cannot plant. 1790. Part II.

In Grenada, the negroes commonly have from 8 to 12 herrings weekly, or ſalt fiſh in proportion; children and infants have half allowance. They have beef and pork at Chriſtmas. P. 144.

In Grenada and the Ceded Iſlands it is cuſtomary, and, in Grenada, there is a law, that proviſions ſhould be raiſed by the whole gang, for the ſick, and for the indolent who neglect their grounds, or who, from caſualties, have not food enough in them; (repeated, p. 179) and pariſh guardians are appointed to inſpect the grounds; and in caſe of want, the maſters commonly buy proviſions.

New negroes are cloathed, and placed with the chief negroes, and regularly feed thrice a day, for a year or more, till they have enough food in their grounds, and can provide for themſelves. Their firſt work is to plant their grounds, and they are allowed, at times, days to weed them. They generally are allowed to ſell the firſt proviſions they raiſe, to attach them to the eſtate and encourage them. Property they can call their own makes them happy, and gives them a better idea of their ſtate. Maſters very often give them poultry and encourage them to rear them. P. 145.

In general, the negroes ſell proviſions, poultry and hogs. A ſlave who makes proper uſe of his time, may ſell produce to the value of from £7 to £15 ſter. yearly. Some induſtrious negroes, who have good land, often ſell from £30. to £40 ſter. Slaves with children have a greater proportion of land than ſingle ſlaves; and, he believes, in the Ceded Iſlands, ½ the current ſpecie is the property of the negroes.

1790. Part II. Negroes are naturally fond of gay drefs, and tho' allowed fufficient working day cloaths, they buy fine cloaths for Sundays. It is very common, in Grenada and the Ceded Iflands, to fee field-negroes in white dimity jackets and breeches, and fine Holland fhirts; and the women in muflins, and 4 or 5 India muflin Handkerchiefs on their heads, at 8 or 10 fh. each. He has often feen flaves give feafts to
P. 146. 100 or 200 other flaves, with every rarity and wines, which he could not have given for £ 60 fter. and they very often borrow their mafter's plate and linen to entertain their friends. Thefe feafts are very frequent amongft the flaves. When large hogs are killed by the plantation-negroes, they are commonly fold to the reft, in fmall quantities.

Negroes with families, or fingle ones, who wifh for houfes, are affifted by their mafters to build them. They are commonly from 25 to 30 feet long, from 12 to 15 feet broad, the fides and tops covered with wild cane, and thatched with cane-tops. They are warmer, drier, and efteemed healthier, than if boarded. At one end there is a hog-pen outfide, and at the other a hen-rooft.

Knows no where a greater proportion of able, experienced, medical men, than in the W. Indies. There are about 40 in Grenada, where they are allowed 7fh. 6d. cur. for each flave, young and old, and paid befides for fractures and operations, and 20fh. cur. per head for inoculation. Sick flaves are immediately fent into the hofpital, where 2 nurfes always attend to nurfe and give them phyfick. The Doctor, if not refident, always vifits them thrice a week and oftener, if neceffary, and the owner or manager, and chief nurfe, examine all the fick every morning. The hofpitals are conveniently divided.
P. 147. There is one on every eftate, obliged by law to be properly kept. Wine and every neceffary is generally found for the fick. Believes the plantation hofpitals, in Grenada, are generally as well attended as thofe in England. If the leaft fore appears on a ne groe's

groe's leg, he is laid up, as it is difficult to cure sores without confinement. Negroes are regularly fed in the hospital. They often remain a day or two in the hospital, with only a dry skin. 1790. Part II.

An estate of 3 or 400 acres, with sufficient slaves and stock, may be worth 30 or £ 40000 ster. The manager ought to have sense, humanity and good conduct. He must study the slaves tempers, and know the care of stock and land, so that he should possess the first abilities. It is the owners interest and care to get such a man. Planters, knowing it the chief point to have the negroes in good heart, look first to his humanity, without which no planter would employ his brother. Managers in Grenada, and the Ceded Islands, have commonly from £ 150 to £ 300 per Annum, which, with the provisions and stock they raise, enables them to live well, and to save most of their wages. If humane, they are generally as much respected as owners, and very often become owners. Are very often gentlemen's sons from Europe, who, having experienced, as overseers, the management of slaves and manufacture of produce, become managers.

Negroes are generally subject to thieving and drinking; and a number of ill disposed negroes coming from Africa often break open stores and rum cellars, steal provisions, quarrel, and run away. These are the causes generally for which masters punish them. All estates are obliged to guard negro gardens, &c. In Grenada, by law, owners or managers cannot order above 39 lashes, on the breech, for any one crime—and overseers cannot themselves punish, or order above 12 lashes. Plantation-punishment is not so severe as 50 lashes given to a soldier, and is soon cured. Great crimes are often forgiven to negroes who have not been punished before, because after several floggings, they consider it as little punishment. Good negroes feel the disgrace more than the whipping. Whipping are more frequent on some estates than others. Owners or managers seldom or P. 148.

ever

1790. Part II. ever puniſh for ſmall crimes; but it is ſometimes requiſite to puniſh, but not too ſeverely—it is the owners intereſt not to puniſh ſo ſeverely as to keep negroes from working: nor did he ever ſee a puniſhment which he could call very ſevere, or more than the P. 149. negro could bear. In the W. Indies, as every where elſe, ſome are more indulgent than others; but he never remembers to have ſeen any cruelties, tho' he has heard of owners ſeverer than others.

In 10 years, ending 1788, he ſaw no beggars or miſerable objects, except at Barbadoes, where he ſaw many whites of that deſcription, ſome ſerving free negroes and ſlaves, who pay a weekly ſum to their maſters.

French domeſticks are very often made companions by their owners. Many of them are their maſters' mulatto children. Their domeſticks are generally better treated than the Engliſh; but they do not feed and cloath their field-negroes ſo well as the Engliſh: they generally work them more and puniſh them more ſeverely.

He thinks the French ſlaves conſiderably better diſpoſed than the Engliſh: they are not ſuch thieves. Being moſtly Chriſtians, they have better ideas of right and wrong. Every evening, out of crop (and on Sunday evenings in crop, p. 150.) they meet of their own accord, and pray, and ſing hymns, with fervency and devotion. (The Grenada negroes are equally devout, p. 150.)

P. 150. All the new negroes he bought ſeemed to be in the ſavage ſtate. Thoſe of the Gold coaſt appeared more tractable and induſtrious. They generally ſhewed themſelves off to be bought and when examined ſeemed diſappointed, if refuſed. On ſeeing their countrymen, on the eſtates, cloathed and comfortable, they ſeemed very happy. He knows not that he ever ſaw one otherwiſe. He has often aſked ſome of his ſlaves, if they wiſhed to return to Africa, and their univerſal anſwer was, "No maſter, me know better". They wiſh not to be thought Africans

Africans, and, with them, " Salt water negro" and "Savage" have the ſame meaning. 1790. Part II.

In Grenada, all the creoles and moſt new negroes are Chriſtians, being generally chriſtened 2 or 3 years after their arrival. They often read the ſervice over their dead. They often attend the churches, Engliſh and Catholick. The clergy, by law, muſt chriſten them gratis, and certain times, yearly, viſit and inſtruct them. Believes the negroes in the other Ceded iſlands are equally religious; tho' there is no ſuch law P. 151.

He had an eſtate 2 years, near the Caribs in St. Vincent, and he has an iſland 5 leagues off, where they fiſh. They have the richeſt land in St. Vincent, and have cleared ſome ſpots where plantanes, tobacco, and caſſada are planted by the women. The men fiſh, get crabs, eggs and birds, and make baſkets, which they ſell among the Iſlands for liquors: are quite idle at other times. They have only a rag round the waiſt, and live in the ſavage ſtate they did in Africa. They generally ſpeak French; and there were always French miſſionaries among them till the Iſland was ceded to us; but they never could convert them. He has often ſeen his negroes feed them out of pity. They are free, and their lands have been confirmed to them by treaty P. 152. with England, when they were ſuppoſed to have 800 fighting men. It is thought they have ſince decreaſed; but believes their exact numbers have never been known.

In 1787, he went from 20 to 30 miles into Trinidad, and ſaw parties of yellow Caribs. The women and children had only rags about their waiſts. They ſeemed perfectly ſavage. The Governor told him they were numerous, and had many parcels of the richeſt land in the Iſland, but not cultivated, except with a few plantane and orange-trees near their houſes which were temporary, as they often changed P. 153. their grounds: alſo that tho' that Iſland was one of the firſt ſettled by the Spaniards, yet the prieſts, with

1790. with all their zeal, never could convert the yellow
Part. II. Caribs. They are free.

Moſt of the free negroes in the Iſlands, have been freed by gift. He has known many repent of their being freed, finding it difficult to ſupport themſelves and get comforts when ſick, equal to what they had before. The women commonly huckſter, and often receive ſtolen goods from ſlaves. Some free tradeſmen work till they can buy a negro, and then leave off. Some live idle on wenches' gains. Never knew a free negro work, nor does he think ſuch would work in the field, for any wages. Their general idea of liberty ſeems to be exemption from work.

P. 154. It is impoſſible for Europeans to ſtand W. India field-work of any kind. Soldiers and ſailors expoſed to the ſun, are liable to diſeaſe. It is cuſtomary to exerciſe ſoldiers before ſun-riſe. Often give overſeers umbrellas to keep off the ſun and rain. White tradeſmen there ſeldom work, in, or out of doors. They direct negro tradeſmen how to lay out the work, and do light, nice jobs. (Repeated p. 173.)

The Ceded Iſlands, being generally very mountainous and ſtony, very little land can be ploughed. Not 1000 acres in Grenada. Steep land ploughed would ſoon be waſhed away. The flat land is moſtly ſtrong clay, and could not be ploughed in wet weather, and, in dry, its hardneſs would make it difficult. Land ploughed would ſtill want ſome negro labour. Lands in the Ceded Iſlands rattoon. The lands can generally be holed by the negroes, after weeding, when they have little elſe to do, and the ſame number muſt be kept to take off the crop. Ploughing would ſave very little, from the difficulty and expence of getting a proper ploughman, the expence of horſes and cattle, and the various ſtructures of ploughs: the charges of ploughing would be double that of holing by taſk-work. Ploughs have
P. 155. often been tried without ſucceſs. Believes the planters would eagerly purſue any mode that promiſed to eaſe their ſlaves. (Believes it poſſible to plant,

after the plough, (without holing) with a good ploughman, but he believes few could plough a furrow ſtraight enough. Knows not that it ever was or can be ſucceſsfully practiſed in the W. Indies, p. 180). 1790. Part II.

Thinks it impoſſible to cultivate a W. India eſtate without negroes attached to it, where 2 or 300 negroes are requiſite for 3 or 400 acres. The ableſt P. 156.
planter cannot tell when the conſtant attendance of the negroes is moſt wanted. Their abſence for a fortnight would be very injurious, and might not be recovered in years. It would be impoſſible, without negroes attached, to hire, lodge, or feed the number requiſite.

Believes women in the W. Indies breed not ſo ſoon, nor ſo long, as in colder climates, ſeldom have above 5 or 6 children, have early and more various connexion, which tends to hinder breeding.

From 27 years experience, and the opinions of medical men, has found, that many infants die of locked-jaw, of worms, and of the putrid ſore throat. Moſt children have the yaws, which, at times, have baffled the firſt phyſicians in England. All the W. India Iſlands are, at times, ſubject to long droughts, heavy rains, calms and cold north winds, cauſing diſorders, and often great mortality. It is generally moſt P. 157.
fatal to the healthieſt, ableſt ſlaves.

In the W. Indies, hurricanes or exceſſive rains, deſtroy the proviſions, from July to November when no ſhips are there; and this country being too diſtant to ſupply them, the ſlaves are forced to eat unripe proviſions, often cauſing great mortality from fluxes, which he has often known attack ½ a gang. Thinks this cauſe deſtroys as many ſlaves as the country diſorders. Formerly they could ſoon get dry proviſions from America; and this evil may be remedied by a trade, in ſmall veſſels, with that country.

Seldom above 3 or 4 years paſs in any Iſland but the whites and blacks are viſited by epidemicks.

1790. Very often an eſtate will increaſe by births for a time,
Part II. and, in 1 or 2 months, loſe $\frac{1}{4}$ or $\frac{1}{5}$ of its ſlaves.
He has an eſtate, with about 200 ſlaves, in the healthieſt part of Grenada, where, from 1766 to 1786, his numbers diminiſhed not above 10: In 1786 they were 12 leſs; in 1787, he loſt 25, moſt of them the ſtouteſt he had, with a liver-complaint. All his neighbours ſuffered equally, and one parti-
P. 158. cularly loſt 47, out of 300, of that diſorder. In 1788, it was fatal, both to whites and blacks, in other parts of Grenada, where it had never been ſo fatal before; but it has ſince been more frequent in all the Iſlands. In the year ending June 1789, his Grenada ſlaves have increaſed 8 by births; but, by letters of October laſt, he loſt, in 6 weeks, 17 by the flux, moſtly able ſlaves. Believes all the Iſlands have ſuffered as much. In St. Kitts and the Leeward Iſlands they loſt a great many ſlaves 2 years ago.

If he could not have bought grown ſlaves to replace his loſs, even 15 or 20 loſt in 170, would have leſſened his crop by at leaſt 60 or 70 hhds. ſugar and 40 punch. rum. Fears, that in ſpite of humanity, rather than ſuffer ſuch loſs, his other ſlaves would have been worked more than if the eſtate had been fully ſlaved, and it might cauſe a greater loſs of ſlaves and crop the next year. But, by buying 20 new ſlaves he ſhould pay this country for manufactures, herrings, &c. duties and freight of 60 or 70 hhds. of ſugar, and of $\frac{1}{4}$ of the rum, above £. 2000, and he ſhould be repaid his loſs in one year; and humanity would be protected, by ſaving his other ſlaves and bringing 20 ſlaves from a ſavage ſtate to be well uſed and made chriſtians of.

P. 159. A weakly handed eſtate, muſt begin crop January 1. and continue till June or July, hence the canes being then watery 2500 or 3000 gall. of liquor will go to 1 hhd. of ſugar; but a full handed eſtate may begin crop in March, April or May, and then 1500 gall. liquor or leſs would make a hhd, with half the labour of ſlaves and ſtock. Newly cleared eſtates, in the Ceded Iſlands, if neglected a year, grow into wood and bruſh 10 or 12 feet high, and if weak-handed, part muſt be abandoned. 1790. Part II.

If the Ceded Iſlands were now fully cultivated and ſlaved, the number of ſlaves would not be ſufficient to continue to raiſe the ſame produce; for now the land there is new and rattoons, and takes leſs dung.

Thinks, if the ſexes were equalized by buying more women, it would ſtill be impoſſible for the ſlaves to be kept up by breeding. P. 160.

His eſtates, as healthy as any in Grenada, having good and abundant proviſion grounds, attended by able medical men, yet, he believes, have loſt 3 per cent. of ſlaves, annually, on an average. From what he knows and has heard, believes the decreaſe in that and the other Ceded Iſlands has been fully as great, and near as great, in the old Iſlands, which are healthier but worſe off for proviſions. (Decreaſe 3 per cent. yearly, moſtly of the able ſlaves, the loſs of labour may be 2 per cent. more, and the increaſe of labour alſo 2 per cent. p. 162, 176). From 1779 to 1784, the loſs in Grenada was eſtimated at 4 per cent. tho' the Iſland was then uncommonly healthy and few whites died. Believes the additional mortality was owing to the ſcarcity cauſed by the war. Is intereſted in 3 eſtates, in a healthy part of Dominica, having plenty of ground proviſions, and a doctor conſtantly reſident; but the decreaſe on them, he believes, has been 4 per cent. No negroes have been put on them ſince 1779. 2 of the works have been abandoned, from the decreaſe, have grown into bruſh and wood, and make not ½ the produce they did in 1779. P. 161.

In caſe of the Abolition, the ſlaves, ſenſible part of the lands growing into bruſh and wood would be unhealthy, and their labour would be harder, would deſpond. Buying new negroes makes the ſlaves happy, as eaſing them and affording them wives. By late letters from ſome of the Grenada legiſlature, he learns that the ſlaves begin to be a little turbu-

 lent,

1790. Part II. lent, saying Parliament would free them, but for their masters. With these ideas the whites might be destroyed in a day. Believes if they knew Parliament meant to abolish a trade so essential to their ease and comfort, and could come at those who should pass such a law, they would not scruple to destroy them.

The Sl: trade, having been almost intirely stopped in the war, the Islands suffered greatly in numbers and cultivation—Grenada lost near 7000, and he believes the others proportionally; and, since then, all our Islands have been and are in great want of slaves. Foreigners have given ½ as much more than we have, and their demand being great, we were obliged to take young and old slaves, setting aside the sick, not being able to get women, and a great many imported are past breeding.

P. 162. The planters creditors are alarmed at the discussion of the question of Abolition, and wish for their money. It has totally stopped loans and sales of W. India estates. The planters holding their property by charters and acts of Parliament, and finding they are likely to be deprived of the only means of preserving it, by acts of Parliament, they consider their estates as in a more uncertain state.

Were epidemicks to carry off ½ the people in this kingdom, the loss could be supplied, from this and the neighbouring kingdoms, and the same may be said of Africa; but, in case of the Abolition, the
P. 163. loss from diseases in one Island, it could not be supplied, from any other, as slaves could not be bought at any price. Hence, in time, the Abolition will ruin the W. Indies and the slaves now there.

His reasons for thinking that, if this country abolish the slave-trade, the other European nations
P. 164. would carry it on and extend it. The French, whose W. India Colonies are not ½ cultivated, have granted bounties on slaves and the ships carrying them. Spain could buy slaves cheaper, were G. Britain to abolish the trade, and has, by a late edict, opened all

all her W. Indian ports, and offered bounties on slaves. By another edict, she has offered freedom to slaves deserting from other colonies. It is well known many English Sl: ships, with English masters and French seamen, have, in the last 2 years, sailed from France, as French vessels, to get their bounties. In case of the Abolition, our Merchants will go to France and Ostend, to carry on the trade with the French and other foreign colonies who, in their turn, will carry slaves to our colonies. Most goods sent to Africa are cheaper in France than England. It is well known, the value of W. India produce, at an under-price, and in a bad year, was £. 9000000, exclusive of exports to Ireland and N. America. Above £. 3000000 in duties freight, and the other £. 6000000 consumed in manufactures and center here.

1790. Part II

P. 165.

The planter, having hitherto considered that he could not be deprived of his property without an equivalent, and seeing his slaves wasting, would think it incumbent on him to get slaves in any way, and at any price. He would be obliged to buy them at the free-ports, and to carry them in small incommodious vessels in which the slaves, in a few days, would suffer more than in a voyage from Africa, and would cost near double the present price. Thinks no Act could prevent the planters from getting slaves; nor does he see, if men of war should seize them, how they could sell them. (Repeated, p. 177.)

P. 166.

Thinks it was stipulated, in the Ceded Island grants, that ½ the land granted should be cultivated, in 20 years, and that there was a penalty for non-performance; but knows of none being inforced.

Most of those who abandoned lands in Grenada were new subjects, and carried their slaves to foreign Islands to avoid paying their debts to British merchants: others from the decrease and non-importation of slaves were obliged to abandon cultivation: others, as no slaves were to be bought, took their slaves off their coffee, &c. estates, and put them on their

P. 167.

1790. Part II. their sugar estates to supply their loss: And some whose slaves had decreased, had not the means to replace them and abandoned their property.

When Grenada was ceded in 1763, the British laws were considered as in force there. In 1764 or 65, a legislature was formed there, which passed laws for the government and protection of slaves; but no law was passed to prevent owners from punishing as they thought proper, it being considered by the legislature, of which he was a member, that no local law could prevent improper punishment so much as the

P. 168. British laws then in force there. All the inhabitants were interested in protecting the slaves, as insurrections might be occasioned by cruelty. The Islands being small, and estates not above 3 or 400 acres, the conduct of masters is generally known. Several masters have been indicted and fined for cruelty, by the Justices, at the Sessions, and one white man was hanged, but whether a master or not, he cannot say.

Some of the many Grenada laws for protecting and managing slaves having been found inadequate, in 1788, a Committee (of which he was one) was appointed to revise and reform those laws. He believes they restricted punishment to 39 lashes, to shew G. Britain, who had been petitioned against the slave-trade, that there was such a law. Thinks

P. 169. the slave was as well protected before as he is by this law; for it certainly was always understood and practised, that the slave was protected by the common law of G. Britain.

The Quantity of slaves grounds depends on their quality and situation. Some having more land than others, give the slaves as much as they can work. Never knew less than an acre given to 6 persons of all ages (exclusive of the common provision-grounds worked by the whole gang, p. 179.) When an estate is said to consist of so many acres, the slaves-grounds are included.

P. 170. In Grenada negroes are not commonly allowed to keep goats. Other things are cheap for that country;

try: Pork about 5d. per lb, fixed by law; a fowl from 18d. to 3s. other poultry in proportion; a roaſt-ing pig 4s. 6d.—all ſterling. Knows no whites who raiſe ſtock, except a little by proprietors, but moſt of it is bought of the ſlaves. 1790. Part II

In the French Iſlands, he believes, the ſlaves have much the ſame quantity of proviſion-grounds as thoſe in Grenada. Has ſeen the Code Noir, and knows the French mode of treating ſlaves. Many regulations of that Code were incorporated into the firſt Grenada ſlave-laws.

French uſe their domeſtics better than the En-glish, but field-negroes of both are on a footing, except that, till the war, American and European proviſions were dearer to the French than the Engliſh, who could and did feed their ſlaves beſt. Cloathing coming cheaper from England, they cloathed them yearly, while the French ſlaves were generally obliged to cloath themſelves, except the domeſtics whom their maſters cloathed for ſhow. The French Iſlands have few eminent doctors; nor are their ſick ſlaves generally ſo well treated as the Engliſh. The French, both in their own Iſlands and in Grenada, work their ſlaves much harder and puniſh them worſe than the Engliſh. But the French now enjoying the American trade, can feed their ſlaves better than the Engliſh. P. 171.

Woollen cloaths, thought more proper, from damps and bleak winds, he never knew given to French ſlaves. P. 172.

Believes the French Procureurs have not attended to their duty to the ſlaves in any one Iſland. Inſurrections have been more frequent in the French than Engliſh Iſlands, as is now the caſe at Martinique, which ſhews that their ſlaves are worſe treated than ours. P. 173.

He never knew but one man in Grenada, who was ſaid to uſe his ſlaves more ſevere than common, but what his property was ruined. Thinks ſlaves are treated

1790. Part II. treated much better than when he first knew the W. Indies.

In most Islands there were laws obliging proprietors to keep a white man for so many negroes, for fear of revolt and invasion, and that proportion of whites being more than what was requisite to direct the estates, white tradesmen were sent from hence to instruct the negroes, which being accomplished, very few whites are employed on the estates, as formerly at Antigua, the wages and expences of a white-man, being double that of a black, the fines for deficiency of whites nearly pay the whole Island expences. He believes the other Islands follow the same custom.

P. 174. Has often changed his managers, but not for 4 or 5 years; except at Tobago, where his attornies have frequently changed his managers, since he left the country.

Owners or attornies generally buy slaves, but with the managers' assistance.

Most managers buy slaves with their savings; but such slaves are seldom kept or hired on the estate he directs. They are generally let to others, the first year, for their maintenance; afterwards they hire them at yearly wages, or in gangs for task-work.

Before the capture of Grenada in 1779, the taxes were partly raised by a poll-tax, sometimes on all slaves, sometimes on those of certain ages: but since the restoration in 1784, the taxes were raised on the produce. On town-negroes, there was a poll-tax from 12 to 18s. cur. per head, according to the exigencies of government. In 1784 a perpetual tax, of 18d. cur. per head, was laid on all slaves, in Grenada, to support the clergy.

P. 175. The roots on which negroes are fed are liable to injury by hurricanes.

P. 176. Domestic and field-slaves are equally healthy: if any thing, the former die faster than the latter, owing probably to their rambling more at nights, especially the young men.

Does

Does not know that the Regulating Bill has in- 1790.
creaſed the price of ſlaves; but it is apprehenſive Part II.
the fear of the abolition, and moſt eſtates being under handed, ſuch as had money or credit to buy, and the demand of foreign colonies being great, prices roſe from £ 40 to £ 50 ſter. for gold and windward coaſt ſlaves, and are riſing daily.

The Britiſh African merchants, having at command Britiſh and India goods fit for that market (which are now ſent to France to aſſort their cargoes
for Africa, at 25 per cent. advance) having greater P. 177.
capitals and knowing the trade better, will certainly keep and increaſe the ſlave-trade, and underſell foreigners.

In Grenada the negroes go to their grounds at 9 on Sunday morning, and return about 12. They then dreſs, and dance, or walk till about 7 o'clock, when they aſſemble to prayers, which they never neglect. After prayers, they paſs the reſt of the evening in their houſes.

Men are uſually preferred for the more laborious P. 178.
plantation-duty.

At the firſt ſettling of the Ceded Iſlands, men ſold conſiderably higher than women, who were not fit for felling trees; but at preſent, eſtates being ſettled and nearly fully ſlaved, women are moſt wanted, and from the age of 15 to 20, fetch full as high a price as the men, generally higher; but, after 25, they ſell conſiderably under the men. Boys and girls, from 12 to 15, ſell at equal prices.

He has a manager and 2 overſeers, on each eſtate, an eminent mill-wright occaſionally, and a doctor attends, but does not reſide. Scarcely knows a ſugar eſtate but has at leaſt as many whites, that number being requiſite. One white ſuperintends each gang, in the field, boiling-houſe, or mill.

In all the Engliſh and French iſlands, he knows, P. 179.
free negroes and mulattoes are conſidered as a nuiſance, as they never cultivate land themſelves, and the women huxter proviſions, ſell rum, and receive

1790. Part II. ftolen goods, corrupting the flaves' morals. Their only ufe is in cafe of invafion.

Thinks the labour now required of the flaves is proper, may be done with eafe, and without hurting their health. Thinks a workman here does more work in 5 hours than the flave in 9.

Witnefs examined—JAMES BAILLIE, Efq. W. Indies,

P. 181. Refident in the W. Indies about 16 years at different times.

P. 182. Purchafed an eftate in Grenada in 1765, and was concerned in the purchafe of another in St. Vincent, which latter was a grant from Government, to General Monckton, and coft £ 33000. The eftate in Grenada was in a very imperfect ftate of cultivation.

Would not have purchafed had he conceived that G. Britain would prohibit the importation of African negroes. Was an attorney for other plantations in St. Kitts and Grenada, and knows the mode of cultivation and treatment of negroes.

His land in St. Vincent is covered with wood.

His purchafe of General Monckton was 4000 and a few hundred acres—Of this about 3000 acres have been fold to different proprietors, and if they can procure African flaves, it may be brought to a ftate of perfection; but fhould the trade be abolifhed, the lands muft return to their natural ftate.

P. 183. About 1400 acres remain unfold, till the prefent queftion is determined. If the abolition takes place, thefe will be entirely left to the proprietors. The land would never have been fold, if it had been underftood at the time that G. Britain would prohibit the importation of African negroes.

Large tracts of land fo fold, particularly in Dominique, are yet uncultivated. Eftates in the Ceded Iflands

Iſlands are by no means in perfect cultivation, and are capable of great improvement, if the proprietors have a market for African ſlaves 1790. Part II.

Large ſums of money have been expended in improvements, and buildings made with accommodations for taking off the crops which the whole of the lands are capable of producing.

Similar improvements have been made on the eſtates bought from the French in Grenada, which iſland never was ſufficiently ſtocked with ſlaves, and the number has been greatly leſſened by exceſs of labour or the French military works during the capture, &c. Thouſands have been purchaſed ſince the peace, but the eſtates in general are far from being ſufficiently handed. Large tracts in Grenada are uncultivated, which may be improved if proprietors are permitted to purchaſe ſlaves. P. 184.

Improvements muſt ceaſe in all the W. India iſlands, without a regular ſupply of African ſlaves. The preſent ſtock is not ſufficient to keep the lands in their preſent ſtate, without occaſional ſupplies from Africa.—Cannot be kept up by breeding—could not do it on his own eſtate, which is a remarkable healthy ſituation in Grenada, where only two whites have died in 24 years. From 1765 to 1771, he was in the habit of improving the eſtate, and increaſed the ſtock of ſlaves from about 140 to 300 by purchaſe. From 1771, till the capture of Grenada in 1779, there was not a decreaſe in the eſtate of above one per cent. per ann. (reckoning the births) though no new negroes were purchaſed. During the French captivity the negroes decreaſed for the reaſons before-mentioned. In the year 1786, a contagious diſtemper, in a few months, carried off 47 of the beſt ſlaves, which number has been ſince replaced by purchaſe, or the cultivation of the eſtate muſt have diminiſhed in proportion.—The P. 185. diſeaſe was a complaint in the liver, and the work of the plantation was in great backwardneſs the whole year it appeared. It laſted from 4 to 6

 months,

1790. Part II. months. No plantation could be better appointed in provifion grounds; there were warm and convenient hofpitals for the fick, and though the negroes had always of their own the greateft abundance of provifions, he always fupplied the hofpital with flour, rice, bread, wine, and other refrefhments. There was a general order to fupply the fick with mutton, and fuch other frefh meats as the eftate afforded. The fick had fuch medical aid as was proper. For the firft 10 years a furgeon was kept for the fole purpofe of attending the negroes, and, during the diftemper, a phyfician went from the town of St. George to attend this eftate, and fome

P. 186. others in the neighbourhood.

Many children die of the Tetanus, or Locked Jaw; but this does not arife from want of care, or excefs of labour in the mothers; for when women are known to be pregnant, their work is gradually diminifhed, till within 2 or 3 months of their delivery, when they pick grafs, and do other light work. During confinement they are comfortably lodged at home, and are attended by able midwives and nurfes. They have proper refrefhments and cordials; (fee p. 202) are allowed 4 or 5 weeks to recover; and it is generally 2 or 3 months after their delivery before they return to the harder labour of the plantation. When in the field, fome elderly women are generally employed in taking care of the children. Believes thefe regulations prevail generally.

P. 187. Negroes are well provided with food and cloathing in all the iflands he has been in; but there is a greater abundance of provifions in Jamaica and the Ceded Iflands, than in the fmaller, when they are more circumfcribed, and the climate more uncertain. Negroes fupply the markets in the Ceded Iflands with frefh provifions, roots, and vegetables, the profits of which they apply to their own ufe. Some of them have property to the amount of 40, 50, 100, or even £200 fterling, which is tranf-

mitted

mitted from one generation to another. Labour is 1790. Part II.
in proportion to ability, and cannot be confidered as fevere, when compared to the labour of the lower order of people in Europe.

Holing of land, which is from Auguft to January, P. 188.
he has always confidered as the hardeft labour on a plantation, during which they have generally a certain allowance of bread, and very frequently fpirits mixed with water.

Punifhments not fevere when compared with the difcipline of the army or navy.

The mortality in the interval between the arrival P. 189.
of the fhips and the fales (which is generally about 10 days) cannot even be eftimated at much more than 1 per cent. on an average, in the Windward Iflands—Knows of no inftance of medical arts ufed to conceal the real ftate of health in the flaves.

Greateft attention is ufed to prevent the feparation of flaves, connected either by relationfhip or friendfhip.

Never knew flaves exprefs a defire to return home.

Slaves in Grenada are generally Chriftians, and in a ftate of comfort and happinefs.

Recollects negro freemen marrying flaves, though P. 190.
they know the children of fuch marriage will be born flaves.

Introduction of new flaves cannot be prevented by any regulation in this country.

France pays a bounty on the importation of flaves into her colonies, amounting nearly to £7 per head. Number of feamen in the French W. I. trade, believes, is upwards of 50,000. Thinks the number imported from Africa to her W. I. iflands, by France, muft exceed 20,000.

Spain is giving every poffible encouragement P. 191.
for the purfuit of the trade in her own colonies.

Infurances are now making on Guinea-men from Bofton, Virginia, and Charles Town, S. Carolina.

A confiderable number of Guinea-men will be fitted

1790. fitted out from Copenhagen the inſtant the trade is
Part II. aboliſhed in this country.

Is of opinion that the groſs value of the W. India and African trade, together, exceeds 7 millions ſterling per ann.

Is of opinion, that if an abolition of the ſlave-trade was to take place for a few years only, it could not be recovered.

P. 192. The abolition of the trade would throw ſlaves in the W. Indies into a ſtate of diſcontent and deſpondency. Every freſh importation is highly acceptable to them. Abolition will produce diſorder amongſt the white inhabitants, and alienate their affections.

Thinks his produce was 240 hogſheads of ſugar per ann. on an average.

Many negroes have purchaſed their freedom.

P. 193. Had a greater proportion of females than were upon eſtates in general, believes they may amount to more than two-fifths, having, when he left the W. I. ſent all his female houſe-ſlaves to his eſtate.

Field-ſlaves are as happy as houſe-ſlaves.

Had a great proportion of deaths among the children within the 9th day, notwithſtanding the ſituation was healthy, and the ſlaves well attended to.

P. 194. Slaves are much better uſed now than formerly—are increaſed in value from £25 to £33 ſterling per head: before the war, to £30 or £40 ſterling. Many cargoes in Jamaica, have averaged lately from £42 to £50 ſterling.

P. 195. Fifty acres of the beſt, out of 400 which his eſtate contained, was allotted for proviſion grounds.

Proprietors of plantations in the French iſlands are much more commonly reſident on their eſtates than thoſe on the Engliſh iſlands.

French field-negroes not ſo comfortable as ours; puniſhment more ſevere; conſumption of ſlaves greater.

The

The number of whites in the French iſlands, is much greater than in the Britiſh; number of white ſervants pretty nearly the ſame.

The Daniſh government have given every poſſible encouragement to the introducing the Chriſtian religion among their ſlaves; and if the government of Great Britain was to pay more attention to the inſtruction of ſlaves, their morals might be very much improved, and it might in the end prove a greater ſecurity to the welfare of the W. India iſlands than people in general are aware of. The Daniſh iſlands, though perfectly cultivated, are under a neceſſity of purchaſing annual ſupplies. P. 198.

Has always conſidered the Regulating Act to be an advantage to the trade. P. 199.

* Lands, in the Ceded Iſlands, were ſold conſiderably beyond their value, and ſettled at a great expence. P. 200.

Plough cannot be uſed. P. 203.

Lands cannot be cultivated by Europeans. Old iſlands more ſtraitened, as to proviſion-grounds; deficiency made up by importation.

There are conſiderable mortgages on eſtates. P. 204.

Accounts of pawns carried off from Cameroons, by Captain Bilby, other Engliſh veſſels ſtop'd thereupon; pawns claimed in the W. Indies, ſent back to Africa, but refuſed. Vide Particulars. P. 205.

The credit of the iſlands is materially injured by the apprehenſions of abolition, in which caſe the ſecurity will come to nothing.

* Prohibition to ſupply foreigners with ſlaves, would much injure the trade and manufacture of Great Britain.

Had a field-ſlave, a driver, worth £ 200.

In Grenada, the ſlaves found there on its ceſſion to us, were all baptized, and continue in the practice of the Roman Catholic religion. And it has an exceeding good effect on their morals. In the old Engliſh iſlands, and in St. Vincent and Dominique, negroes ſhamefully neglected as to religion. P. 206.

Thinks it will require ten years to get any conſiderable return from a new ſettled eſtate.

Never

1790. Part II. Never was on the coaſt of Africa, and therefore cannot ſay whether the negroes imported from Africa are taken from a more happy ſtate to be placed in a worſe; but believes, from information, that they are more comfortable in the W. Indies than in their own country.

Proviſions in the iſlands are of quick growth.

Witneſs examined,—MR. JOHN CASTLES.

P. 207. Reſided in Grenada from 1766 to 1788 (except one year) as a ſurgeon till the laſt 2 years.

Purchaſed ſome uncultivated land, and furniſhed it with negroes from Africa.

Population, he thinks, will diminiſh every year, without recruits from Africa: becauſe negro wo-
P. 208. men are not ſo prolific as women of this country, owing to early, exceſſive, and promiſcuous concubinage. Children are ſubject to the tetanus, or locked jaw, ariſing from an irritability of conſtitution induced by the warm climate; the wound on the laceration of the navel-ſtring, retention of the meconium, bad milk, and ſudden expoſure to cold. No remedy for jaw fall. Fatal epidemical diſtempers.

$\frac{1}{3}$ of the children die within the month. Few im-
P. 210. ported women breed.

Gave all attention to raiſing children on his eſtate. It was his intereſt. Negroes injure their health by
P. 211. night viſits and dances more than by labour. Ill treatment of negroes not the cauſe of the want of ſpecies by breeding.

P. 212. Would not have bought the eſtate had he underſtood the means of ſupplying African negroes were to be cut off. Has kept up his number, but not his ſtrength.

If the Planters cannot recruit his numbers he muſt be ruined.

Condition of negroes much more comfortable than that of the labouring poor in England.

Brought two negro ſlaves to England, who, after ſtaying about 3 months, begged to return. Said they did not like this country; it was dull. They pined after their dances and other cuſtoms. He ſent them both home, where they remain contented. 1790. Part II. P. 213. P. 214.

They were exceedingly ſtruck with the number of beggars in the ſtreets, and uſed to ſay, " Buccra not good".

On their return, one of them (the man) had the option of what trade he would be put to. The woman was hired to hawk merchandiſe about the country. P. 215.

Two males are imported to one female. Loſt by deaths about 6 per cent. per ann.

Planters always go upon the ſyſtem of breeding ſlaves; it is their intereſt. P. 216.

Adults alſo are ſubject to tetanus. P. 217.

Has heard they are not fond of ſelling, in Africa, thoſe women beſt adapted for breeding.

Fancies negroes in Africa do very little work, muſt be habituated to labour by degrees; in 2 or 3 years are ſaid to be " ſeaſoned." Not many die within 3 years, though more afterwards. Relations always ſold together. The loſs of field ſlaves would be ſupplied in a very trifling degree by ſending houſe ſlaves into the field. P. 218. P. 220.

Witneſs examined,—John Greg, Esq.

Was in the W. Indies for about 20 years, from the year 1764. Was in the Ceded Iſlands 2 or 3 times each year, twice in Jamaica, at Antigua, Hiſpaniola, Martinique, and St. Lucia, but reſided moſtly in Dominique. Secretary to the King's Commiſſion, and Auctioneer in diſpoſing of the lands in the Ceded Iſlands. Sold 174000 acres for £.620000, under a covenant for the purchaſer to cut down, clear and cultivate one acre out of 20, every year, till half P. 221.

1790. the uncleared land ſhall be cleared; under penalty of
Part II. paying 5 per ann. for every acre neglected. Vide Grants.

P. 222. The greateſt part of St. Vincent and Dominique remains in wood. More than ½ of each have been diſpoſed of.

P. 223. The lands, in numerous inſtances, were ſold far above their apprehended value.

P. 224. Immenſe ſums have been laid out in buildings and other works, in ſome inſtances more than the purchaſe money. Number of negroes in Dominique and St. Vincent, a year ago, was about 27000. Judges the preſent number inadequate for the lands already cleared, without large annual ſupplies. Some plantations are falling back to a deſert ſtate, from the high price of negroes cauſed by the rumour of aboliſhing the trade. 120000 additional negroes would hardly be ſufficient to clear and cultivate the uncleared lands.

Had it been apprehended that the ſlave trade would be aboliſhed no perſon would have purchaſed theſe lands.

P. 225. There will be a great deficiency of labour, from the preſent full grown negroes growing paſt their work. Has obſerved negroes in all the Iſlands much happier in general than the lower people in England. Recollects no beggars, or deſerted ſlaves.

P. 226. Number could not be kept up by breeding: This not the effect of ſevere treatment.

Effect of abolition would be general ruin of the whites, and deſtruction of the blacks.

Beſides common cauſes of mortality, negro-women plunge in rivers immediately on delivery, and under other improper ſituations, put on wet cloaths, which bring on complaints unfavourable to propagation.

All poſſible means have been attempted to counteract the ſeveral cauſes of mortality.

P. 227. The negroes apply hot linen to the navel ſtring, which produces irritation and brings on the fall of the jaw.

Some

Some eſtates in Dominique were begun to be worked with capitals unequal to the enterpriſe; beſides which, uſurious loans, an impoſition of 4½ per cent. on the produce, and a duty of 30s. on every imported negro, ſerved to complete the ruin of the adventurers. 1790. Part II. P. 228.

French houſe negroes better, field much worſe treated than our own. P. 229.

The price of negroes in 1765, was £. 26 10s. per head. At preſent they are £. 50. Before the report of an abolition prime negroes ſold at £. 35 to £. 38. P. 230.

The relief held out by Parliament in caſes of famine, by permitting the Governor of any Iſland to import proviſions from the foreign Iſlands, is futile; becauſe no ſtores of proviſions are, or can be, kept there. Hurricanes have done great damage. P. 233.

It is the maxim, and the intereſt of Planters to raiſe Creoles.

Witneſs examined,—John Anthony Rucker, Esq.

Is a conſiderable proprietor of lands in Grenada, Cariacau and St. Vincent. P. 235.

Would not have adventured his property if he had underſtood that Great Britain would prohibit the importation of negroes; wiſhes he had not. Has lent large ſums, which he would not have done, had he apprehended abolition of ſlave-trade. Has not ſufficient numbers to keep up the preſent cultivation. Cannot poſitively ſay, whether the ſtock may, in future, be kept up by breeding, having never been in the W. Indies, but is informed by his agents they cannot.

Abolition will have a dreadful effect, as we muſt have recourſe to foreigners to ſupply us with ſugar, which will cauſe a balance of trade againſt Great Britain of 1000000 to 1200000. The loſs of ſhipping would alſo be great.

1790. Part II. P. 237. The credit of W. India property was very bad before the agitation of this queſtion, and it is now grown much worſe. The ſecurity of the large debt from the W. Indies to G. Britain would be materially injured.

The purchaſes he made in the W. Indies were particularly fortunate and advantageous.

The experience of 25 years has taught him the ſtock of negroes cannot be kept up by breeding.

Witneſs examined,—JOHN HANKEY, Eſq.

Is a very large proprietor of lands in the Ceded Iſlands, ſince 1764, has alſo very large ſums outſtanding. Would neither have purchaſed lands nor lent money, had he conceived the importation of negroes would have been prohibited.

P. 239. His eſtate can by no means be cultivated without negroes, nor has he, at preſent, a ſufficient ſtock, nor can he keep up a ſtock without ſupplies from Africa.

Believes the defect of population not owing to ill treatment or exceſſive labour.

Effect of abolition will be the gradual decay and, at laſt, ruin of the Iſlands.

The agitation of this queſtion has injured the credit on W. India property, and if the ſupply of negroes be ſtopped, the ſecurity of the large debt of the planters to G. Britain will be very materially injured.

P. 240. Never was in the W. Indies—W. India credit was very good before the war, and ſince would have revived but for the queſtion of abolition.

Amount of the advances of this houſe on W. India property, was about £ 250000, at 5 per cent.

Witneſs examined,—WILLIAM TOD, Eſq.

P. 241. Is a merchant of London, and proprietor of lands in Grenada and the Grenadines, ſince 1774 or 1775.

—Is

—Is alſo a creditor on the ſecurity of W. India eſtates. 1790.
Eſtates cannot, in his opinion, be cultivated but by negroes. Part II.

Would not have purchaſed, or lent, if he had underſtood that the importation of negroes would be prohibited.

Eſtates have not a ſufficient ſtock, nor could that be kept up without ſupplies from Africa.

Defect of population not owing to ill treatment, nor exceſſive labour.

Effect of ſtopping the importation from Africa, in his opinion, would be fatal.

Has refuſed to lend money on W. India ſecurity, till he ſaw the event of the queſtion of abolition of ſlave trade.

The ſecurity of the debt from the W. India planters will not be ſo good as it was if the trade be ſtopped.

Never was in the W. Indies.

Witneſs examined,—Mr. Robert Thomas.

Reſided about 9 years in St. Kitts and Nevis as a P. 246.
ſurgeon, and attended between 4000 and 5000 negroes annually.

A ſurgeon's attendance expected once or twice a P. 247.
week, or daily, if neceſſary. On moſt eſtates 6s. per head annually allowed, beſides extra charges for capital operations, &c. and night viſits.

Had every opportunity of obſerving how negroes were treated, worked, fed, lodged and cloathed. They are divided into three claſſes or gangs, the 1ſt or great gang able-bodied negroes (excluſive of tradeſmen and watchmen) who do the moſt laborious part of the work. The 2d, or weeding gang, from the age of 12 to 18 or 20, ſuch as are weakly or ailing, and employed in light work. The 3d gang, from the age of 6 to 12, employed in picking graſs for the manager's or proprietors ſtock.

1790. Part II. P. 248. Negroes in Nevis appear in the field about 6 o'cl: work till about 9, when they breakfaſt; at ¼ before 10 reſume their work, which is continued to 12, they are then diſcharged till 2, in this interval, out of crop, the major part of the gang are expected to bring a ſmall bundle of graſs, during crop: the cattle fed with ſliced cane-tops. At 2 o'clock they enter the field again, and work till 6, and about 7, if out of crop, a few bundles of graſs are again thrown. Once a week allowance given out to the head of each family, either at 12 at noon, or about 7 at night.

Women with children at the breaſt have many indulgencies, as coming an hour later into the field, never throwing graſs, retiring to ſuckle their children; pregnant women, on moſt of the eſtates, when 3 or 4 months gone with child, if in the large gang, are uſually removed to the ſmall one, and in their 7th month excuſed from all labour, going where and doing as they pleaſe.—A negro midwife attends the lying-in women in natural caſes, but in preternatural a ſurgeon, who has a handſome fee, about £9 ſterling. A nurſe waits on the woman, when delivered, and her infant, till ſhe can attend to it herſelf; every comfort afforded which that ſituation required, and not expected to work till the end of 4 weeks, and not then if the ſurgeon thought a longer indulgence neceſſary.

P. 249. For the cloathing of negroes eſtates, having a credit in England, uſually ſet a ſufficient quantity of coarſe baize and oſnabrugs with worſted caps and proper hats. Each negro man receives a quantity of baize for a blanket, and of oſnabrug for a ſhort jacket and trowſers, and each female enough for a ſhort wrapper and petticoat, with a like quantity of the baize. The younger negroes receive a proportionable quantity. Eſtates having no credit in England, buy theſe articles of the ſtore-keepers at a high price.

For many of the negroes, who are idly diſpoſed, and not truſt-worthy, the proprietors or managers have thoſe articles made into cloaths, and given them.

For

For the negro infants many owners either ſend 1790.
out annually a couple of ſuits of baby cloaths or, Part II.
if reſident, have them made up for them by negro ſempſtreſſes.

The food uſually diſtributed among the negroes conſiſted of rice, coarſe flour, rye-meal, dried peas and beans, American corn, and alſo of ſalt proviſion, viz. herrings, ſhad and other ſalt fiſh; they had alſo the Iſland proviſion, viz. potatoes, yams, Indian corn, bananas, plantanes and caſſada; but theſe three laſt articles were the produce of their own proviſion ground, their private property. The quantity of proviſion allowed was moſtly from 7 to 9 pints a week for each negro, of any of the above articles, and the ſame number of herrings or ſhads, or a pro- P. 250.
portional quantity of ſalt fiſh; the above quantity was given on many eſtates to every child as ſoon as weaned. This food, in his judgment, proper for the negroes, and though a bare ſufficiency for their ſupport, the weekly allowance is not wholly depended on, the induſtrious having many advantages from their proviſion ground, the produce of which furniſhes them with conſiderable ſums; as well as raiſing hogs, goats and various ſpecies of poultry. Negroes near towns derive advantage from ſelling graſs and fuel to the inhabitants. Hence they have food amply ſufficient for their ſupport, inſomuch that many of them purchaſe fine cloaths, and frequently die poſſeſſed of what may be called large ſums of money to them.

Seldom any reluctance to give whatever the ſurgeon thought proper to negroes in ſickneſs, ſuch as chicken or mutton broth, or even wine, which articles the manager regularly made a charge of to the owner.

The loſs of negro children occaſioned by dentition, worms, eating dirt; alſo the putrid ſore throat, P. 251.
which uſually carries off numbers; but the principal cauſe is, the neglect of the mothers. Has known few inſtances of the tetanus or locked-jaw in children,

1790. Part II. dren, but adults very liable to it from lacerated wounds or injuries in the tendinous parts.

There was an annual diminution of negroes on an eſtate, whoſe owners gave a pecuniary reward and other indulgencies to every mother, who reared her child to the age of 2 years.

Pregnant women during the time of their lying-in and afterwards, certainly not under greater diſadvantages than the lower claſs of white women in this country, being exempted from hard labour during pregnancy, and proper care taken of them after lying-in. See 248.

P. 252. The cauſes of the decreaſe of adult negroes on the ſugar plantations very numerous. 1ſt. The free and eaſy intercourſe of females with males. 2d. The frequent abortions which the women deſignedly bring on themſelves. 3d. The chronical diſeaſes to which women in warm climates are more ſubject than in colder ones. 4th. Putrid fevers, ſore throats, and fluxes, the laſt occaſioning vaſt mortality. 6th. The immoderate uſe of ſpirits, and many diſeaſes contracted in their nightly rambles and dances. Laſtly, too long ſuckling, viz. about 2 years, beſides many diſeaſes prevalent in cold climates.

Except in caſes of atrocious offences, corporal chaſtiſement is now ſeldom inflicted.

Never called upon, in his medical capacity, to negroes after ſevere puniſhment.

Reſident in St. Kitts, about 12 months commencing in 1776.

P. 253. Reſident in Nevis from 1777 to 1785. In 1788 paſſed 8 months in Nevis and St. Kitts, but not as a medical man.

The preceding evidence relates to the treatment of negroes in St. Kitts, as well as Nevis.

Preſumes a greater proportion of African negroes may die in the firſt three years after their importation than afterwards, and that the change of climate produces very great effects on the conſtitution of the negroes

groes, many dying under the greateſt care and attention, though put to no laborious employment. 1790. Part II.

Believes labour of ſlaves by no means tend to ſhorten their lives, as they always appear chearful during crop time when they work the hardeſt. P. 254.

The Creole negro generally induſtrious, the African uſually very indolent.

A woman of equal health and ſtrength with a man, he conſiders far more valuable, becauſe her increaſe benefits the proprietor; ſpeaks not of field-negroes.

Negroes are not allowed ſhoes, nor do they wiſh to wear them. P. 255.

St. Kitts and Nevis are liable to ſevere droughts, by which almoſt all vegetation is ſtopped, and the uſual produce of the Iſlands diminiſhed.

Thinks $\frac{2}{3}$ at leaſt of the infants born, die under a twelvemonth.

The office of watchman is to keep cattle from intruding on cane-pieces, whilſt the plants are young, and when mature, to guard them from depredations of negroes. Watchmen alſo attend ſtores, &c. where any valuable effects are depoſited.

While reſident in Nevis from 1777 to 1785, an epidemical putrid ſore throat prevailed once or twice, which carried off many children, and almoſt every year during the rainy months, fluxes were fatal to a great many full grown negroes, eſpecially ſuch as were weakly. P. 256.

The rains commence about Auguſt, and end with November or the beginning of December.

Air impregnated with moiſt particles, tends to give a certain check to the perſpiration, which being thrown upon the bowels, is very apt to end in a flux. Fluxes are apt to prevail after heavy rains, from the water that is commonly drank coming down from the mountains impregnated with noxious particles. In 1786 a putrid fever prevailed in both Nevis and St. Kitts, which ſwept off many black and whites. The ſlaves in that and the former year were more

1790. Part II. than usually unhealthy, fluxes and fevers of a putrid kind prevailing more than common.

P. 257. Thinks the colonial laws restrain the master from exercising any undue authority over his slaves. Any owner ill treating them would certainly be despised, and not admitted into the society of respectable men.

The planters in Nevis more usually reside on their estates than in most other Islands.

The owner of an estate, if resident in England, names an attorney, who appoints a manager, whose conduct is often enquired into by the attorney, and when guilty of a breach of trust, or of any severities to the negroes, he is discharged.

As to whether it was generally believed in Nevis and St. Kitts, that the law of England extended its protection to slaves in those Islands? He says, before the framing of the Colonial laws of the different Islands, the master had an absolute authority over his slave; but as self-interest is a predominant passion, and that as it is contrary to every owner's interest to be cruel to his negroes, he presumes that they were used as mildly as they now are.

The allowance given to the slave is just a sufficiency for his support, the superfluity arising from this and the produce of his provision ground, which is not very great, is converted into money for slaves private purposes. The usual quantity of ground allotted each slave, besides that about his house, may

P. 258. be about ¼ of an acre, and generally some mountain-land. The ¼ acre is always planted with potatoes or some other vegetables for the slave's use. The allotment of mountain-land is always increased in proportion to the family of the slave, but not the ground round the house. Many estates have no mountain ground, the owner then gives a greater allowance of food. Where there is no mountain-ground, believes the greatest allowance to be 11 pints of any kind of grain per week, besides an equal number of herrings; the allowance out of crop time being greater than during the crop season; the reduction of allowance may

may be from 9 to 6 or 7 pints; but at this time the 1790.
negroes have many advantages, ſuch as a ſupply of Part II.
hot ſyrup, a liberty of eating canes, and are in better condition and health than at any other period of the year.

The negro-women lie-in in their own houſes.

Never ſaw much whipping, and on his laſt viſit P. 259.
to the W. Indies found it was almoſt diſuſed, confinement being attended with better conſequences, for a negro would rather be whipped than confined. And this diſcontinuance of whipping he thinks to the intereſt of both maſter and ſlave.

From the intereſt of the Planter depending on the ſlave, the tyrannic acts of oppreſſion and tortures ſaid to be inflicted on the negroes, are ſurely ſuch abſurdities as are ſelf-apparent.

Is very certain the cultivation of ſugar eſtates cannot be carried on by Europeans.

Is perfectly ſenſible it is the intereſt and wiſh of the Planters in general to rear as many negro-children as they can.

Has poſitive evidence that the ſlaves in the W. P. 260.
India Iſlands, have a decided ſuperiority, as to every comfort of life over the common labourers and poor people of Ireland and Scotland, by being regularly ſupplied with every neceſſary of life, cloathing, food, comfortable houſes, protection in health, the beſt advice in ſickneſs, and, on their deceaſe, having a father and protector for their children.

1790. Part II.

Witneſs examined—JAMES TOBIN, Eſq.

Has lived 10 or 12 years in the W. Indies at different times, chiefly in Nevis. Has often been in St. Kitt's, and occaſionally in moſt other Engliſh and ſome French iſlands. Knows the manner of culti-
P. 261. vating W. Indian eſtates, and has an eſtate in Nevis. Thinks it impoſſible to cultivate W. India lands by any other than negro labour. Sees no reaſon why free negroes ſhould not do as much work as ſlaves, but never knew a free negro do field labour. In St. Vincent are many free negroes, (improperly called Caribs) and there negro labour is very dear; but were they diſpoſed to work, the planters would give them very great prices; they live, however, like ſavages. In Jamaica there is a good number of free negroes; but he does not find that any of them work in the field for hire.

Does not conceive it poſſible to cultivate ſugar plantations by whites.

Does not think that the number of negroes ſufficient to cultivate ſugar eſtates can be kept up by propagation, for theſe reaſons—more males imported than females, from the Africans being all Polygamiſts,
P. 262. and of courſe unwilling to part with their females—the early and promiſcuous intercourſe of the ſexes—the venereals—young females procuring abortions, to preſerve their perſons—the obſtructions, &c., the female negroes are ſubject to from their irregularities—the negro women ſuckling too long—the premature debility of the men by ſpirits—the little care too many of the negro women are apt to take of their children—the many diſorders to which negro children are peculiarly ſubject, as fluxes, worms, and the fevers incident thereto, the lock'd jaw, and eating dirt. On his eſtate has had 2 males to 3 females, of whom remarkable care has been taken—a free woman conſtantly attends the ſick and breeding women; yet, for theſe 4 or 5 years, he has but juſt ben able to keep up his number.

Has

Has never found the lock'd jaw ſo frequent in Nevis as in St. Kitt's, and ſeveral other iſlands. 1790. Part. II.

Negroes, infant and adult, are ſubject to fluxes, putrid fevers, and ſore throats, beſides the ſmall-pox, meaſles, &c.; and has no reaſon to think the loſſes from theſe diſeaſes would be counterbalanced by breeding.

Negroes are uſually fed with flour, Indian corn, rye meal, biſcuit, Guinea corn, and other grain; and yams, potatoes, &c., when to be had: they have beſides, ſalt herrings, ſalt fiſh, &c. The proviſions allowed may be ſufficient; but it is always underſtood that they are to add to their allowance by their own induſtry, which they can do, having always land to plant, and leave to raiſe goats, hogs, and poultry, to ſell for themſelves; alſo graſs and wood, which they ſell in the towns. During his reſidence in the W. Indies, perhaps 2-3ds of the freſh proviſions he uſed were bought of his ſlaves, or thoſe of others. P. 263.

The negroes have Oſnabrugs, or coarſe linen, for a jacket and breeches for the men, and a jacket and petticoat for the women; with ſome woollen cloth, and generally hats and caps, at leaſt once a year. The children of all ages are allowed cloathing.

Negroes' houſes are built by themſelves, with the maſters' help, with, at leaſt, two rooms, one to ſleep in, the other for common uſe; many of their houſes have 3 or 4 rooms, with cook rooms detached.

The houſes are generally thatched and wattled, and many plaiſtered; but many head negroes, particularly in St. Kitt's, have boarded and ſhingled houſes. They ſleep on raiſed benches ſpread with matts and blankets. P. 264.

On all eſtates there are regular ſick nurſes, and generally a ſurgeon employed by the year. Sick ſlaves have ſago, portable ſoup, wine, freſh meat, &c. Poultry and mutton are often killed to make them broth. He knew a convaleſcent ſlave have 16 lambs, each worth 2 dollars, killed for his uſe.

A negro woman, 4 or 5 months gone with child, works

1790. works not in any of the gangs, but picks graſs, at-
Part II. tends the children in the field, or does ſome light
work, more to keep her in exerciſe than for profit.
In lying-in ſhe has the ſame attention as the ſick.
A midwife is generally on the eſtate; but in caſes
of neceſſity an eſtabliſhed practitioner is called at a
very heavy expence; as midwifery, night viſits, or
capital operations, are paid for extra. They have
always 4 weeks to lye in, and more, if neceſſary; and
after coming out, are allowed to come an hour or two
later into the field whilſt nurſing. Never recollects
ſeeing a negro woman far gone with child put to any
hard labour.

Lame, incurably diſeaſed, and aged negroes, have
the ſame food, clothing, and accommodation, as if
P. 265. perfectly ſerviceable. He is warranted to ſay, that
the puniſhments of ſlaves are mild, compared to
thoſe of Britiſh ſoldiers and ſeamen.

From obſervation he has no doubt but the ſituation of the W.-India ſlaves (puniſhments apart) is preferable to that of the labouring poor in Europe, the climate giving an obvious advantage to the ſlave; for in a cold climate two of the greateſt luxuries are warm lodging and warm clothing, both which the labouring poor can ſcarcely procure; but in the W. Indies cool lodging and cool clothing are two of the greateſt indulgencies, both which the negro can eaſily obtain.

The labour expected from the negroes varies with their ſtrength, and, in ſome meaſure, with the ſeaſons. They are generally divided into 3 gangs; the great gang conſiſts of the ableſt men and women; the ſmall gang, of the younger and leſs able; and the graſs gang, of children under an old woman, to keep them out of miſchief, and uſe them to employment. The great gang hole the ground; in weeding and in crop the two gangs are generally united.

The negroes are generally called into the field by
a bell about 6 o'clock; about 8 they have ½ hour for
P. 266. breakfaſt, generally in the field; in about ¾ of an

hour they resume their work, which they continue till noon; but in very dry seasons (being out of crop expected to bring grass at noon) they are generally discharged at about ½ past 11. At 2 o'clock they return in the field, and continue till about 6, when they are discharged to bring more grass; in crop, when the stock is fed on cane-tops, and little or no grass required. A few attend the mill and boiling house some hours after dark; and on some estates being divided into proper spells, they attend them most of the night, so that on the whole the crop may be called the season of hardest labour; and yet the slaves are always then heartiest. On the whole, he is convinced that the labour of a negro through the year is by no means so severe as that of an English labourer. 1790. Part II.

Out of crop the negroes can generally go to rest by 7 o'clock; but this partly depends on themselves, as they are sometimes backward in bringing their grass, and generally come to get their allowance at that hour. As it is dark between 6 and 7, it could answer no purpose to keep them out of crop, from their houses, after that hour.

The cultivation of a sugar estate bears a much nearer resemblance to that of a garden, than to that of an English farm. Planters who have kept this idea in view have generally made the most of their property. W.-India lands require very nice preparation. No produce is sown; every thing, even grain, being planted: the plough and other European implements are therefore excluded: they have, he believes, been tried on estates level enough to admit the experiment, but, he is well informed, without any good effects. The young cane sprouts are remarkably tender, and require repeated hoings, to be done most carefully of course by hand. Manure in the W. Indies is not spread as in England, but is carried and carefully placed round each plant separately; so that wheelbarrows or carts could not be used after the canes are come up; but the manure is gene- P. 267.

1790. Part II. generally carted, and made into heaps at proper diſtances on the land before holing, to ſave as much of the work as poſſible to the negroes. In Nevis and Montſerrat it would be impoſſible, from the rocks, (except a very few ſpots) even to try the plough. The ſevere droughts, to which the ſmall iſlands are ſubject, would alſo be an invincible impediment to the plough, as lands, if they could be ploughed, would require a long time to mellow. The planters are ſo ſenſible of the value of negro labour, that they have left very few experiments untried that were likely to leſſen it—it being a maxim among all prudent planters never to employ a negro in doing ſuch work as can be done otherwiſe.

In St. Kitt's ſtaking cattle, to provide manure and ſave negro labour, prevails more than in any iſland he knows. In Nevis they uſe moving pens, ſomewhat like ſheep folds; by which dung is made where it is uſed.

There are very few places where ſmall light dung carts, drawn by mules, cannot be uſed; but in places too ſteep for ſuch carts, the manure is carried out in horſe-hair bags, on mules, to ſave negro labour.

P. 268. Moſt planters certainly prefer Creole ſlaves to Africans, and therefore pay all poſſible attention to breeding.

Knows in Nevis, that a pecuniary reward is given to the mother on rearing her child to be 2 years old; and that freedom from all labour is granted to every negro woman who is the mother of 6 working children.

From reading, and from converſing with men well acquainted with Africa, and from occaſional converſation with Africans themſelves, has every reaſon to think that their ſituation is better generally in the W. Indies, than it was in their own country; and it is very ſingular, that there never was an inſtance of a negro (even an African) who had obtained his freedom, ever returning to Africa, or even expreſſing a wiſh

wish to do ſo. This has been ſaid to ariſe from the connections they have made in the W. Indies; and if ſo, it proves that they can form connections there equally, if not more, agreeable to them than thoſe they quitted. It is a general miſtake to ſuppoſe that negroes in the W. Indies are very anxious to procure their freedom; if ſo, many of them could buy their freedom with the money they ſave. Has known freedom offered to ſlaves on the moſt moderate terms, and refuſed, becauſe they ſhould loſe their friends and protectors. Has little doubt but thoſe negroes could have bought their freedom at the ſum propoſed; is poſitive in one inſtance, as he (the ſlave) has bought his ſon's freedom, and ſlaves for his ſon's uſe, himſelf (who was a fiſherman, 280) ſtill remaining a ſlave.

1790. Part. II.

P. 269.

It is very common for free negroes to marry (in their ſenſe of the word) women ſlaves, though they know that their offspring would be ſlaves.

Has reſided in England as a W.-India merchant ſince 1784.

Has great reaſon to think that the agitation of the queſtion for aboliſhing the ſlave trade has had effects on W.-India credit, very baneful and very extenſive. The houſe he is concerned in, and, he believes, many greater houſes, have been deterred by this conſideration alone from making advances.

P. 270.

Was moſtly in the W. Indies from 1758 till 1766. His father poſſeſſed the family eſtate for that time, and for a great part of it renter of another pretty conſiderable property; in the management of both which he was chiefly employed. In 1766 he returned to England, remaining there till 1777, when he went back to the W. Indies, and ſtaid till 1784. Did not particularly attend to his gang till he laſt left the W. Indies, being before that time employed in getting rid of ſome of the worſt, and in procuring a gang, likely to increaſe. In 1784, had 72 males and 100 females; in 1785, 72 males and 98 females; in 1786, 73 males and 98 females, having this year

 bought

1790. Part II. bought one; in 1787, 77 males and 102 females, 6 new negroes being bought—the increase this year was 3; in 1788, 77 males and 102 females, having with such a superiority of females barely been able to keep up the number, but cannot state the births and deaths in that period.

P. 271. In St. Kitt's the land is so very valuable that the negro houses stand very close; the negro grounds, therefore, are generally at some distance from their houses. In Nevis, where land is not so valuable, the houses stand farther asunder, and there is generally a lot of land to each house; but in both believes it is usual (in Nevis it is) to allow them one crop from a piece of cane land, besides the land round their houses and the negro provision ground. The distant land is generally either mountain land, or gutsides.

Had about 260 or 270 acres in cultivation, of which in general he planted yearly about 90.

The whites in his service were a manager, an overseer all the year, and a distiller in crop—he hired a free Mulatto woman to attend the sick and the lying-in woman; and the same number were employed in his absence.

Never knew any sensible planter who did not think it for his interest to breed, rather than buy slaves.

Thinks the general treatment of slaves to be better now than it was 30 or 40 years ago; but knows of no particular alterations of late.

The protection enjoyed by the slaves in these two islands was that of the laws of England—he does not recollect any colonial laws in Nevis interfering with
P. 272. these. In St. Kitt's he believes there is a law to punish the maiming of slaves, passed in 1783.

Apprehends it to have been the general opinion, that the English law extended to slaves in Nevis and St. Kitt's.

Instances proceedings in Nevis in the case of a supposed murder of a negro by 2 white men, carried on, as he apprehends, under the laws of England: and another of a white overseer, supposed to have wantonly murdered a negro of the estate he lived on, who was capitally indicted and tried; but the proofs not appearing satisfactory, found guilty of manslaughter—sentenced to a year's imprisonment.—Vide particulars. 1790. Part II.

Can't say it was commonly understood that the slave was secured by the laws of England from immoderate punishment by his master; but knows it to be a general-received opinion, that all the laws of England are in force in the W. Indies, where they are not counteracted by particular colonial laws. P. 273.

Rooms were not generally appropriated for lying-in women, as many planters, in the old islands, hold even hospitals to be more detrimental than useful, by increasing epidemicks; and where the negroes are mostly Creoles, the sick and lying-in women find themselves more at ease in their houses.

There is a poll tax in Nevis and St. Kitt's, which, he believes, commences from the birth.

Few of the slaves pretend to much religion—their morals, probably, as good as those of the very lower order in England.

The regulating act, he has been informed, has raised the price of slaves; and to it he chiefly attributes the late advance. P. 274.

Has reason to think, that the situation of field negroes in the French islands is by no means better than in the English, especially as to punishment—the house negroes seem to be treated with more familiarity than in the English islands, but doubts whether that materially benefit them. The Code Noir appears to be well calculated to secure good treatment to the slaves; but he believes it is far from being rigidly enforced, and sometimes it is impossible for the planter to comply with it, particularly respecting provisions. Believes the French planters oftener reside on their estates than the English. P. 275.

The negroes are not likely to be better used by the proprietor, than by a prudent manager, because the former feels immediately the expence of an ample

1790. provision and necessaries, which the latter does not;
Part. II. and it is a particular pleasure to the manager, redounding much to his credit, that the negroes under him look well.

P. 276. Does not recollect any managers discharged for shewing too great indulgence to the negroes in food and labour.

Information, as to their true interest, is equally accessible to to the French as to the English planters; but from observation thinks the former in general not so well educated as the latter.

The greatest time the negroes have to cultivate their own land is all Sunday—sometimes, and in seasonable weather, when a little extra time is likely to be particularly useful to them, they have Saturday afternoon; and he believes, on some estates, they generally have it; besides there are holidays, 2 or 3 at Christmas, Good Friday in general, and on many estates, a day at the finishing crop, the other times are such as they chuse to take from their rest; the 2 hours at noon is seldom employed in preparing a regular meal, their chief meal being supper; so that they often work their ground then.

The allowance from the master generally, he thinks, is regular and settled, but sometimes affected by the scarcity or plenty of provisions to be bought.

The allowance differs in some measure on different estates; the average may be stated at about 6 to 9, or 10 pints of grain or flour for each negro per week, including every weaned child; besides this they have 6 or 8 herrings per week, or salt fish, &c. in propor-
P. 277. tion; in addition to which, on many estates, and on all which he directed, they had out of crop, a regular breakfast served them in the field, of a biscuit, molasses and water, qualified with rum in rainy weather. Whenever from indolence or inattention to dressing the provisions served out, any negroes fall off, they have more victuals served out to them dressed. Negroes thus fed with dressed victuals, are called the pot gang; and it is a reproach for a negro to be so

careless

careless as to be obliged to be fed that way. On most estates a pot is boiled daily for the children, weak and convalescent negroes, and those under confinement. 1790. Part II.

The negroes may neglect their provision grounds; but on some estates they are obliged by their masters to cultivate such grounds, though this is not common. The character of negroes as to indolence or industry, as various as that of whites, and depends much on the part of the coast they come from.

Has found it easy to persuade some negroes to adopt such alterations in managing their own concerns as might tend to their advantage, but in general they are obstinately wedded to their own customs.

Not to be supposed that many negroes possess con- P. 278.
siderable property in a small island, like Nevis; besides they are very jealous of letting their owners or managers know it.

A sum sufficient to buy a field negroe's freedom, would not be deemed a considerable property, if he chose to save the money he could earn instead of spending it in fineries for himself and his wives, and other superfluities.

His property depends chiefly on the quantity of stock and poultry he may raise.

The pastures of the estate, if extensive, are generally more than enough to keep the master's stock in wet, but not in dry weather.

Severe droughts are common in Nevis and St. Kitt's, especially Nevis. In those droughts the master's cattle are often with difficulty furnished with sufficient grass, yet it is very remarkable, that from some cause or other, the negro stock seldom or ever appears affected by such droughts. The managers are not in general allowed to keep stock, at least such as go into the pastures; such stock out of crop are fed with P. 280.
grass or shrubs gathered by grass gang generally.

Surgeons, for their attendance in these two islands, have usually 6s. per ann. for each negro, young and old; but such annual sum is the least part of their profit, as they charge for every night visit 3l. 6s.; for

1790. Part II. for every midwifery caſe (in Nevis) 5 times that ſum, and for all capital operations in the ſame proportion; they alſo charge ſeparately for inoculation. With ſome of the moſt uſeful medicines (bark eſpecially) they are generally ſupplied by the planters, or charged ſeparately by the ſurgeons. Currency varies from 160 to 187½ per cent.

It is not very common for field negroes to have more than one wife.

Apprehends that taking the coaſt of Guinea altogether, the W.-India iſlands may be ſaid to be in a healthier climate; and yet, from experience, the change of the climates has very bad effects on the negroes, on their firſt arrival.

Doubts very much whether, if the negroes in the W. Indies were to be freed, they would be nearly as

P. 281. happy as they are now; but to ſuch of them as have induſtry and prudence to make a proper uſe of it, freedom is preferable; but thoſe who abuſe it, are leſs happy than a good ſlave.

In the preſent ſtate of the iſlands, and few as free negroes are, they can earn more by ſundry trades, fiſhing, &c. with the ſame time and induſtry, than by hiring themſelves to do field work on eſtates at the uſual price; but were a general emancipation to take place, or the number of free negroes greatly increaſed, it might probably be otherwiſe; it cannot therefore be expected, in the preſent ſtate of the iſlands, that free negroes ſhould offer to do field labour.

P. 282. The communication between the W. Indies and Africa not very frequent, but veſſels are occaſionally ſent from the iſland to trade for ſlaves.

Believes few managers keep negroes to let as jobbing gangs, either to their maſters or others.

The cane pieces, proviſions, and other ſtores, are generally watched.

For the protection of free negroes from ill uſage, every law is as much open to them as to Whites.

P. 283. Suppoſes an African cannot lay by a ſum to buy his freedom in a ſhort time after his importation, and in his comparison of the state of slaves in the W. Indies, and negroes in Africa, and also of the former and the labouring poor of England, he has alluded to the tolerably industrious slaves, which, in fact, are the majority. The profligate and incorrigible are generally apt to run away, to sell their clothes, and to neglect the food allowed them, are often loitering about the towns, and strolling along the bays and sea side, half naked, and apparently half starved; and from such wretches he thinks the state of the slaves in the islands has been described and published in England, by people who have transiently visited them, without knowing the management of estates, and the treatment of the slaves. 1790. Part II.

Three persons have been tried, convicted, and punished, for ill treating their own slaves, under the common law of England, in St. Kitt's; and of such convictions authentic transcripts have been sent home for the information of the H. of Commons. Such documents evince how much the police of Nevis and St. Kitt's has been misrepresented by assertions that, in those islands, there was no law to interpose between the tyranny of the planters and their defenceless slaves. P. 284.

The slaves, neither before nor after the surrender of Nevis to the French, shewed any disposition to revolt, but quite the contrary.

In St. Kitt's, when attacked by the French in 1782, the slaves eagerly desired arms to defend their master's property; and, on some estates, where the whites were insulted by the French soldiers, the negroes took the most ample and savage revenge.

The instances of conviction and punishment of persons for ill treatment of slaves in Nevis referred only to the two murders before specified.

The instances of conviction and punishment of masters for ill treating their own slaves, mentioned to have occurred in St. Kitt's, were, since the passing of P. 285.
the act for punishing offenders for particular kinds of ill treatment; but the indictments under which

they

1790. Part II. they were convicted and punished, were under the common law of England. Knows of no similar convictions and punishments in St. Kitt's previous to this period. Does not recollect having heard the particulars of the several cases of conviction and punishment in St. Kitt's, except the case of Strode for slitting a negro's ear.

P. 286. By custom the master supposes he has the right of exacting labour from the slave by compulsion, the master being the judge of the labour exacted; but knows no law that gives him such right. And the statute law of England supposes that right to exist in the master, as clearly as any colonial laws, as many acts of parliament relating to the colonies, would be absurd, without supposing such right actually to exist.

P. 287. Thinks the mode adopted in prosecuting Strode and Burke on the common law of England, and not on the new-island statute, demonstrates, that, in the opinion of the prosecutors for the crown, the statute created no new indictable offence; but that an act of wanton cruelty by a master on his slave was a misdemeanor indictable at common law in that island, before the statute passed.

Witness examined—ALEXANDER DOUGLAS, Esq.

Resident in St. Kitt's from 1749 to 1771, except a few months; leased part of an estate, managed two estates besides his own, and was attorney to several
P. 288. estates of absentees. Had under his care about a 6th or 7th part of all the negroes in the island. Could not keep up the negroes without importation.

On the estate he leased are 100 males and 115 females, but in general, believes the males exceed the females. The stock has not been kept up by breeding,

ing, even on the eſtate he leaſed. To increaſe the negroes by breeding, was a particular object of his attention. 1790. Part. II.

Thinks it impoſſible for whites to undergo field-work in the W. Indies, and free negroes are too idle to do it for hire; never knew an inſtance of it.—— Does not think it probable that the proprietors could keep up the neceſſary ſtock of negroes by breeding, having himſelf tried it and failed. Does not ſuppoſe it owing to over-working, neglect, or ill treatment.

Women ſix months gone with child, do as they pleaſe, and their indolence has been deemed one cauſe of the children dying of the locked jaw, within the ninth day. They are attended by a midwife P. 289. and ſick nurſe, and have every thing neceſſary in their condition, alſo the aſſiſtance of a plantation ſurgeon, if required. Should the mother be too indolent (which ſometimes happen) to provide baby cloaths, moſt people, he believes, ſend for them to England. Added to the produce of their own grounds, the general allowance to negroes in St. Kitt's, was from 6 to 8 pints of flour, beans, and Indian corn, or a baſket of yams. With 12 to 15 acres of cane land planted in yams, he has been able to feed the negroes, ſometimes for 9 months together; but the produce depends on the weather. Each ſlave has alſo 6 or 8 herrings a week, or ſalt fiſh in proportion; and at Chriſtmas ſalted beef; but their allowance is more or leſs, as the maſters ſee requiſite. Good negroes live in plenty; the vagrants often want, and it is impoſſible to prevent it. Good negroes have very large quantities of graſs, wood, poultry, pigs, roots, &c. to ſell.

In crop, negroes that grind all night, divide their gangs into 3 or 4 ſpells, but of late, on moſt eſtates grinding in the night is left off. Out of crop, they are generally diſcharged about 6 or 7 at night, and called out in the morning at daylight, about 6.

Thinks the negroes in St. Kitt's have from 9 to

1790. 11 hour's reſpite in the 24, and they are univerſally
Part II. healthier in crop than at any other ſeaſon.

The texture of the land at St. Kitt's is looſer and eaſier holed than the other iſlands. A creole is put into the holing gang, according to his growth or ſtrength, at 16, 17, or 18 years of age.

As to maſters, in their behaviour to ſlaves, being actuated by a conſtant jealouſy, not to be ſatisfied by any exertion, or ſoftened by any attachment of the ſlaves, the idea is perfectly new to him; never knew maſters treat their ſlaves in St. Kitt's with ſpiteful ſeverity; thinks all maſters treat their ſlaves with compaſſion, as their moſt valuable poſſeſſion, and recollects no inſtance of ſeverity. By accounts received, thinks the treatment of negroes in St. Kitt's better, if any thing, than while he was there. Every proprietor, of common ſenſe, wiſhes to breed as many negroes as he can.

291. A Creole negro of equal age and ſtrength, would, he thinks, from the knowledge of his good quality, be worth 2 at leaſt, perhaps 3, of new negroes, whoſe qualities the proprietor muſt be ignorant of.

Managers, in the proprietors' abſence, have no reluctance, nor ſhew any inattention, to rearing and breeding negro children.

The planters generally prefer a ſingle to a married manager, unleſs the wife happens to be remarkably careful of the negroes.

Does not conceive any want of attention to breeding is conſequent on the abſence of the proprietors.

Of the 6 eſtates mentioned in the paper the Rev. Mr. Ramſay delivered in to the Privy Council, he believes about four of the proprietors never were in the W. Indies in his time; of courſe, their affairs were left to managers and attornies. Mr. Molyneux was there for about a year, he believes; Mr. Crook, after living long in England, ſpent a few of the laſt years of his life in St. Kitt's, where he died.

4,781 was the amount of the Treaſurer's account of negroes in St. Kitt's in 1768.

20,435 was the number of negroes in St. Kitt's in 1788, as sent by the island, and given in to the Privy Council. 1790. Part II.

Thinks the negroes have certainly more comforts than the labouring poor of Europe: they do not work so hard, and have a master to take care of them and their children when sick. P. 292.

Thinks the effect of the abolition of the slave trade on the negroes now in the colonies, would be sedition, from a fear that their labour would be greater as the gang decreased, and there being no hopes of assistance from Africa, as heretofore.

Thinks no act could prevent the importation of negroes into the English islands; every man would naturally assist his neighbour in the common cause.

Thinks, from 6 to 8 pints of flour, beans, &c. per week was given to each negro, and herrings from 5 to 8.

Recollects no criminal proceedings against whites for offences against slaves, while he was in the W. Indies, but one or two being threatened with prosecutions, left the island.

His whole gang was 215; his estate about 250 acres.

They lost a great many infants, and there were a great many very old people on the estate when he came into possession; the estate is healthy. P. 293.

Very young children, he thinks, have half allowance; recollects having a complaint from some mothers, that they had not time to dress their children's food, but having always looked on the breeding women as the most valuable of the gang, from their sobriety, and always keeping at home, he determined to have victuals dressed for their children daily. They came for this food punctually, a week or two, or longer; but at last they dropped off one by one, and he left off the practice.

Whilst he was in St. Kitt's, Mr. Thomas lost, in a year, by a flux, 34 of his best negroes, out of 170

1790. Part II. to 200; and Mr. Thomas, he believes, was remarkably careful of his negroes. Does not believe that losses of negroes by epidemics are uncommon in St. Kitt's, and knows no means by which these losses could be supplied but from Africa.

Witness examined—THOS. NORBURY KERBY, Esq.

P. 299. A native of Antigua—left it in 1762—returned February 1780—staid till July 1788; was a Member of Assembly till early in 1784, then received a mandamus from home to a seat at the Council.

Has 2 sugar plantations; has been attorney for friends at different periods; cannot exactly say how many years the estates had been in his family—but a considerable time—and descended to him.

P. 300. Thinks most of the estates in the island want slaves; one of his estates is sufficiently handed, the other not: as to those he is concerned for, some are sufficiently handed, others not.

Thinks there may be as many born as die; but by no means raised to maturity. On one of his estates, the increase equals the decrease; on the other, does not: on one for which he is concerned it is equal, on the others not; cannot exactly tell the numbers raised, where the increase equals the decrease, but certainly not all, as many die within nine days of the tetanus.

Believes many die from inattention of the mothers, as they are apt to think young children a burden, and great bar to their pleasures, and to nocturnal meetings and dances.

Having been very unsuccessful in raising children on one of his estates, he built a lying-in hospital, hoping to have the women, lying in, more immediately

diately under the manager's eye, and ſo greater care would be paid to the little comforts they wanted.— But from the ſlaves' diſpoſitions, and their great diſlike to all confinement, his endeavours had not proved, when he came away, very beneficial; and he is apt to believe his loſſes ſince have ſtill been in the ſame proportion.

1790. Part II. P. 301.

On arriving in the W. Indies, he found that the ſlave-houſes on the eſtate, where they decreaſe, had formerly ſtood expoſed to the N. wind, and that medical men had adviſed re-building them in a different ſite, which was directly done; yet his loſſes ſtill continue, though he is confident no eſtate has greater attention paid to the ſlaves in every ſituation, particularly to mothers and children.

The negro women are very partial to their own midwives. A ſlave in labour, on his own eſtate, was reported to him as in danger: he directly went to her friends, and told them he had ſent for a doctor to give her every help. The anſwer was, if he came he ſhould not attend her, as ſhe preferred the eſtate midwife. She was delivered before the doctor came. Doubts not, loſſes are ſuſtained from want of ſkill in ſome midwives. Whenever a difficult caſe cocurs, believes a medical perſon is always employed.

It is the practice on his eſtates, and thoſe for which he has been concerned, to pay the midwife for every child born;—to encourage the mothers, he has alſo made them ſome preſent, generally about Chriſtmas.

Certainly does not aſcribe the failure of increaſe and rearing of children, to hard work, harſh uſage, or improper food of the mother, while pregnant or afterwards. As ſoon as a ſlave ſays ſhe is with child, and that hard work would hurt her, every attention is paid her. P. 302.

Believes it general to relieve from all hard work a ſlave 4 months gone with child; ſometimes they do not lie-in for 6 or 7 months after. They are always

1790. ways attended by the nurse of the estate and some fe-
Part II. male friends; and care is taken that they have every
necessary. He allows such baby-linen as is wanted.

Makes the women bring their children to him at the end of the 4th week, then orders them to such work as he thinks they can bear. Believes a woman never goes to hard work till the end of 6 weeks.—Children of careless mothers are always put under one of the nurses, who pay them every attention, while the mother is in the field.

To the children of other mothers every attention as to food and lodging is paid, though they are not taken from them. The work is always proportioned
P. 303. to the slave's strength. The estates in general, and his own, have not a proportionate number of females. Cannot at all times get out of a cargo, the breeding females wanted: the proportion brought from Africa is very inadequate.

Thinks it would be impossible to keep up the present stock without supply from Africa; and is confident it would be impracticable, if they had an equal number of women, considering the disorders to which persons in the W. Indies are subject, and the dreadful ravages often caused by epidemical ones. In 1779, it was generally thought in the island, and from his own losses verily believes, $\frac{1}{5}$th of all the negroes died of a dysentery. In 1782 many died by an epidemical pleurisy; in 1783, by the measles; and in 1786, there were heavy losses by the small pox and chin-cough, though every attention was paid to inoculation.

Generally speaking, thinks they may, with propriety, be put to the hardest field-work from 18 to
P. 304. 20; some are more capable of labour sooner. If he should lose any able slaves, before the Creoles reached this age, if the African trade was abolished, a proportion of his land must be uncultivated, or his young negroes be worked too soon. If the trade was not abolished, he would certainly look to Africa for

for ſupply. Thinks every negro brought forward to work beyond his ſtrength, muſt be worn out very early. His loſſes in 1779, 82, 3, and 6, have not been repaired; though he conſtantly bought ſlaves, when he could, from Africa or elſewhere, as far as he was able; but, from many bad years, few planters were able to repair their loſſes. 1790. Part II.

The crops in the iſland in 1779, 80, and 81, were generally very bad: he did not make, in 3 years, what he ought to have made in 1.

Thinks, if the crop had been large in 1780 and 81, and there had been no ſupplies from Africa, it would have been impoſſible for the ſlaves then on the iſland to have done the work. If the African trade ſhould be aboliſhed, and the iſland again have ſuch calamitous years as 1779, 82, 3, and 6, great part of the land now cultivated muſt be neglected.

It has been generally found, that eſtates which are beſt handed, make in proportion the largeſt crops. P. 305.

Thinks, were the ſlave-trade aboliſhed, all the ſlaves would be very ſorry, as they would be certain the work would fall wholly on themſelves: It is very well known, they expreſs much ſatisfaction when they hear of the arrival of ſlaves, and often aſk their maſters to buy a few more help-mates.

In July 1788, he paid 42l. for the ſame kind of ſlave, which in 1787 he bought for 36l.—Which he attributes entirely to the report of the abolition, which had reached the W. Indies; but ſhould certainly prefer a Creole, even at an advanced price.

Thinks every planter, who ſtudies his intereſt would prefer the breeding of ſlaves to buying Africans. Believes planters conſtantly pay new negroes every attention, and give them neceſſary time to recover from the fatigue of the voyage.

Slaves are lodged in ſtone, wattled and dawbed, and wooden houſes, built and kept in repair by the maſter, or by allowing the ſlave time to do it:—Clothed by him (ſpeaks of his own eſtates and thoſe

he

1790. Part II. he directs) with 1 suit of woollen, and 1 of Osnaburgs annually.—He always allows from 8 to 12 measures of grain per week to each slave—from 26 to 36lbs. of yams or eddoes;—from 4 to 8 herrings according to the age, or from 2 to 3lbs. of salt-fish. They have also dry salt. Every estate gives each slave yams or flour, with salt beef or pork at Christmas, beyond the weekly allowance, and 3 holidays. Believes it a general rule on every well-regulated estate to give any slave that applies for additional food, such help as he appears to want, without respect to weather. In bad weather, the whole gang have grog,—and when working hard.

He gives allowance to every one on his estates, and those under his care, according to their ages. On every estate land is allotted for the slaves, which
P. 307. they cultivate for their sole benefit. All may raise small stock, goats and hogs, which they dispose of entirely as their own. Never knew a case where the money arising from them was considered but entirely as the slave's own.

Men of war, and merchant-ships are constantly supplied on Sundays with vegetables, the slaves property;—on other days it is usual to send vegetables to market by the slaves, on the owner's account;—the small stock, goats, and hogs are chiefly the slave's property, and with which the shipping is chiefly supplied.—The people of St. John's have their small stock and vegetables chiefly in the same way as the shipping.—It is common for masters to buy stock from their slaves, and pay as much as other persons.

Remembers a slave giving 200l. for his freedom: Also knows many who spend annually from 10l. to 15l.

One afternoon weekly is allowed to the slaves out of crop, to work their own grounds,—sometimes in crop, but not constantly.

They hold every Sunday a market to sell their produce and stock.

Every

Every estate has an hospital for the sick, who are attended by a medical man and proper nurses,—supplied with every requisite, and never sent to work without the doctor's sanction. A doctor is constantly employed at a certain rate for each slave; attends twice a week, is liable to be sent for whenever necessary—paid also for fractures, midwifery, venereals, &c. 1790. Part II.

Thinks the slave enjoys full as many comforts as the English labourer, in some respects more; as he is sure of being taken care of in sickness, and has not the anxiety of providing perhaps for a wife and young family.

The usual punishment of slaves is, whipping for petty thefts, such as breaking open negro-houses, stores, and stealing from other slaves;—for higher offences they are tried by 2 justices, one being of the quorum, and 6 white jurors balloted for out of 12, and punished according to the offence. A master generally inflicts from 10 to 39 lashes for the offences he takes cognizance of.

Believes no planter ever thinks of engaging an overseer, without enquiring his character, and if cruel, he is never employed. P. 309.

An overseer is never allowed to punish except by an occasional lash at work, and that generally over the clothes;—on ill behaviour he complains to the manager. Every man tries to get a manager of information and education, with whom to trust his property, and he is generally associated with by gentlemen. Has himself discharged an overseer and a manager for cruelty;—the last could get no employment afterwards, and was obliged to leave the island.

Thinks holing (which lasts about 3 months) and dunging the hardest work; though in crop the slaves work many more hours.

The dung is carted to the land's side, and thence carried by the slaves in small baskets, on their heads, to the holes. The slaves carry them with the greatest

1790. Part II. apparent eaſe, as that is the uſual mode of carrying weights.

P. 310. It would be impoſſible to diſtribute the dung any other way.

Heat appears congenial to the ſlaves—never knew one complain of it—has often ſeen them baſk in the ſun in the heat of the day, when they might have been in their houſes.

Thinks it morally impoſſible for Europeans to do the neceſſary field labour—for he twice made trial; one with a gardener, the other a carter—after a very ſhort time, not above a fortnight, they each gave up their offices, finding the climate too ſevere.

Knows the military always complain of the heat, if kept out any length of time. It is the opinion of all the officers with whom he has converſed, that it is too fatiguing for the men to be out, except evenings and mornings. Recollects the regt. quartered in Antigua were obliged to carry their proviſions from the king's ſtores to the barracks, and in a few weeks it was neceſſary to give them a cart, the work being too ſevere, though it was not ¼ of a mile on level ground.

Knows the plough has been uſed by ſome, but found not to anſwer.

P. 311. His ſlaves coſt him 5l. per annum each, beſides the yams he raiſes, which generally feed them all between 4 and 5 months; and wine, freſh meat, &c. for the ſick.

Were it poſſible by the plough, &c., to leſſen in the leaſt the ſlave's labour, or the expence, certainly the planter would moſt readily adopt it.

Recollects another ſlave, worth 180l., partly inherited, conſiderable part got by his induſtry—he thinks, becauſe he was a valuable tradeſman, and had conſtant employ. He who gave, as mentioned, 200l. for his freedom, was a maſon.

P. 312. When he ſpoke of many ſlaves ſpending from 10 to 15l. per annum, he alluded to field, as well as houſe-

house-slaves. The last acquire their property from selling their stock, roots, and fruit. These sell at a moderate price, compared with the same or similar articles here. 1790. Part. II.

One of his estates consists of 120 acres of cane land, the gang 152; the other of 222 acres, gang 137.

Cannot state the proportion of infants, &c.; but thinks there are about 22 domesticks on the estate where he resides, besides about five more, who wait on the manager and overseer; on the other, about 8 attend on them.

Were he to speak of the acres in an estate in Antigua, he should include every part.

The proportion of slaves' provision-grounds varies P. 313. in almost every estate: on one of his, the provision-ground is large; on the other, very small.

The ground-provision is the produce of a part of the master's land allotted for raising provisions for the whole gang. Every negro family, he believes, has a piece of ground for raising provisions, universally through Antigua.

On one of his estates, where there are the most slaves, he thinks the land for the whole gang not above from 2 to 3 acres; on the other, about 4. Some of it adjoins the negro huts, or within a stone's throw; the rest is at some little distance.

As far as he saw, each hut has between 14 to 18 feet square, which is the quantity on his estates on which the slaves generally allot to stock-pens, and not provisions—some plant fruit trees.

The provision land, divided among the slaves, is seldom the best, but answers for provisions.

Believes a slave sells full as much provision of his own growth as he uses; but as they are generally fond of new provision, they often sell their allowed grain, and eat part of the provisions they raise themselves. In 82, many of his own told him, they often got a dollar a week for the vegetables they sold in the hurricane months to the shipping.

1790. Part II. While he lived in the W. Indies, he often knew the slaves' provisions, as well as the masters', much hurt by bad weather and winds—in that case they have an extra allowance.

The slave commonly gets his property by selling his produce, allowed grain and stock, and, from his industry in the time allotted him to rest, has often known field slaves earn ½ a crown a day as porters; particularly Sunday, that being considered as entirely his own.

P. 315. No field work is ever allowed on Sundays. Mechanics, he believes, work almost every Sunday, if they can get work. It is very usual in crop for slaves to thatch, on Sundays, negro houses.

No master has a right to exact any work, ever so trifling, from his slave on a Sunday without pay.

In crop the slaves' hogs are generally fed with the canes they carry away; the goats with grass, &c.; the poultry with grain. He speaks of canes, ground and unground, especially the last; though slaves are not allowed to take a large quantity of canes not ground, it is done very constantly.

Considers the yearly expence of 5l. each slave, exclusive of ground-provision, to begin nearly from the birth, as he regularly gives food and cloathing from that time; but it was on an average, of old and young.

P. 316. The chief articles in this estimate are food, clothing, doctor's charges, and parish and public taxes, which begin at birth, continue through life, and are considerable.

Some free negroes work as tradesmen in towns, but in general they prefer sedentary business.

Has bought new negroes, in various lots; the largest, he thinks, not above 16. Bought as many females as possible, and preferred young persons. Thinks the last 2 lots were all under 15. Many were only fit for children's work.

It is not very common to get a lot of slaves, all young;

young; nor ſhould he, had not a friend wiſhed for adults; they therefore accommodated each other. 1790. Part II.

The buyer may reject any ſlaves out of any lot; and the ſeller never obliges him to take more than he wiſhes; but then the price is often raiſed. Believes near relations, appearing to be ſo, are never parted. Is confident no near ones were parted by his and his friend's purchaſe; but in his lot there were 2 ſiſters and 2 brothers. P. 317.

Thinks a Creole ſlave ſo much more deſirable, as being attached to the ſoil, than an African, that the expence can never be worth any planter's attention; though he believes by the time a Creole comes to maturity, he coſts as much, if not more.

Believes the motives for preſſing an act for regulating the trial of criminal ſlaves by jury, originated from all the magiſtrates thinking it too great an undertaking to ſit, both as judge and jury, on any perſon's life.

Never heard any bad effects reſulted from the former modes of trial.

It certainly was generally underſtood that ſlaves were protected by the common law of England. A ſlave of his had been ill-treated by a young man without any provocation: he thought it his duty to apply to a magiſtrate: the man was bound over; but through ſome of his friends the matter was made up, at the particular requeſt of the ſlave, to whom he made ſatisfactory recompence: but for this he ſhould certainly have proſecuted him to the utmoſt. The ſlave was a cooper, and coming home from St. John's, the young man very wantonly rode againſt him; and on the ſlave's remonſtrating, beat him. P. 318.

The ſlave applied to him directly.

From every information he has gained, the regulating act has certainly tended materially to raiſe the price of ſlaves.

Speaking within his own knowledge, does not know any alteration in the treatment of ſlaves.

The

1790. The Moravian and Methodiſt preachers have ap-
Part II. plied themſelves very zealouſly and ſucceſsfully in the converſion of negroes in Antigua; and having built
P. 319. proper meeting houſes, all the ſlaves are encouraged by their maſters to attend.

The general effect on the converts has been a more decent behaviour and religious attendance; and moſt are become Chriſtians.

Before the Moravians and Methodiſts came to the iſland, the negroes very generally attended all the churches, and they conſidered themſelves as influenced to purſue the doctrine they heard; but from their having had greater attention paid them by the Moravians and Methodiſts, he thinks, they are much more enlightened than they were.

Managers have often ſlaves, (their own). Some wait on them: others are often hired to work with the gang of the eſtate they manage.

The lives of ſlaves are full as long as thoſe of free negroes, but not quite ſo long as that of whites that do not work. Has know negroes live to a great age.
P. 320. Doubts not ſlaves would live much longer, if leſs debauched.

From the ſituation of his eſtate cloſe to the ſea, where there are moſt ſlaves, they want land leſs than on the other, by being moſt plentifully ſupplied with freſh fiſh from the ſea, and the guts adjoining.

A young healthy Creole ſlave is generally put to the hard work of an eſtate at Antigua, about the age of 18.

The iſland is ſubject to frequent long droughts, ſometimes ſucceeded by great rains. Recollects no rain of conſequence from Feb. 80, when he arrived
P. 321. there, to Oct. and he underſtood, before his arrival, the iſland in general had wanted rain many months; he has juſt received from thence ſimilar accounts. Various epidemicks often follow ſuch a change from drought to moiſture.

Underſtands epidemicks have lately raged there, and many have died. On ſome eſtates it has been more

more fatal; on one eſtate, of 240 ſlaves, 12 died in very few days; and at differeat times from 20 to 30 lay dangerouſly ill. 1790. PART II.

Certainly does not think it poſſible, under ſuch circumſtances, for a planter, the moſt ſucceſsful in rearing Creoles, to carry on his uſual cultivation without interruption, unleſs he can buy new ſlaves to ſupply the occaſional loſſes of ſlaves by theſe epidemicks.

Witneſs examined.—Doctor SAMUEL ATHILL.

Was born in Antigua. Firſt left it 1764, returned to it 1779. Was in the aſſembly 5 years, and appointed counſellor 1786. P. 321.

Practiſed phyſic there, and attended from 8 to 9000 negroes. Had ſo much per head yearly, and bound to attend when called on (at times, twice a day) beſides 1 or 2 viſits weekly. Had extra pay for laborious deliveries, fractures, &c. P. 322.

Poſſeſſes 2 eſtates in Antigua.

By far the greater part of eſtates there were underhanded. Some few perhaps had more ſlaves than they wanted. P. 323.

As a medical man and a planter, thinks births may equal deaths, but the number raiſed does not equal the decreaſe; negro children are liable to the jaw-fall; few had it on his own eſtates; on thoſe which he attended, he was never called for it, death following ſo quickly: Thinks the cold and damps they are expoſed to, by their mothers night rambles is one great cauſe why children are not reared; which the owners cannot remedy; they do what they can by exempting nurſing women from throwing graſs at night, or other work which the reſt are occaſionally forced to: Many other cauſes prevent children being reared; unhealthy ſituation of an eſtate, its nearneſs to a town or port: On one of his

 eſtates

1790. Part II. estates far from town, his slaves increased; on his other estates near English harbour, fewer children are born and raised, from the excesses of both sexes,
P. 324. at that port.

Great attention was paid to rearing children on all the estates he attended; a good slave, when settled and had several children, is always careful of them, and is encouraged by her master; many owners give midwives rewards on births. He gives a dollar. Pregnant women seemed more likely to suffer from indolence, than hard work: As soon as they feel themselves with child, and often long before, they withdraw from work; and he has found it difficult to get them to attend the field merely to look on; which he always insisted on, to prevent their carrying heavy burdens to market, or doing other injurious work for themselves. When brought to bed, on most estates, she has any nursing woman she chuses, to attend her the first 9 days: She has sugar, oatmeal, &c. daily, and often candles and other indulgencies: Never works till her month is up, and then she does not turn out till the sun is well up, and retires before it is down: She has the child with her in the field which she attends, as it cries; so that the work of
P. 325. a nursing woman is very trifling indeed.

Where he has ordered wine, animal food, or other indulgencies, has no reason to think they were ever withheld.

The dysentery was epidemic in Antigua 1778, 9, 1780, and carried off nearly 1 5th of the slaves. On his estate, east-part of the island he lost few, being a healthy situation, on his other estate he lost more.

Every medical exertion was used to stop the progress of this distemper.

Has known food scarce from a long drought; if the owner gave less food, the work must have been less, and his wants kept pace with the slaves wants; for his last 5 years residence, the island has been more flourishing, and he has seen no signs of scarcity.

The

The ſcarcity from the drought mentioned, was in war-time, when the whites alſo ſuffered very much. 1790. Part. II.

Has in the courſe of his practice, generally found the negroes in health, ſpirits, and ſeemingly content, and when he noticed their houſes want repair, on mentioning it to the manager, it was done.

Does not recollect being called to attend any ſlave in conſequence of a puniſhment; though had it happened, thinks he muſt have known of it. For great faults they are oftener confined, which they mind more than chaſtiſement.

New ſlaves are generally very much indulged. From the want of ſlaves, he thinks there is not enow of females.

The abolition of the ſlave trade would certainly increaſe the difficulty of keeping up the ſtock; a few eſtates on the iſland, not very much weakened by mortality, may never require an African ſlave, but ſuppoſes thoſe muſt originally have had moſt women.

The loſs of 1779 is not yet repaired, the bad crops which followed diſabled moſt from buying, till within theſe 2 or 3 years.

Many muſt have ſtopt cultivation, had the African trade been aboliſhed, as taſk work would have been ſo high as to prevent them from doing it that way, nor could the cultivation have been carried on even by this mode. For taſk work being at 7l. 10s. per acre, inſtead of 4l. 10s. as prior to 1779, the iſland muſt be concluded ſtill very much underhanded.

As a medical man and a planter, thinks the ſlaves could not be kept up by breeding; ſome eſtates are unhealthy, and have other circumſtances unfavourable, which makes him doubt if, by any means, the encreaſe could be made equal to the decreaſe: the planter would conſtantly prefer breeding, Creoles being preferable to Africans.

Thinks eſtates could not be cultivated otherwiſe than at preſent: The number of ſlaves required in crop, could not be otherwiſe ſupplied: Whites could not

1790. do the work: Plough-men and boys were brought
Part II. out to eſtates where the plough was tried; but they
could not ſtand the labour there.

P. 328. Never heard a negro complain of heat, but often of cold.

Thinks the plough cannot be uſed in Antigua; where it has been tried in ſituations moſt favourable, it has always been given up. The planter would certainly adopt any mode tending to leſſen expence and his ſlave's labour.

In crop, the firſt work in the morning is cutting canes, in which all that can be, are muſtered; when there is enough cut to put the mill about, 3 able men attend it, and 5 or 7 younger hand them canes; when 2 coppers of juice are ground, 2 more ſtrong men are called as fire-men, and 2 boilers; as more juice is collected, more men are called, and there are generally 7 boilers, and 4 fire-men on a moderate eſtate with 9 coppers; amounting, with thoſe in the diſtillery, to 20 or 30, when the work is briſk; ſo that few are left to cut canes, drive the cart, and do the other work, except on very well-handed eſtates: Such an eſtate with 9 coppers, ſhould pro-
P. 329. duce 200 Hhds. of ſugar a year.

The number of ſlaves in the boiling-houſe is not proportionate to the ſize of the eſtate, the produce, or number of ſlaves; for, ſome, over-rating their property, may have erected buildings for 200 Hhds. when perhaps it does not turn out 60; but ſtill, the coppers being there, are uſed and attended.

On eſtates weakly handed, the canes are cut by the whole gang one day, and manufactured the next.

Canes ſhould be cut juſt when ripe, when let ſtand longer, 'tis to the Planters great loſs: If not ground immediately, in a few days they ſour, and are fit only to make rum.

It often happens, that the perſons who are em-
P. 329. ployed in cutting the canes, attend the boiling-houſe
afterwards to a late hour; but they do not in ge-

neral turn out with the gang to hard labour the next morning. 1790. Part II.

Though cane cutting is laborious, he does not think it one of the hardeſt ſervices of the plantation; it is done with ſuch alacrity and good ſpirits that it ſeems trifling; women do it with as much ſeeming eaſe as the men; The inſtrument uſed is a bill, a good cane is from 5 to 8 feet long, it is cut down at P. 330. the root, then the top is taken off, and, if too long to go into the cart, cut in two; young ſlaves and women with young children, attend to bundle up the canes as they are cut.

Diſtilling begins 10, 15 or 20 days after the firſt canes are cut, and laſts through the crop, conducted by a ſkilful negro, with 4 aſſiſtants under the direction of the manager.

The act intitled "An act for ſettling and regu-"lating the trial of criminal ſlaves by jury" was paſſed, to relieve a hardſhip complained of by magiſtrates, two of whom (one being of the quorum) ſat in judgement upon the ſlaves for all crimes, thus acting as judge and jury; it was alſo thought more effectual juſtice would be done the criminal by a jury.

Aſcribes tetanus in young children to a premature expoſure to cold, but is of opinion that ſo many do not die of it even as owners think; none die within the 9th day, but it is ſaid to be of the jaw fall; though it is natural to ſuppoſe that many die from the ſame cauſes which cut off white children.

His eſtate on the windward part of the iſland is 400 acres; 200 in canes, 30 in proviſions, the reſt paſture: his other in Falmouth diviſions, near Engliſh harbour is 220 acres; 100 in canes, 20 in proviſions, the reſt paſture. On the largeſt he has 220 ſlaves, of which about 80 are field ſlaves, on the other 110 or 115 ſlaves.

Some of the proviſion ground is planted with Guinea corn by the whole gang, and the produce ſtored for the uſe of the eſtate; the reſt is divided among the ſlaves at the rate of about 70 feet ſquare

1790. Part II. per head; as he had ſo much land, his proviſion grounds in general were larger than common, and they had more if they pleaſed; yams and eddoes were beſides annually raiſed in the cane land.

Beſides the produce of their own grounds, they had from 8 to 12 meaſures (of about a pint each) per head, or 26 to 30 pounds of yams each, a week; ſuch as look ill are fed twice or thrice a day; at dinner they have a very full meal.

P. 332. From the produce of their grounds, their goats, hogs, and poultry, an induſtrious family both live and dreſs well.

The paſture ground is allotted for feeding cattle, mules and ſheep: a large herd of cattle requires 2 men and 2 young boys, mules one man, and ſheep 2 boys. On his windward eſtate he had fewer by one man, on the other he kept no ſheep, and one man and 2 boys were enough to attend the cattle and mules.

It requires an able and truſt-worthy ſlave to attend the paſture grounds.

The potatoe raiſed by the ſlaves is thought to exhauſt the land more than any other root; on eſtates where almoſt the whole land is in canes, the proviſion ground is taken in exchange for the ſame quantity of new land once in 2 or three years, to the mutual advantage of owner and ſlave: the ſlaves are always pleaſed with the exchange, as new land yields them more.

When their ground proviſions fail, which is often,
P. 333. their allowed ſood is increaſed; he never gave, as a general allowance, more than 12 pints, but generally gave what more was aſked.

Thinks the annual expence of a ſlave from 5l. to 8l. currency; in war it was fully 8l.

On his eſtate at windward, his ſlaves increaſe; on the other at Falmouth, he placed 20 ſlaves in the laſt 9 years, and the number does not now exceed what it was then.

Never bought more than 8 Africans, and thoſe in

1 lot;

1 lot; 7 males and 1 female, all about 15 years of age, from the windward coaſt.

Never heard it doubted, that breeding is more profitable than burying to the planter.

In the ſcarcity before mentioned, large orders for provisions were ſent to Great Britain, and ſupplies tried to be got from the neighbouring iſlands: quantities of beans, flour, and Indian corn were got from Euſtatius, bad, and exorbitantly dear. P. 334.

He deſires, in conſequence of more maturely conſidering a calculation made and communicated to him by the late Alderman Oliver, to ſtate ſterling for currency in his preceding eſtimate of a ſlave's annual coſt for maintenance in war time, when every article of food is dearer, as is alſo the freight and inſurance. P. 335.

The various ſorts of ground proviſions, are yams, the moſt material, and moſt productive in a light ſoil, ſuch as the eaſt, north eaſt and north weſt parts of the iſland; eddoes, which do beſt in a ſtrong or clay ſoil, Guinea and American corn, which grows in either, and Plantanes, which do beſt in rich and moiſt bottoms and near rivulets, cannot therefore be raiſed with advantage in Antigua as a material article of food; worms hurt every ſpecies of proviſion but it.

In caſe ground proviſions fail, planters have generally a quantity of beans from England, for an emergency, which are kiln dried, and keep a long time: In peace never knew Indian corn altogether wanting at market; it is ſubject to be hurt by the weevil, and ſoon gets muſty.

The W. I. iſlands ſuffered much when the American ports were ſhut; and even the average price of grain from thence is nearly double what it was before the war; then it might be had for 5s.; now they aſk 8s. 3d. or 9s. per buſhel. P. 336.

Slaves have not ſuffered from this circumſtance; believes they never were better fed in Antigua than for the laſt five years: more yams and eddoes have been raiſed, more beans imported, and there has been

1790. been always American grain at market, though at a
Part II. higher price than before.

The cane requires regular rains, the yam will do with lefs; but in October, when appling, it muft have rain; the eddoes require much rain: the uncertainty in raifing American corn makes it, he thinks, come higher than buying: the paftures require conftant rains.

P. 337. Guinea grafs is raifed in particular fpots, and in the intervals between cane pieces; being more attended to than the general pafture, it can do with lefs rain, but continued dry weather often kills it.

Does not know there has been any material improvement in the economy and management of a fugar eftate of late years.

In cafe of the abolition of the flave trade, thinks a confiderable number of flaves could be introduced into ours, from the neighbouring iflands.

Slaves live to as great an age in the W. Indies as whites: on moft eftates old age is fpent in a comfortable and eafy way.

When they deem themfelves fuperannuated, they
P. 337. do no work for their mafter; before that, their work is light; they act as affiftant nurfes for the fick and for children, and wafh or cook for the overfeers: he had 15 or 16 of the firft defcription at Windward, an old fettled eftate, and the gang chiefly Creoles; on the other, he had not about two; being near Englifh Harbour, the flaves there lead a more debauched
P. 338. life than the others; are not fo healthy, nor live fo long: of the fecond clafs, can't fay how many he had.

Slaves are often long lived in Antigua: never knew a flave abandoned by his owner, becaufe unfit for labour from age or difeafe.

An able field-flave watches canes, &c.—an old flave fometimes lives in the negro grounds and plantain walks to guard them; in that cafe, his hut is made more durable and comfortable than the common watch-houfes.

The

The late advance of price on slaves, he believes, has been on males and females alike. 1790. Part II.

Formerly, he believes, the slves thought little of religion, and few were Christians; many now attend churches and meetings, and most are baptized, from the settling of Moravian and Methodist teachers in the island; the former have two good chapels, are attentive to their duty, and lead exemplary lives.

Impossible to keep up stock without importation. P. 339.

Never knew a black ploughman in Antigua. P. 340.

It is from the excessive heat that he thinks a white incapable of field labour in the W. Indies. Thinks the medium heat at Antigua may be about 80° of Farhenheit.

Several estates have a white overseer, who turns out with the slaves in the morning, calls a list, and sees that each is at work, attends the great gang part of the forenoon, when, from the great heat, he retires, and if at a distance, has a mule to carry him home; in the afternoon, he calls the list again, and overlooks the work.

Never saw a white whom he thought could hole; is certain they could not stand the office of fireman, or boiler.

White domestics have so many negroes about them, that they soon become gentlemen; and believes they are generally deemed useless: knew but two cases where they were tried, in both they became sots, and were sent back.

For one European blacksmith in a shop, there are 3 blacks, who do the drudgery; they are not healthy nor long lived. P. 341.

The cutting of canes is so easy, that often more than one cane is brought down by a stroke of the bill.

Though in crop the slaves work harder, yet are they incomparably more chearful than at other times, and are much healthier after a long than a short crop.

In

1790. Part II. In Antigua, they cool down their coppers every night, but not immediately after ſun-ſet; at an average about 9 or 10 o'clock; ſeldom begin boiling before ſun-riſe; hence the ſlaves have time to reſt, if they chuſe.

Townſpeople who have no plantations, and keep horſes, are furniſhed with provender by the negroes of the neighbouring eſtates, who carry it in for ſale
P. 342. at noon and evening, to a great amount; graſs, ſo bought, will coſt 2s. 3d., or 2s. 6d. ſterl. a day for a horſe, beſides oats.

Thoſe townſpeople, alſo the troops and ſhips of war, are furniſhed with vegetables, hogs, and poultry, by managers, by ſome owners who make it an object; but chiefly, he believes, by the ſlaves; ſome poultry is imported from America.

Slaves have the entire property of what they get by their induſtry; never heard of an owner interfering in any degree with the property of a ſlave ſo acquired.

From the obſervation he has made of the labour, treatment, and general ſtate of the ſlaves in Antigua, he ſcruples not to declare, that he thinks the negro and his family happier, and much freer from cares and miſery, than the peaſantry in many parts of this country.

ALEXANDER WILLOCK, Eſq.

P. 343. Reſided 36 years in Antigua, (except in England 18 months, p. 356); had eſtates there, and was attorney for others; returned to England in 1781.

Moſt eſtates wanted hands, eſpecially after the fatal year 1779, before which his eſtates were full handed. His ſtock at firſt was moſtly Africans; increaſed by births till 1779, when on two of his eſtates, of above 500, he loſt 50 by fluxes from Aug.

to

to Nov. The general loſs was computed at 4,500 or more. 1790. Part II.

Several negroes have been ſince imported, but there is ſtill a great deficiency: he happened to be ſo well ſtocked as to want no ſupply. Leſs ſugar muſt have been made, had no new ſlaves come; and ſhould a ſimilar misfortune befall the iſland, and the ſupplies from Africa cut off, ſeveral perſons muſt abandon their eſtates. P. 344.

He has been lately informed from the iſland, that Dec. and Jan. laſt were remarkably ſickly, and many ſlaves were loſt: in confirmation, he produced an extract of a letter from a Mr. Lovell to his wife, dated Antigua, 14th Jan. 1790, which ſays, that all Dec. had been dreadful ſickly among the negroes: on ſome eſtates more fatal than on others; and that at Mr. Brookes's eſtate (Pope's Head) 12 out of 240 were loſt; 30 or 40 down together on the Wood eſtate. P. 345.

Says, that in the ſickneſs in 1779 every attention, medical and other, was ſhewn; that himſelf called two ſurgeons, in aid of the proper one of the eſtate, and told them, that they could not put him to too much expence for the negroes. P. 346.

Does not think eſtates in general have females enow; he bought a great many.

Thinks the preſent ſtock of ſlaves in Antigua could not be kept up by breeding.

Breeding is more profitable than buying, one Creole being worth 3 Africans.

Slaves are, in general, fed, cloathed, and lodged, by their owners; their food is corn, beans, rice, herrings, at times pork, flour, biſcuit, or beef; they have alſo proviſion grounds, and are allowed to keep as many fowls and hogs as they pleaſe. He allows his ſlave generally an afternoon a week (which was not the general practice, p. 354) to work their grounds, where they often employ a part of the hour and half they have at dinner time. P. 347.

1790. Part II. Has known ſeveral ſlaves acquire money: a female ſlave of his bought of him two ſlaves.

A ſlave of his refuſed his freedom, ſaying, white men would beat him, and he ſhould have no maſter to help him.

Has known many ſlaves reach old age.

He takes dunging, in baſkets of about 25lb. in all, to be the hardeſt field work: they always do it
P. 348. cheerfully, for he generally gave them grog. The baſket of dung is not the greateſt weight a ſlave may be required to carry—a firkin of butter will weigh 70lb.

Their houſes are from 25 to 30 feet long, with two rooms: they are provided with cabins to ſleep on and covering.

Produce depends conſiderably on the number of hands. He bought an eſtate with 120 ſlaves, and made about 70 hogſheads of ſugar; there is now 350 ſlaves on it, and it averages 150 hogſheads.

P. 349. Breeding is not obſtructed by hard labour or ill uſage; he exempts his women, when they declare their pregnancy, from all hard labour; lying-in they have every indulgence, and any negro they chuſe to attend them; he gives the midwife a dollar (8s 3d. currency) for each child that lives 9 days. Moſt aſſuredly the maſter does his utmoſt to preſerve the children.

As to the effect the abolition of the ſlave trade may have on the negroes, he dreads it above all things; thinks that ſo ſoon as they knew that there would be no more imported, they would deſtroy the whites; there are, he reckons, 15 to 1 in Antigua.

Negroes rejoice on the arrival of a ſhip which happens to have ſlaves from their part of Africa aboard.

He carried out 2 ploughs from England in 1770 by advice of a Mr. Baldwyn, but they did not ſuc-
P. 350. ceed. No whites could ſtand the climate in field work; never employed any; never knew a corn hole dug by a white; has known ſome employ white gardeners, were obliged to give it up. The lower whites

whites are ſo drunken, there is no dependence on them. 1790. Part II.

Dung could not be carried through the cane fields in carts, (to eaſe the ſlaves), the carts would deſtroy the cane holes.

Has 2 ſugar eſtates in Antigua; one in the Body Diviſion of 450 acres, 250 in canes and 200 in paſture and proviſions, (p. 352) bought in 1768, with 120 ſlaves; he continued to add to theſe by purchaſe till 1781; with an increaſe of 230 ſlaves and 30 mules he highly improved it, and raiſed the produce from 70 hogſheads a year to 150 hogſheads on an average of 7 years, (p. 353). His other eſtate in Pope's-Head Diviſion is of 130 acres, 90 in canes and 40 in paſture and proviſions, bought in 1777, with 130 ſlaves; loſt 25 in 1779; bought none; there is now 100, which are ſufficient, the land be- P. 351.
ing light, work eaſy; (the proportion of cane land on each the ſame as when bought, p. 352.)

Had more males than females; men are neceſſary for boilers, tradeſmen, carters, and watchmen.

Thinks the planters are fortunate who, upon an old ſettled eſtate, have two-thirds of their ſlaves workers (including the graſs gang) from 6 or 7 to 55 years old; of the other one-third, one-fifth may be ſuppoſed above 55.

Was factor for all the ſales at which he bought P. 352.
ſlaves; never bought more than 50 at once; always choſe them between the age of 10 and 25, but if any old parents in the lot, bought them; never ſeparated relations. As a factor, never ſuffered a family to be ſeparated; if a buyer had laid out a lot of ſlaves, and it was afterwards known they had relations in the cargo, he inſiſted the buyer ſhould take theſe alſo, or give up the others. Has bought ſlaves from Bonny, the Windward Coaſt, and chiefly from the Gold Coaſt.

On his largeſt eſtate his ſlaves have 10 to 15 acres proviſion ground, and often a cane piece of about 10 acres for further proviſion. On the other eſtate P. 353.

 they

1790. Part II. they have about 10 acres. At both the manager lays out the ground in proportion to each family. Cane holes are 2 feet, ſometimes 4 aſunder. His working ſlaves had generally from 12 to 14 pints of corn, with about 5 herrings, per week; the others from 8 to 10 pints, with about 4 herrings: about one-third of the gang were generally fed from the pot; thoſe ſo fed may have about 21 pints of corn or beans, with herrings, beef, or pork, in the pot per week; ſometimes they have rice twice a day, which is deducted from the 21 pints of grain. (The ſtouteſt of the pot gang had alſo proviſion ground. The overſeers were directed, when any negro had neglected to bring his breakfaſt to the field with him, to ſtop his allowance, and feed him from the pot: this, though they got more food by it, they reckoned a diſgrace, as treating them like new negroes. p. 354.)

After great damage by a hurricane in 1772 he enlarged his works.

P. 354. The exceſs, over the uſual allowance which the pot gang had, was much more than equal to the produce of the ordinary lots of proviſion ground.

Slaves near towns can pick graſs, and ſell it in the market from 2d. to 6d. per bundle.

General allowance of food in Antigua not equal to his; but where he directed, he kept it up as much as he could.

When the ſupplies from America were cut off, he did not give an ounce leſs food to his ſlaves, though the article ſometimes coſt him thrice the price.

The ground proviſions are, yams, eddoes, Guinea and Indian corn, potatoes, and caſſada; all which often fail in droughts, to which they are ſubject; but the proviſions and indulgences he gives his ſlaves are ſufficient without them.

The hardieſt ground proviſions are caſſada, Guinea and Indian corn.

It was not general in Antigua to allow the ſlaves an afternoon to themſelves.

P. 355. Heretofore he thinks there was no protection for the

the ſlaves againſt maſters and others; but ſince he came home he is told there is an act in the iſland, that whites, uſing a ſlave ill, are brought to ſeſſions, if the owner proſecutes. Has known ſlaves beat by whites (not their maſters) without redreſs; but ſlaves are now much better uſed than when he firſt went to the iſland in 1745, and their good conduct deſerves it, as they are much more civiliſed, and often go to church and methodiſt meetings on Sunday. 1790. Part II.

Has heard the ſlaves inſtructed at methodiſt meetings to be attentive and obedient to their maſters, with other good advice: never knew the regular clergy pay any particular attention to them. (Has heard that the Society for propagating the Goſpel ſent miſſionaries out to convert the ſlaves, p. 357.)

Thinks a humane maſter cannot do worſe by a ſlave than to free him.

Had 33 domeſtics on the Body-Diviſion eſtate, P. 356. (none on the other), viz. 5 footmen, 2 cooks, 8 waſherwomen, 3 ſempſtreſſes, 5 ſmall ſtock-keepers, 2 grooms, 6 women with child, and 2 aged females; no town houſe; had many more than was generally kept by people of the ſame rank, owing to his having many children. (Thinks no family in the iſland kept ſo many domeſtics, p. 358.)

Reared moſt of his negro children from the encouragement to the midwives, and attention to the mothers.

Slaves of 6 or 7 years are put under the charge of a careful old woman, and pick graſs merely to keep them employed.

From the increaſe of ſlaves and the mules upon P. 347. his eſtates, he planted more canes than his predeceſſor.

Proviſions have advanced in Antigua 150 per cent. on an average, ſince the ſupplies from America were cut off.

The ſlaves near the towns and Engliſh Harbour have a good deal of traffic by their ſmall ſtock, yams, &c.: they ſupply alſo the troops and ſhips of war.

W. INDIES.—Witness examined—R. HIBBERT, Esq;

1790.
Part II.
P. 360. A native of this country, resided about 18 years in Jamaica, left it September 1789, was a merchant, knew the management of plantations there, was owner also of estates there, and has had charge of others.

Is certain Jamaica cannot be cultivated by Europeans; for no European could bear constant exposure to the heat, still less when labouring. The soldiers are allowed black pioneers to carry wood, water, &c. The officers have told him the mortality has since decreased much.

P. 361. A sugar estate, at the present prices, could not afford proper food and accommodation for the necessary number of European labourers.

There are a great number of free negroes and tradesmen, of whom many do nothing.

There is occasionally a necessity for more than can be done by the plantation negroes. Never knew free negroes offer to do field labour; has known them offer themselves as tradesmen.

The plough is used in Jamaica, he thinks, whenever it can advantageously, from nature of soil and surface, &c. in most of the islands it cannot be used; where it has been long used, has known it often worked by negroes. Such parts as may be cultivated with advantage, are far from being all so.
P. 362. Many estates with full value paid, and extensive works built, are only partly settled; must be thrown up, or continued with loss, if owners are deprived of the means of cultivation. Much land is uncultivated.

Thinks some uncultivated land unfit for sugar, or coffee, cotton, &c. but a large part would do well for coffee.

Lessening

Leſſening the duties on Britiſh plantation coffee 1790. Part II.
has cauſed many, who could not ſettle a ſugar plantation, to buy ſome wood-land and a few ſlaves, and open and till it ſucceſsfully. Thinks they ſhall thus gain many uſeful citizens of the middle claſs, who will add to the ſafety and happineſs of the iſland, and increaſe the commerce and revenue of the mother country. Such ſettlements cannot be made without negroes. Thinks the old ſettlements, if ſtripped for this end, muſt ſuffer in proportion; and thinks the new ones, moſtly in their infancy, P. 363.
muſt be thrown up, or cultivated to certain loſs.

Believes the preſent cultivation of Jamaica cannot be kept up without annual importation of negroes. The negroes generally decreaſe on ſugar eſtates; for, in moſt, males exceed females. Infants are ſubject to the locked jaw, in a few days after birth; and the young women have indiſcriminate intercourſe with the men. The adult are ſubject to the yaws, and every diſorder as Europeans. Fluxes are often cauſed by improper food; and ſometimes after hurricanes proper cannot be had. Recollects great mortality among the negroes from ſuch cauſes; loſt about a ſixth of about 120 in two or three weeks, on a ſmall eſtate in pariſh of Clarendon, by a flux ſo cauſed, though the beſt help in the iſland was applied. Does not recollect, if confined to his own eſtate, or general at that time; but it P. 364.
was general after every hurricane he ſaw. If ſuch diſorders, with putrid fever, are common, after every rain ſucceeding long drought, he thinks they ariſe from improper food. Some die of them.

The Jamaica report, of 1788, proves the proportion of imported males and females has been for many years as 5 to 3. It differs much on ſugar eſtates; in general, males exceed one fourth at leaſt, which is certainly one cauſe of the decreaſe.

Cannot ſtate the general proportion of deaths and births; has had many years eſtates of his own, and others

1790. others under his care, and does not recollect one
Part II. case of births equal to deaths, though all attention
was paid, and no excessive labour required.

Thinks every attention generally given to pregnant women, on plantations known to him. There may be instances to the contrary: knows none.

In general, the locked jaw among children is
P. 365. fatal.—A native is of more value than an African:
certainly for planters' benefit to encourage their rearing. Slaves are often so reduced by diseases, &c. as to make it needful to purchase or hire fresh.

Thinks such estates could not be kept up without fresh imports. Sugar estates so reduced, could not be put to other use with equal profit; in some cases might do for pasture, or cotton, but the works and appendages would be of little or no use. Thinks coffee, indigo or pimento could not be raised on old sugar land; that it must be thrown up as such, not to be used in another way, to any thing like the same gain.

Never heard domestic negroes in the island computed. In towns, the principal families he knew, have from 10 to 30; in the country, in general,
P. 366. barely what is necessary.
Does not think if all the domesticks were turned into the field, fresh importations would be unnecessary. It is mostly thought a punishment. Many would be so hurt in their spirits by such change, as to be of very little use, even if their numbers were greater.

He is a member of the assembly.—A duty of 30s. currency on every negro imported is imposed by their legislature; 20s. paid by buyer, 10s. by importer; makes part of the island fund for subsistence of the king's troops; quite independant of their English pay. Believes, if Great Britain should forbid importation of Africans, they would want rather power than will to continue it; that the plantations only partly settled, must depopulate the small settlements, or be thrown up; and that the full-handed plantations

plantations (the ſexes being in general badly aſ- 1790.
ſorted) would naturally, in time, decreaſe in Part II.
produce, and a total ſtop be put to improvement.
The whites have very ſeldom any other domeſtics P. 367.
than negroes. Upon plantations in general no more, he believes, than are neceſſary.

The full-handed plantations are ſo badly aſſorted as to ſex (5 to 3) becauſe men are ſuppoſed capable of more labour; knows not what it is alſo owing to the deficiency of procuring females in Africa, or diſpoſing of them in the Weſt Indies: Knows nothing of the trade on the coaſt of Africa; Sugar planters chiefly chuſe males.

Believes the number of negroes annually exported and imported from and to Jamaica, very accurately ſtated in the report of the aſſembly; cannot now call it to mind: They differ greatly.

When a plough is firſt uſed, a white man is P. 368.
moſtly employed.

On ſuch plantations as he has had care of, the annual uſual decreaſe has been about 5 per cent. increaſe 2 and ½. No true judgement can be formed whether the decreaſe is greater or leſs on cotton or coffee plantations being new. Rather thinks the proportion of ſexes more equal there, as the work is lighter.

Believes inſtances of inattention to pregnant women very rare.

White ploughmen and tradeſmen have very high wages. Never knew the ſun oppreſſive to
negroes in full health; does not recollect one ſuch P. 369.
that complained.

Believes many diſeaſes brought on negroes by nocturnal ramblings and dancing.

Their food is in general good and ſufficient. They are protected and provided with food and raiment by law: Thinks the laſt conſolidated ſlave-law indiſputably ſhews the legiſlature of the iſland diſpoſed to give them every neceſſary comfort and protection.

W. Indies.—Witneſs exd.—John Wedderburn, Eſq;

1790.
Part II.
Is a native of Great Britain; has lived between 26 and 27 years in Jamaica; left it the beginning of laſt
P. 370. May; was a planter, and has property there: had care of ſeveral plantations; of full 5000 negroes.

Thinks they are treated with humanity; are in general in a happy ſtate; are attended when ſick by a doctor, who preſcribes every medicine proper for them; have proper nurſes, often proviſions of the beſt ſort from owner's or overſeer's table. They have often alſo wine, and whatever other neceſſary the doctor thinks proper. Has known in dangerous caſes the medicines given by whites, who often loſe their night's reſt by it. Negroes by age or infirmities, incapable of labour, moſtly live in a comfortable negro-houſe; have every allowance and attendance, as if ſtill of the greateſt value, are ſtill fed and clothed;
P. 371. never knew one ſuch diſcarded by his maſter.

The Africans have a remarkable ſaying in their diſputes, to ſhew that the ſtronger can take no advantage of them; "this no for we country, this for "Buccra country; Buccra country every body have "right;" i. e. in their own country, the ſtronger often uſe the weaker as they pleaſe, whether juſtly or not.

The negroes have lands to cultivate for their ſole benefit; raiſe much more proviſions than they uſe, and ſell poultry, hogs, and various kinds of fruit, and have the profits. Many might be rich; numbers ſpend their money in fine cloaths, and ſalt meat from England; others buy cows and heifers: Has known
P. 372. on different eſtates from 10 to 40 taken care of promiſcuouſly with their maſters, who take no part. They ſell them when they will. He has bought from different negroes, young ſteers, and paid them from £10 to £13 per head.

He

He has known different negroes wiſh to buy their freedom themſelves, and a few friends poſſeſſed of money ſufficient. Recollects an eſtate where there were 300 ſlaves, the owner, in eaſy circumſtances before the hurricane of 1780, by that calamity, other ſtorms, and perhaps ſome little imprudence, became embarraſſed: A writ was iſſued the marſhall came to the eſtate to ſecure him, and left it diſappointed. In the evening a few of the chief negroes came to their maſter, told him what they had heard, and brought him between £200 and 300. He refuſed it with thanks. 1790. Part II.

Such land in Jamaica as may be cultivated to advantage, is not, by many thouſand acres.

He thinks the lands now in canes cannot be uſed to advantage in coffee and cottons; if it could, the loſs to many planters would be great, having bought lands and ſtocks, raiſed buildings, and had various ſtores from England, only to cultivate the ſugar-cane; thinks cane-land in general not adapted to thoſe articles, and that to oblige the owner to this change, would be much the ſame as taking part of his property without paying for it. P. 373.

Thinks Jamaica cannot be cultivated by Europeans. They could not bear the neceſſary labour, and the mortality he thinks would be ſo great as to ſtop the attempt.

Thinks the ſun's heat not hurtful to the negroes health, and that it affects them little at work; has ſeen them often at it, and ſtood with them hours at a time; They ſeemed to him to feel no inconveniences.

Jamaica cannot be cultivated by the plough: It is uſed in many parts, but after ploughing they are forced to dig the cane-holes with hoes, to plant the canes, and often to trench the land to dry it.—Great part, ſteep and hilly, does not admit the plough; many thouſand acres have ſtones and rocks ſo intermixed with the ſoil, that the plough cannot turn it up.

1790. Part II. Many estates are cultivated so, that the canes are not stocked up, but it is a rule to keep them on the stock as long as possible. The plough could be of no use there only the hoe.

When the plough is used, the same number of negroes are requisite; but it is of infinite advantage
P. 374. to them by breaking the soil, and taking a part of the hardest labour from them: But supposing fewer at ploughing season, the usual number would be necessary in crop-time.

Has heard the legislature of Jamaica has encouraged inventors of machines for saving manual labour. Planters have readily adopted all they thought advantageous, or that have stood the test of experience.

An overseer has commonly from 6 to 10 domestics, mostly unable to support field-labour; the most weak and delicate, are generally put to domestic uses.

Thinks the present cultivation of Jamaica cannot be kept up without annual imports; not that the negroes are used ill; the women do not breed there, as the labouring ones of Great-Britain; greatly from promiscuous intercourse, causing venereal disorders,
P. 375. often destructive of the constitution. Many die by yaws, fluxes, ulcers, and pleurisies; infants besides the disorders to which they are subject in Great-Britain, are liable to the locked-jaw, of which he thinks ¼ die.

Supposes the loss in 20 landed in tolerable health, about 5 in the first 3 years; if with yaws, or other disease, double at least. Thinks they would be dissatisfied in having no more recruits from Africa, having often heard them wish for such help; and that the slaves now in Jamaica would be worse used, because most sugar-plantations being at so great expence, are obliged to borrow of the British merchant, and make him annual consignments, and payments; deprived of slaves, they could not; The merchant would be disappointed—the connec-

tion,

tion unprofitable to him. He may, to be ſure, take 1790.
ſteps, compelling the planter to puſh his ſlaves be- Part II.
yond their ſtrength, to pay him, in hopes of keeping
up his crops, and preventing the ruin of himſelf, and P. 376.
family.

Slaves labour about 11 hours out of crop-time; in crop-time, though the time of labour with ſome is longer, they are moſtly happier, and in better condition, from the canes they eat, and the liquor they drink.

Thinks, if the ſlave trade was aboliſhed, many planters could not pay their debts. Some ſmall trifling ſettlement might be practicable; none of much importance.

There are many free negroes in Jamaica, ſome of them tradeſmen; but moſt idle. The eſtates often require the help of other negroes, beſides the owner's; has known the free then employed as tradeſmen, but in no other way. Many eſtates, where expenſive works have been erected, and much money laid out, are only partly ſettled; no further progreſs can be made, without ſupplies from Africa;
unleſs thoſe, who have jobbing gangs, were to ſell P. 377.
them; then the loſs of their help to different eſtates, would be very diſtreſſing, and no other eſtates could be ſettled with propriety.

Native negroes, are much more valuable than imported; it certainly is the planter's intereſt to encourage raiſing them, and they do.

Many diſeaſes are brought on the ſlaves by night travelling, feaſting, and dancing.

Except after ſuch calamity, as the hurricane 1780, they have plenty of wholſome food.

If an act of parliament for aboliſhing the ſlave-trade, ſhould only transfer that trade to other nations, the Africans would not be benefited, or the cauſe of humanity advanced, as far as he is capable of judging.

Is

1790. Part II. Is convinced the ſlaves there would ſuffer exceedingly, as their labour would naturally be encreaſed; thinks it would tend to depopulate Jamaica, leſſen its cultivation, and prevent its improvement. Thinks it would not be attended with

P. 378. ſatisfaction to the planters, and other whites there; is confident it would produce alarming diſcontents.

Quantity of land, negroes, and produce, on as many eſtates as he can recollect, are as follows:

	Acres.	Negroes.	Hhds. Sug.	Pun. Rum
Meſopotamia	2600	310	315	230
Grange	1500	175	165	70
Gleneſley	1800	230	110	80
Caledonia	3000	180	75	45
Blue Caſtle	1800	245	240	140
Blackheath	1100	110	180	80
Mount Eagle	1000	165	160	80
Spring Garden	2600	250	165	90
Green River	1000	240	240	115
Richmond Vale	700	220	155	80
Providence	1000	106	110	75
New Foreſt	2000	180	—	—

New Foreſt is now improving in Cotton and Coffee, Sugar-Work being in a Manner given up.

Theſe eſtates can make annually the quantity of ſugar juſt ſtated, if there are no ſtorms, and they have the ſame ſupport of ſlaves as now; by more ſtrength they can make much more.

P. 379. Meſopotamia is level land, and great part only adapted to paſtures; many of which are over-grown with logwood, and require more ſlaves to improve them. The Grange is hilly, of rather poorer nature, and one of thoſe, where the plough is uſeleſs.

Believes Gleneſley produces the leaſt ſugar of all, from the moſt land. Its cane land has been ſo exceedingly injured by the hurricane of 1780, that it does not yield well; about 200 acres are in canes. On many of theſe eſtates, the canes lie contiguous; on others, the paſtures are diſperſed with the canes; the lands in wood, and ruinated, lie moſtly by themſelves.

Does

Does not know that the value of any of theſe 1790.
eſtates could be eſtimated from the quantity of ſugar Part II.
produced, except Green River, and Providence: The others (ſome of them in particular) have very valuable land, fit for ſugar, and when improved, would become exceedingly valuable.

The mode would be to buy more ſlaves, without P. 380.
which it is impoſſible to improve them; it would require much labour and expence, but would pay very amply, he thinks; great part is at preſent in wood, moraſs, or ruinated.

Cannot ſtate the number that would be neceſſary to cultivate fully all theſe eſtates; but as to his own, is convinced, that it's valuable land, fit for ſugar-canes, would require 200 more, and without them, the preſent cultivation cannot be extended, were they to continue nearly the ſame, as to ſugar, paſture, wood-land, &c. Thinks the preſent ſtock of ſlaves, if kept up, not tolerably ſufficient. Many of thoſe eſtates now require more labour than formerly, when the land was new.

The general proportion of male and female ſlaves P. 381.
in Jamaica, ſuppoſed 5 to 3.

On a very few eſtates there are Moravian parſons, but in general no attention is paid to any religious inſtruction. The Society for propagating the Goſpel has not, to his knowledge, employed any perſons in converting the ſlaves.

He has no calculation by which to eſtimate the ordinary expence of maintenance of ſlaves at various ages. They have as much food as they can eat, except after ſuch a calamity as that of 1780, when the allowance was not ſo liberal. Three large plantanes are thought as much as they can eat at a meal; when ſmall, they get more. They in general live on the produce of their own proviſion grounds. They are naturally lazy and neglectful of themſelves; are fed plentifully by their maſters. A few eſtates excepted they have more land allowed than they can cultivate.

Refers

1790. Part II. Refers to the late consolidated act for the legal protection of the slave from ill-usage by his master, or other whites. Thinks the effect in Jamaica, of stopping the intercourse with America, was the loss of many thousand lives for want of a supply of provisions, rice, corn, &c. particularly after the hurricane of 1780.

Indian corn and cassada are cultivated in Jamaica with good success.

Has often bought slaves soon after their arrival from Africa; the chief part have been deliberately chosen from the whole cargo. They generally employ one day in each fortnight, and Sundays, in cultivating their own grounds, and have often other days allotted to them, when it appears necessary to their employers.

Doubts not, if a law were to pass here to forbid the importation of slaves into Jamaica, they would be secretly brought in, and that most of the planters there would encourage it.

P. 383. Thinks the late regulating act has been attended with much advantage.

The slaves for the plantations are in general bought by the owner, or his attorney.

Many estates in Jamaica are so steep, that the plough would be destructive, by the violent rains peculiar to it washing away the soil.

Thinks an African's constitution perfectly well adapted to bear heat: never knew a slave in health complain of it. Pleurisies are often got by being out at nights; the healthiest and stoutest field-slaves are more subject to them than others: has known many very fine valuable ones die of them. The Owner generally prevents those nocturnal rambles, as far as possible.

The produce of the estates before-mentioned, was exceedingly reduced by the hurricane of 1780, but cannot say exactly in what proportion. The produce was much less than in 1789.

Whether

Whether the crop is great or small, the expence of cultivation is the same, and often increased, particularly by such a calamity as that of 1780; but when the crop is smallest, the expence is greatest, only in particular cases; in storms, a long continuance of dry weather, when the cane-stalks are hurt by it; if the crops of corn and provisions are on the ground, they are destroyed; but the provisions taken early, before the hurricane months come on, are safe. The hurricane of 1780 destroyed the plantains, and in many respects, the ground provisions. The proprietors bought on this account provisions from England and America 1790. Part II. P. 384.

Never knew but one free negro desire to return to Africa; he went to see his friends, and returned again. As far as he can recollect, he was a Gold Coast slave.

If the estates in an incompleat cultivation for want of sufficient slaves, could be cultivated to their extent, he thinks the increase of produce would be a very great addition to the revenue, commerce, and manufacture of the mother country.

It is not usual in general for slaves to obtain their freedom, till after a long residence in the West-Indies.

Witness examined.—GEORGE HIBBERT, Esq;—

A merchant of London.

The house he is concerned in, has had considerable dealings with Jamaica (as factors to the planters) and to whom the house is considerably in advance. P. 385.

They import from 5000 to 6000 hogsheads of sugar, besides other articles, the gross value of which may be from £ 200,000 to £ 250,000.

From the concurring evidence of planters, others who have lived in the islands, and from his expe- P. 386.

T rience

1790. Part II. rience gained in the course of business, he believes the abolition of the slave trade will greatly injure the population and produce of Jamaica, and consequently himself as a merchant and creditor.

Any estimate of his, of the debt of the sugar islands to Great-Britain must be from partial inadequate grounds: but could never make it less than £ 20,000,000. Lord Sheffield conjectures such debt to be one-third of the value of the colonies, which has, since he wrote, been estimated £ 70,000,000.

Speaks from experience, that the creditors of West India property include these classes, each to a considerable sum, especially the 2 first. 1st. Merchants who have advanced money, to get consignments, support old correspondents, or protect old engagements. 2d. Morgagees who have advanced money on interest. 3d. Annuitants by purchase, will, or marriage-settlement. 4th Legatees, many under old bequests. 5th. Consignors of goods to the West Indies, captains and mates of ships, &c. 6th. Shippers of goods for the stores, to order. 7th. Creditors on bond, note, &c. 8th. Representatives of the deceased of the above classes, or whose concerns are assigned to others. Their engagements are chiefly under the first class.

P. 387. A considerable part of their capital is lent to creditors, part in settling new, and extending and improving old, estates; and, he believes, part in new machinery and modes of manufacture; also a very considerable part in advances made to repair damages by hurricanes, and to feed the negroes in drought and famines. Their books contain some debts which have existed from 40 to 50 years: and he believes had they not protected these debts by advances to buy negroes and other relief, the estates, now their security, would have been long ago ruined. Believes, that when by short crops, low markets, or other causes, the planters have been distressed, they are generally relieved by British loans. In most of their

their concerns, they have underſtood the buying new negroes to be abſolutely neceſſary to carry on the eſtates, and have advanced money for that uſe. 1790. Part II.

Several planters have aſſured him that they wiſh for new negroes, not to extend eſtates, but merely to eaſe their preſent ſtock. P. 388.

In Jamaica there is a conſiderable number of ſtore-keepers, and importers of Britiſh goods, and who are not land-holders: Advances to ſuch reſt on the ſecurity of the produce; Agriculture in the Weſt-Indies, eſpecially in Jamaica, is the baſis of their returns and ſolvency.

Their ſecurity reſts intirely on the produce of eſtates cultivated by negroes. Real ſecurity is either an eſtate with negroes, or negroes alone. Land without negroes, or an immediate proſpect of buying them to work the land, would be conſidered by a merchant here, as no ſecurity.

Such Weſt-India properties as give ſecurity for Britiſh loans, he thinks, may, with a very few lucky exceptions, be comprized in 3 claſſes. 1ſt. Long ſettled eſtates, which, thro' depopulation, or accidental calamities, need ſupplies of negroes. 2d. Eſtates, in a progreſſive ſtate, prudently adding a few negroes yearly to their gangs, till their ſettlement is compleated. 3d. Eſtates newly ſettled, or by accidents almoſt without negroes, but which would be an ample ſecurity to their creditors, if furniſhed with negroes cheap.

Several Jamaica eſtates mortgaged to them, have portions of uncleared land, which are ſome ſecurity, while negroes may be bought to make them productive. On ſome of them the cultivation has been advantageouſly extended.

Believes minor's eſtates leaſed, with but few negroes, have been often improved by ſuch leaſing, when the minor came of age. Knows a renter of a minor's eſtate, who, on the minor's taking poſſeſſion of it, carried off a good gang of negroes, and ſettled an

1790. Part II. entire new estate, which with a small addition to that gang, promises to turn out very well; but the proprietor has in his late letters to them expressed great anxiety about working his own estates; and if he can't buy new negroes, will find his present fine canes of little value, and his estate worth almost nothing. Believes the estates of infants, or others, so situated, could not possibly be improved or kept up, without new negroes.

Had their house expected or believed that the slave trade would be abolished, they certainly would not have made the great advances or engagements stated. He never thought of the abolition, as not believing it probable; but knew that his trade, the West-India estates which secure his advances, the African trade which supports those estates, and even the very loans he has made, have been encouraged and sanctioned by repeated acts of parliament, of which he

P. 390. produced a list as follows, viz. 1st. Acts encouraging and protecting the sugar colonies, 15 Cha. II. chap. 7; 22 and 23 Cha. II. ch. 26.—7 and 8 Will. III. ch. 22.—6 Anne ch. 30 and ch. 37; 8 Anne ch 13.—4 Geo. II. ch. 15; 5 Geo. II. ch. 24; 6 Geo. II. ch. 13; 12 Geo. II. ch. 30; 19 Geo. II ch. 30; 21 Geo. II. ch. 30.—5 Geo. III. ch. 45; 6 Geo. III. ch. 52; 27 Geo. III. ch. 27. The leading feature in all these acts is encouragement to the sugar colonies, as inhabited by British subjects, and very advantageous to Great-Britain.

P. 391. The 2d division of acts on the slave trade, and stating it necessary for the West-India colonies. Royal charters of Cha. II. of 1664 and 1672.—9 and 10 Will. III. ch. 26.—10 Anne ch. 27.—The Queen's speech, June 1712.—23 Geo. II. ch. 31; 25 Geo. II. ch. 40.—4 Geo. III. ch. 20; 5 Geo. III. ch. 44; 23 Geo. III. ch. 65; also, tho' quoted before, 27 Geo. III. ch. 27. Also the proceedings of the House of Commons from 1707 to 1713, during all which time the slave trade was under

their

their consideration; and it was recommended, by a 1790.
message from the Queen, to consider its nature; and Part II.
no publick censure was then passed on it; but it was
repeatedly voted advantageous to Great Britain, and necessary for the sugar colonies. And, tho' the various bills brought in, and some of which passed the Commons, failed from disputes between the chartered company and private traders, it does not appear the restriction, much less the abolition of the trade, was ever thought of.

The 3d head of acts encouraging loans to the West India proprietors, from British and foreigners, viz. 5 Geo. II. ch. 7; 13 Geo. III. ch. 14, and 14 ch. 79.

The inspector general of imports and exports, P. 392.
has stated to the Privy Council, the imports from the West-Indies to Great-Britain in 1787, at

	£.	s.	d.
	4,945,387	19	10

And from the West-Indies in 1787, was exported to Ireland, value

	£.	s.	d.			
	127,585	4	5			
The U. S. of America	196,460	8	0			
British Col in America	100,506	17	10			
Foreign West-Indies -	18,245	12	6			
Africa - - - - -	868	15	0			
				443,666	17	9
Grand total				£ 5,389,054	17	7

The inspector general states these to be mercantile values formed on the prices current published at Lloyd's. This trade employed 1815 vessels, 242,721 tons, and 21,1 4 seamen. That the exports from Great Britain to the West-Indies in 1787, in British goods, &c. amounted to £ 1,638,703 : 13*s.* : 10*d.* and from Ireland, besides what is shipped in vessels cleared out from Great-Britain £ 20,160

The witness believes the annual average of slaves imported and retained in the British West-Indies may be 15,657, amounting at £ 35 per head, to £ 547,995.

The

1790. The inſpector general has alſo ſtated the quantities,
Part II. and cuſtom-houſe values of imports from the Weſt-Indies to Great Britain only in 1788, whence he has, with all the care and exactneſs he could, eſtimated their groſs mercantile value, (taking the opinion of experienced brokers on the average prices of that year) and which on a very moderate calculation, amounts to £ 6,800,000 of which he finds that

the cuſtoms and exciſe received about	£ 1,800,000
Ship owners for home freight, about	560,000
Britiſh merchants and brokers, for commiſſions, about - - - -	232,000
Under-writers for inſurance, about - -	150,000
Wharfingers, &c. including primage or freight, about - - - - -	95,000
The whole of which is - -	£ 2,837,000

P. 393. The reſt, being ſomething leſs than 4 millions, is the net proceeds paſſed to the credit of the planters, by the Britiſh merchant; but from which muſt be farther deducted the value of Britiſh goods exported to the plantations, with freight, inſurance, commiſſion, and port charges thereon; alſo the ſum paid the African merchants annually for ſlaves; and when to this is added the intereſt of the debt due from the colonies to Great Britain, there can be no doubt but the whole £ 6,800,000 reſted in Great Britain. In confirmation, can aſſert that tracing the groſs produce received through their houſe, for many years, in his time and his predeceſſors, (no inconſiderable value) there is a very ſmall part of it indeed, which he cannot follow home to one or other of the above heads.

The tonnage in the Weſt India trade, in 1787, has been ſtated 242,721 tons; and though in that eſtimate, ſome veſſels are included which muſt have made more than one voyage a year, and their tons are counted for each voyage, yet in many caſes, the eſtimated tonnage is ſomewhat under the real: taking therefore that quantity, and eſtimating the Weſt India ſhips, with all their expences at ſea, at only £ 10 per ton, the amount is £ 2,427,210. 1790. Part II.

The amount paid by the Britiſh Weſt-India trade to ſhip owners, for freight alone, may be eſtimated as follows:

Homewards to Great-Britain, as above -	£ 560,000
Outwards on Britiſh manufactures, &c. about	120,000
On Iriſh manufactures exported, and proviſions in ſhips clearing out from G. Britain	22,000
On exports from the Weſt-Indies to Ireland	14,000
On exports from ditto to Britiſh America, and the United States - - - - - -	25,000
On imports from America to the W. Indies, including ſhips clearing out from G. Britain	200,000
Total freight ——	£ 941,000

To which add the freight paid, in the price of negroes, to the African ſhips, and this Article alone will be found above a million ſterling. Moſt certainly the diminution of Weſt-India produce, will affect the quantity of freight; and if the ſhips now employed in that trade don't get other employ, it muſt affect the price. The ſame cauſes will reduce the tonnage, and number of ſeamen. The increaſe of price of the Weſt-India produce will be neceſſary to counterbalance it's diminution, to make the eſtates as productive as at preſent. A diminution of Weſt-India produce, if cauſed by any difficulty of getting negroes, will raiſe their price, when to be had. The increaſe of price of produce, will certainly diminiſh it's conſumption, and the export of it from Great-Britain. P. 394.

Having never been in the Weſt-Indies, he can only ſpeak from facts well authenticated, or generally admitted. The committee of council in Jamaica ſtated, he believes from the tax-rolls, that the ſlaves there in 1768, were about 167,000. Governor Keith in

1790. Part II. 1774, about 193,000. Governor Clarke in 1787, at 256,000. The aſſembly in 1787 ſtated the ſlaves at 240,000, at the leaſt: But obſerves that the number on the tax-rolls, was only 210,894. Governor Keith ſays, his number in 1774 was from the tax rolls; but there were at leaſt 10,000 more, as many jobbers and

P. 395. others gave not in their numbers. The witneſs thinks, the only fair calculation can be from the tax-rolls, according to which, he gave in this ſtatement:

	Slaves
In 1768, the number was about - - - -	167,001
Left in the iſland to 1774, incluſive - -	41,038
Left in the iſland from 1774 to 1787, incluſive	87,624
	295,662
Deduct on the tax-rolls in 1787 - - - -	210,894
The deficiency in 19 years is - - - - -	84,768

or 4,461 annually, i e. 2.34 (in decimals) per cent. per annum, on the medium number.

1768 ——	167,000
1774 ——	193,000
1787 ——	210,894

3)570,894(190,298 is the medium N°

The calculation of loſs in the firſt 6 years, will be:

In 1768 the number was - - - - - -	167,000
Left in the iſland to 1774, incluſive - -	41,038
	208,038
Deduct on the tax-rolls in 1774 - - -	193,000
The deficiency in 6 years was - - - - -	15,038

or 2.506 per annum, i. e. 1.4 per cent per annum, on the medium number.

1768 ——	167,000
1774 ——	193,000

2)360,000(180,000 is the medium N°

The

The calculation of loſs the laſt 13 years will be: 1790. Part II.

In 1774, the number was	- - - - - -	193,000
Left in the iſland to 1787	- - - - - -	87,624
		280,624
Deduct on the tax rolls in 1787	- - - -	210,894
The deficiency in 13 years was	- - - -	69,730

P. 395.

or 5,364 per annum, or 2,65 per cent. per annum, on the medium number.

1774 —— 193,000
1787 —— 210,894

2)403,894(201,947 is the medium N°

The laſt 13 years was marked by war and repeated hurricanes, from which for the firſt 6 Jamaica was exempt. The whole 19 years form no unfair average of the circumſtances of the iſlands; and it appears, the population of Jamaica for thoſe 19 years, has diminiſhed more than two and one-third per cent on the medium number; that it has diminiſhed in an increaſing ratio, and not increaſed in a growing ratio, as has been ſtated; that admitting 15000 ſlaves to have periſhed in the above periods, from hurricanes, the diminiſhed population in Jamaica alone will remain nearly 70000 in 19 years; that a loſs of two and one-third per cent. upon 450,000 ſlaves, ſaid to be in the Britiſh Weſt Indies is 10,500 and may be computed as the immediate annual diminution of the number, ſhould the ſlave-trade be aboliſhed.

He is certain that an abolition of the ſlave-trade would be followed by an immediate decay of the credit of the Britiſh merchants who have conſiderable engagements with the Weſt Indies, and that they would be obliged, however unwilling, to preſs their debtors, and to foreclose mortgages, to the ruin of many plantations, whoſe value would be affected by the quantity of ſuch property at market, P. 397.

 and

1790. Part II. and the notoriety of the cause of their sale. The British merchants, finding their profits diminish with the diminished produce of the islands, must necessarily lessen the expence, by which they contribute to the revenue, and must look forward to the ruin of the trade, that they and their families have depended on. He believes many rich West India planters, whose estates are large and full-handed, might for a while feel little injury from the abolition, and even receive a temporary benefit from it, while the present system of colony regulation is continued, as by the ruin of smaller planters, whose slaves they would buy, their rivals would be diminished; but that they and the kingdom at large, must soon feel the ruinous event of the abolition, in the total decay of the sugar colonies, and in the dependance of Great Britain on foreigners for her immense consumption of their produce.

P. 398. In lending money on a West India estate, the annual produce is more considered than the nominal value.

The London merchant has 2½ per cent. commission on the gross sales of produce, the same on amount of supplies shipped, and ½ per cent. on making insurance on each.

Much of the Jamaica rum is sold on the estate, or at the next shipping port. What is sent home by the planter, is generally consigned to him to whom he sends his sugar.

P. 399. Insurance outwards or homewards, is always made on a policy, deliverable to the planter on demand. If the merchant stands part of the risk, it is as an under-writer, as an individual, not in the firm of the house.

The West India merchant is often the husband of ships, and holds his share of them. The share of the merchant in general is supposed much less now, than it was some years ago.

The

The eſtates do not require ſupplies in proportion to their produce. 1790. Part II.

The planters often draw bills on the merchants to whom their produce is conſigned, to pay for the ſlaves they may buy. The planter has often credit in the iſland for the ſlaves he buys. When he draws on his merchant, at the expiration of that credit, he draws at the iſland uſance, or, if for a longer time, intereſt for ſuch time is included in the bill. P. 400. Bills from Jamaica are uſually drawn at 90 days ſight, they may be, on an average, 2 months on the voyage.

In all caſual buſineſs, the merchant reimburſes himſelf from the ſale of the ſugars, for the ſums advanced to the planter, for ſtores ſent out, commiſſions, &c. but where there is a connection (and in ſuch there is commonly an advance) ſuch exactneſs in keeping the account balanced cannot be expected.

In the war, it was certainly difficult to ſell Weſt India eſtates to advantage; and he thinks the agitation of the queſtion of the ſlave trade has in part renewed that difficulty. The facility of borrowing money on Weſt India eſtates has certainly increaſed ſince the peace; and, if not entirely prevented by P. 401. the agitation of the preſent queſtion, he believes it to be becauſe they who well know the value of the Weſt India trade, cannot believe the abolition of the ſlave trade, on which that commerce depends, will take place.

As to eſtates which have kept up their ſlaves without importation, he can recollect but one, among all with whom his houſe was connected, that of Lord Dudley, which he underſtands, is peculiarly fortunate in ſituation, eaſy of labour, number of ſlaves and proportion of the ſexes. In 1776, their number was 637, in 1788 it had increaſed only 31, in that time it was exempt from any of thoſe calamities that affected the neighbouring eſtates, yet

1790. Part II. there were two years in which there was decreaſe, of one year they have no account, and in one year there was neither increaſe or decreaſe. In 1788, there was 222 men, 220 women, 59 boys, 41 girls 126 children, 668 in all. The late Lady Dudley ſaid, that the eſtate did not pay her above 3 per cent. on the capital advanced. He is not certain, but believes, that in the period juſt mentioned, no new negroes were bought for Lord Dudley's eſtate.

In 1787, Jamaica did not make its average crop. The importation into London only, was 10,000 hogſheads leſs than in 1785. and 13,000 leſs than in 1788. Has always underſtood the leeward iſlands made much leſs than an average crop in 1788.

P. 402. the year on which he calculated for all the Weſt Indies.

In Jamaica of late years there has been conſtantly a premium paid to drawers of bills on Great Britain, at uſance from 5 to 10 per cent. A large debt due from Weſt India iſlands to Foreigners, contracted, as he believes, on the faith of parliament, their being an act expreſsly encouraging it.

A very conſiderable quantity of herrings is ſent from Scotland, Ireland, and Newfoundland, to the Weſt Indies for negroes.

The ſeamen employed in thoſe fiſheries are not included in the above eſtimate, except ſuch Newfoundland ſeaman as may occaſionally carry the fiſh to the Weſt Indies.

P. 403. When he ſtated that the rich planter, whoſe eſtate is large and full handed, may find a temporary benefit in a greater price, ſhould the abolition of the ſlave trade diminiſh the number of his rivals at this market, he preſumed on his being able to keep up his ſlaves and produce during ſuch temporary benefit. Thinks the diminution of produce from the abolition muſt increaſe in compound progreſſion, and that a price could not be afforded here any way adequate to ſuch a diminution. If the price was much higher, he he believes, an equal consumption could not be expected, for it was generally thought much affected by the high prices last war. 1790. Part II.

Has heard lord Dudley's estate is separated from others, in a particular way. Has often heard persons who lived on it say, this peculiar situation keeps the negroes from rambling at night, and getting venereals, pleurisies, &c: which tend to lessen population. And also from being infected with the small-pox, &c. The attorney or manager informs them that when by a late contagion, many of the neighbouring estates suffered, that estate lost none, and had but few ili of it.

Witness examined. — Admiral SHULDHAM.

Lord Shuldham (Admiral) has observed the behaviour of masters to their negro slaves, in the islands where he has commanded, to have been mild, gentle, and indulgent, equal to that generally shewn by masters to their servants in this kingdom. The slaves were decently clothed, and properly for the climate, and seemed perfectly satisfied with their victuals, and lodging: He never heard them make any complaints; they are in all respects perfectly satisfied, so, that when a midshpiman, he envied their condition, and often wished to be in the same situation. P. 404.

In his opinion, the West-Indies could not be cultivated to advantage by Europeans, it must be attended with immense expence, and the loss of a greater number of lives, from effect of climate on European constitutions.

French West-Indiamen he considers as one of the principal sources of the French naval power; these ships he does not think remarkably fine vessels; they are of about 3 or 400 tons, and manned pretty much as our own; but it is 27 or 28 years ago, since he was in that part of the world. P. 405.

1790. Part II. Admiral Barrington has obſerved, that the maſters, in the iſlands where he has commanded, have always behaved to their ſlaves with the greateſt humanity. The ſlaves appeared properly fed, clothed, and lodged; and more labour did not ſeem to be required of them than they could properly bear. They are, in general, perfectly ſatisfied with their condition, ſo much ſo, that when being miſerable himſelf, (from being 4 months Commander in Chief, without an opportunity of revenging the inſults of France) he has ſeen them ſo happy, that he wiſhed himſelf a negro; but when he had his full revenge, he never wiſhed himſelf a negro afterwards.

He does not conceive the plantations in the Weſt-Indies could be cultivated to advantage by Europeans.

P. 406. Ships employed in the French Weſt-India trade, he conſiders as one of the principal ſources of the naval power of France; they are remarkably fine veſſels; have, he ſuppoſes, double the number of hands that our ſhips have, and are as large or larger than ours in the ſame trade. He conceives the French have of late years encreaſed their Weſt-India trade, and alſo the number of their Weſt-India ſhips.

The Britiſh Weſt-India trade is no doubt a conſiderable nurſery for ſeamen. He holds it by all means important to keep up, and encourage the ſlave-trade: its abolition, will tend to reduce the Weſt-India trade, and conſequently to leſſen the number of ſhips, and ſeamen.

In the laſt war, he was three months at Barbadoes, and on ſhore every day, where he had continual opportunities of obſerving the ſituation of the negroes,
P. 407. and conduct of their maſters; he never knew any act of cruelty, by the owners, on their ſlaves, nor ever ſaw a puniſhment; but one, which was that of a negro woman by her own huſband.

The

The ſlaves in Barbadoes are more comfortably lodged, and much cleaner than the labouring people of Ireland, and in general in the Weſt-Indies they appeared happier than the labouring poor in Ireland, and many parts of Great-Britain. 1790. Part II.

Whether by proper regulations the ſtock of negroes could be kept up without importation from Africa, is a queſtion he cannot anſwer; he has heard, that ſome very few plantations may keep up their ſtock;—for example, Comiſſioner Martin's.

Witneſs examined—Adm. MARRIOTT ARBUTHNOT.

Admiral Arbuthnot having commanded on the Weſt India ſtation, has been frequently in plantations, both in St. Kitt's and Jamaica, and never obſerved the leaſt cruelty to ſlaves; has ſeen them puniſhed, but neither inhumanly nor wantonly, and by no means ſo ſeverely as a Britiſh ſoldier or ſailor; they are clothed according to the climate, and fed with the utmoſt care, having ground allotted for that purpoſe, beſides other Proviſions from America, and conſtantly from England; in point of lodging, and accommodation, they are better off than the labouring poor in Ireland. No more labour is required of them than they can properly bear, their labour is not equal to that of ſeamen in a man of war, in heaving down or clearing; ſo far are they from a deſponding ſtate, that they have as joyous moments as any of us: He has been very happy amongſt them. P. 408. P. 409.

He calculates, in Jamaica, there are 16,000 whites, and 200,000 blacks, and that it is impoſſible for this country to ſend out 200,000 in their room; therefore the plantations in the Weſt-Indies cannot be cultivated to advantage by Europeans. Says, that in 1730, he was midſhipman to a 40 gun ſhip, that carried out 2 regiments

1790. Part II. regiments to Jamaica, where the colonel died in a fortnight, the greateſt part of the officers, and three-fourths of the regiment in little more than a year.

The ſhips in the French Weſt-India trade, he does not conſider as a principal ſource of their naval power, but of great conſequence to them; he knows nothing of the veſſels, nor how they are manned.

The Britiſh Weſt-India trade, he thinks, is a nurſery for ſeamen, and that important to be kept up, and that the abolition of the ſlave trade, will aſſuredly tend to reduce the Weſt-India trade, and leſſen the number of ſhips and ſeamen; and the grounds of this opinion are

P. 410. a certainty, that if all the ſeamen employed in any trade, do not die by unhealthy climate, thoſe that return, will be uſeful to their country. The ſeamen from Guinea ſhips were of great uſe laſt war in manning our fleet, but at what period, he does not know, not having been at the Windward iſlands, where the ſhips received great recruits from Africa.

He does not know whether any regulations would keep up the ſtock of negroes, without importation, but, thinks it impoſſible that any improvements or better regulations can be made: Our labourers earn their bread with greater difficulty than the negroes.

The negroes are beyond compariſon better treated now, than when he firſt knew the Weſt-Indies in 1763; in particular, they are much improved in Jamaica, where they are treated more humanely, and in general appear comfortable. He anſwers that their clothing

P. 411. is well adapted to the climate; they want for nothing, and ſeemed ſatisfied. Every plantation of 150 negroes had a ſurgeon.

During the laſt war, he was not in the Weſt-Indies, he was in the Weſt-Indies in the year 1763, and being aſked on what grounds he thinks the ſlaves better treated now than formerly, he anſwers, that he only confines himſelf to the year 1763.

Witneſs

W. Indies—Witneſs examined—Admiral Edwards.

1790.

Admiral (Richard) Edwards ſerved in the Weſt- Part II. Indies in 1731, 1753, 1760, and 1761. Has not been reſident in the iſlands, and does not know any P. 411. thing very particular of the behaviour of maſters towards their ſlaves; does not recollect any particular cruelties; and in particular eſtates has obſerved a ſhare of humanity to the negroes; he never heard any complaints of their proviſions, and as to their clothing, he has moſtly obſerved them naked, ſome inſtances P. 412. excepted. He never knew any inſtance of more labour required of them than they could bear. He by no means conceives the Weſt-India plantations could be cultivated by the labour of Europeans.

He has been on the coaſt of Africa, and when there received and redreſſed a few complaints of the men on board African ſhips, of want of proviſions, and other caſual matters; thinks the ſeamen treated in this as in other trades; never was any where but men and maſters made mutual complaints: believes, if the ſlave trade were aboliſhed, the French and Dutch would engroſs the trade of the Gold Coaſt.

He believes the ſlaves treated better now than when he firſt was in the Weſt-Indies; thinks moſt ſlaves on the Gold Coaſt are ſupplied from the Along-ſhore-coaſt, from the different forts, and the boats which go often for a week or longer trading from the ſhips; P. 413. thinks the numbers ſold to other Europeans would be increaſed on our aboliſhing the ſlave trade, and that we ſhould be forced to buy of them. He never heard of an African ſlave in Weſt-Indies expreſs a wiſh to return home. The ſlave trade, as combined with the Weſt-India trade to England, he apprehends, is of equal conſequence in manning the Britiſh navy, in time of war, as any trade he knows; thinks the abolition of, or a check to either of theſe trades would

1790. Part II. produce no good to the navy. As to preventing the ſmuggling of new negroes into the Weſt-India iſlands, it could no more be prevented than ſmuggling any where elſe. The ſlaves in all the iſlands furniſh the ſhips of war with live ſtock, &c. for they have bum-boats, as we have at Spithead, and elſewhere; but not being a judge, he cannot ſay that this traffic amounts
P. 414. to any conſiderable ſum. The African trade by itſelf is of conſequence to the manning the navy; he ſays, he could have no converſation with any one, as to the inclinations of negroes to return home, becauſe he never knew any thing of their inclinations for it.

W. Indies.—Witneſs examined—Admiral HOTHAM.

Admiral (William) Hotham has known the Weſt-India iſlands from a boy, and never found the conduct of maſters to ſlaves otherwiſe than very proper. The treatment of ſlaves was mild and humane; they ſeemed properly fed, clothed, and lodged; he never thought more labour was required of them than they could properly bear; they did not appear deſponding, but very well ſatisfied with their condition, and always very chearful. Judges it impoſſible to cultivate the
P. 415. Weſt-Indies by Europeans,—their conſtitution would not bear it.

The ſhips in the French Weſt-India trade he thinks a principal ſource and nurſery of the naval power of France; ſays they are fine ſhips, as large or larger than Britiſh Weſt-India ſhips, but knows not how they are manned. He thinks the Britiſh Weſt-India trade a conſiderable nurſery for ſeamen, the African trade alſo a nurſery; theſe two trades are advantageous in ſupplying ſeamen in time of war, and they ſhould therefore be kept up; thinks the abolition of the ſlave trade would reduce the Weſt-India trade, and leſſen its ſhips and ſea-
P. 416. men. He has been often on ſhore in the Weſt-Indies,

and

and frequently obſerved the condition of ſlaves, and the behaviour of their maſters towards them; was on Sir Wm. Coddrington's eſtate, for 6 weeks or 2 months, and had daily opportunities of obſerving their treatment, and has been occaſionally on other eſtates, on all of which they were well treated; with no particular ſeverity; he has been five or ſix years in the Weſt-Indies, at different times, and does not recollect to have ſeen more than 3 or 4 puniſhments, and is far from thinking the planters may be juſtly accuſed of cruelty or wanton ſeverity.—The ſlaves in all the iſlands carry on a conſiderable traffic in ſupplying the fleets with proviſion, who pay them more with ſhips proviſions in exchange, than with money; but theſe proviſions he believed were for the perſonal profit of the ſlave. On the abolition of the ſlave trade, he ſhould think it almoſt impoſſible to prevent the ſmuggling of new ſlaves into the iſlands: What number of ſhips could prevent it he cannot judge, nor can he ſpeak to the inefficacy of the regulations made to prevent the introduction of American proviſions into the Weſt-India iſlands, not having been there ſince that time. P. 417.

W. Indies.—Witneſs examined—Captain Lambert.

Captain (Robert) Lambert has ſerved in the Weſt-Indies, at different times, 8 or 9 years, particularly in Jamaica; he ſerved firſt in a king's ſhip, afterwards as commiſſioner at Port Royal. He never obſerved ill uſage to the ſlaves, but thought they generally ſeemed happy, and ſaw nothing to the contrary of their being properly fed, clothed, and lodged; it did not appear to him that more labour was required of them than they could properly bear, always ſaw them chearful after leaving work; thinks he ſees more deſponding people in this country, than among the negroes: is ſure the Weſt-India plantations could not be cultivated P. 418.

1790. Part II. to advantage by Europeans. From number of ships and the number of men carried, he thinks the ships in the French West-India trade a principal source of their naval power. Their West-India ships are extremely fine, large, and well manned. The British West-India trade forms a considerable nursery of seamen in time of war; he never had any other means of recruiting his ship than from West-Indiamen; imagines it highly important to keep up and encourage
P. 419. the West-India trade. The abolition of the slave trade would undoubtedly tend to lessen the West-India trade, and the number of ships and seamen. Were the slave trade abolished, it would not be possible to prevent the running new slaves into the islands. He thinks he left Jamaica in 1784; says only from hear-say, that the population cannot be kept up without continuing the importation of African slaves; was obliged to have the king's slaves under his direction replenished, to carry on constant work; these were mostly men, who had wives, but neither their wives nor children belong to the king. He has known a greater number of men come to the navy from Guineamen than from other ships, because they carry a greater number. Does not know of any considerable number of plantations able to support their stock of slaves, without purchasing recruits.

W. Indies.—Witness exam[d]—Commodore GARDNER.

P. 420. Commodore (Allan) Gardner has served in all the West-India islands, and returned from Jamaica August 1789. Cannot point out any particular impropriety of conduct of masters to slaves, as in all countries there may be good and bad; in Jamaica he believes the treatment in general humane and mild. He believes slaves have sufficient food for their work. Little clothing is necessary in tropical climates, but once or twice

twice a year he believes a certain proportion of cloaths is in general diſtributed to every ſlave. For their lodging, huts are provided, the comfort of which depends on themſelves. No more labour is required of them than they can properly bear; a labouring man in England does twice the work of a negro. Thinks them not in a deſponding ſtate; as in this country, there are ſome conſtitutionally of a melancholy turn; from their chearfulneſs out of work-time, and readineſs to engage in diverſions, he believes them perfectly ſatisfied with their condition. Firmly believes the Weſt-India plantations could not be cultivated by Europeans, having known Jamaica 24 years; he reſided the laſt three as commander upon a penn allotted to the admiral, and attended to the cultivation of about 80 acres. During the hurricane months he employed perſons ſkilful in farming, from the ſhips, to plant corn, to mow and make hay; they worked only in the morning early and in the cool of the evening, and yet, though allowed extra proviſions and grog, were unable to go through this buſineſs: he therefore ſubſtituted negroes. From this circumſtance, and obſerving that book-keepers, when attending to negroes, ſtand under umbrellas, he is ſatisfied Europeans cannot ſtand the climate. He thinks it cannot be doubted, that ſhips in the French Weſt-India trade are one of the principal ſources of their naval power; they are conſiderably larger than our own, and better manned. The Britiſh Weſt-India trade is a nurſery for ſeamen, and extremely advantageous for ſupplying men in time of war; it is important to keep up and encourage it, ſo long as the iſlands are thought worth keeping. He conſiders, if the ſlave trade were aboliſhed, there is an end of the colonies, as the negroes are the very ſinews of the planter. He thinks it impoſſible to keep up the ſtock of ſlaves without importation from Africa; and grounds this opinion on the diſproportion of females to males, promiſcuous cohabitation, the diſeaſes thence ariſing

1790. Part II.

P. 421.

P. 422.

1790. Part II. arising, and the diseases they bring with them from the coast of Guinea. Supposes there are three males to two females in Jamaica. A greater proportion of males than females has always appeared to him. He is confident they are much better treated now than when he first knew the island; their burden grows daily lighter, and they are better fed, clothed, and
P. 423. attended to. Believes there are very few if any plantations able to support their stock without new recruits. Has not made this an object of enquiry. Has resided, except 6 or 7 weeks, for 3 years on shore at Jamaica; is of opinion, if estates had kept up their number without importation, he should have heard it remarked. On the arrival of a cargo, the planters are all anxious to purchase, and many involve themselves in debt by so doing. They can purchase negroes only because they consider them necessary to the cultivation of their estates. As a proof that the settlements of estates are much encreased since he first knew Jamaica, he says, that there are now 50,000 more negroes there than there were then. He believes he has heard in conversation, that there may be eight or ten estates in Jamaica that have kept up their stock without buying imported negroes.

W. Indies.—Witness examined—Lord MACARTNEY.

P. 424. Lord Macartney was upwards of 3 years in the West-Indies, as governor of Grenada, the Grenadines, and Tobago, from 1776 to 1779. Treatment of negroes there depends much on the temper of the master, whose behaviour is greatly regulated by his own interest, connected with the well-being of his slave. Thinks in general their behaviour is mild and humane; has heard of a very few bad examples, but not known them. A bad master is always much despised by his fellow planters.

Slaves

Slaves in general ſeemed properly fed, clothed, and lodged. Intereſt of maſter and exertion of ſlave are ſo connected with theſe things, that great attention is always paid to them. Thinks no more labour required of ſlaves than they can well bear. Some parts of cultivation require more labour than others; but thinks a labouring man in England works full as much as a negro. 1790. Part II.

Deſpondency of negroes depends on the countries they come from. They are brought from an extent of coaſt of 40 degrees of latitude. In ſome of the countries he has underſtood they were ſlaves before exportation; in others the government is different. Some, as the Coromantees, living he believes under a leſs deſpotic government, are high ſpirited, and not very ſubmiſſive to their condition. Has heard there is one nation of negroes which are prone to ſuicide at home, and have conſequently given the examples of the ſame diſpoſition when brought to our iſlands. P. 425.

He believes many ſlaves, after having been ſome little time in our iſlands, would not go back if they could.

Thinks that no man, who has been a year in Weſt-Indies, through all the ſeaſons, can think it poſſible to cultivate Weſt-Indies to advantage by Europeans. Without great care they can ſcarcely preſerve their health, without labor.

Never having had a plantation, he cannot well anſwer the queſtion, whether preſent ſtock of negroes, in the iſlands he governed, could be kept up without freſh ſupplies from Africa.

The preſent ſtate of reſidents there he does not know; when he was governor, many perſons of large eſtates were reſident, and many abſent; but having loſt his papers, when the iſlands were taken, he cannot at once aſcertain the proportion. P. 426.

Recollects having heard a gentleman in Grenada had calculated the comparative expence of breeding, and that of buying imported Africans; and that he

was

1790. Part II. was of opinion, it was more for his intereſt to work out his ſlaves in a few years, and ſupply their places by freſh purchaſes, than to work them moderately like his neighbours. Whether he reduced his opinion to practice he does not know; but poſſibly he did: he was a new ſubject, not an Engliſhman, and but little reſpected in the colony.

Does not recollect the laws of the iſland give any effectual remedy to a ſlave againſt his maſter; one fact of remedy he knows, viz. a little before his arrival a white man was hanged for murdering a black woman. He repeats, that in general, he believes ſlaves are not ill uſed, it being contrary to the intereſt of their maſters.

The number of white perſons on an eſtate muſt depend on number of negroes; on a large plantation there ſhould be and uſually are a manager, under-manager, and a doctor: on many eſtates there are more.

Does not recollect what legal protection free negroes enjoy, but conceives they might be redreſs'd by a magiſtrate in the uſual manner:—he is not certain.

As to a white perſon, deſirous of committing an act of violence on a ſlave or free negro, being able to find an opportunity, when all the whites ſhould be out of the way, of executing his purpoſe without fear of legal conviction, he thinks he might, in the ſame way as
P. 427. againſt a white, if all the whites were out of the way, conviction depending on a jury, if brought to trial. Does not recollect any inſtance of negro evidence being admitted.

He conceives the ſtate of a negro, excluſive of liberty, which is a ſentiment felt by every Engliſhman, and which few negroes feel in the ſame extent, to be very comfortable. Being in general well fed, well clothed, taken care of when ſick, and having every thing provided for him, he fears no creditors, which on the whole renders his ſtate, excluſive of the idea of being a ſlave, perhaps as comfortable as a peaſant in this country.

To

To the best of his recollection, the whites on the island were 1,400, and the negroes 33,000. 1790. Part II.

Not having had either a plantation or any considerable number of negroes, cannot tell whether they look forward in general to a state of freedom with anxiety. Those of his own family were so happy, that he believes they never had, at least, they never signified a wish to him to be free; he made them free on his arrival in England, and they returned as free to Grenada. Conceives many field negroes desire P. 428. to be free, but knows not what would become of them if they were: he imagines they would wish to return to their former state. In some cases freedom is held out to them in the clauses of some of the acts, as a reward or a temptation. But no negro can be made free in Grenada without great expence,—he believes 100l. currency to his master. Does not know whether the protection of their masters is the best security that negroes enjoy against ill treatment from other persons: it is one undoubtedly; it may be the best.

Being asked whether he does not imagine, that as negro evidence is not in any case taken, numberless opportunities of gratifying a disposition to ill-treat negroes may occur to a white man, without any fear of legal punishment, answers, that though he said he does not remember negro evidence ever admitted at Grenada, he does not know that cases may not occur, in which it may; he heard that on Mr. Franklin's trial in Tobago, attempts were made to introduce it, but it was not received. Cannot say what operated on the minds of those British subjects who P. 429. purchased lands, and extended large capitals in Grenada (whether they were led to it by a dependance on the faith of parliament, for their protection and cultivation, or not.) Supposes they expected their profit from the same mode of cultivation as had been practised before. Has understood they have borrowed large sums of money from Foreigners, and believes

Y they

1790. Part II. they did so under the faith of parliament; he supposes that if from the want of cultivation, the estates became of no value, some other provision would be made by the legislature to indemnify the creditors. Wishes to avoid giving any opinion as to whether the abolition of the slave trade must necessarily make those estates of no value.

He has heard instances of worse treatment of negroes in Grenada under the French government than after it came under the English government, but does know the facts himself.

Not having any estate of his own, and living chiefly in town, he cannot from his own observation say, that when the proprietor of slaves becomes distrest in his circumstances, the slaves suffer for such embarassment by a diminution of their subsistence, or increase of their labour; he thinks it possible, and believes they may have suffered just as servants do here by the distress of their masters.

W. Indies.—Witness examined.—Sir John Dalling.

P. 430. Sir John Dalling Bart. resided as soldier and governor in Jamaica, off and on from the taking of the Havannah till 1781. Great attention is paid by masters to slaves. The worst master is the freed negro. Treatment of slaves is in general mild and humane, particularly of the field negroes. They are well fed, and though sometimes unfavourable seasons make a scarcity, the planters, from humanity, as well as interest, seek provisions for them at any expence. Their clothing and lodging are well adapted to the climate. The general work of negroes is not to be called labour, according to the acceptation of the word here; a well regulated plantation is not an unpleasant object to the eye and mind. Great attention is paid them in sickness; and in old age they are put to to ſlight work. A deſponding negro is generally a being that from refractorineſs or diſinclination does not chuſe to work. Among ſuch numbers there muſt be many of ungovernable temper as among us; in the military line the diſguſting puniſhments are generally divided among 20 or 30 in a regiment from 500 to 700 men. A well minded negro looks forward to ſomething better than his preſent ſtate. That they are in general ſatisfied, may appear from their not having been incited to deſolation and murder long before this period by the public conduct of this country, which has doubtleſs been exaggerated to them through various channels. 1790. Part II. P. 431.

In the mountains of Jamaica an European might, by his labour, poſſibly produce enough for his conſumption, but no where in the iſland any of the ſtaple commodities. Great-Britain could not bear the conſumption of men to cultivate the plantations; the young people ſent out for book-keepers can ſcarce be kept alive, though without work. Umbrellas were neceſſary for them when ſtanding out, and would be more ſo if working; and a negro or white perſon muſt be obliged to hold it over them.

He is ſure the preſent ſtock of negroes cannot be kept up without an annual importation from Africa. The abolition of the ſlave-trade would by degrees prove the ruin of every proprietor, and produce beggary to his deſcendants, and by degrees alſo, he fears bankruptcy to this country.

Cannot ſpeak poſitively to the annual decreaſe of a given ſtock of negroes not recruited by purchaſe, but it uſually depends on ſituation. Imported negroes bring many diſorders with them; excluſive of ſuch, in happy ſituations, the conſumption is trifling, but in unwholeſome ones, which are many, it is great. Some of the diſorders of imported negroes, ſuch as yaws and flux, are infectious. He infers the impoſſibility of keeping up the ſtock by breeding, under proper regulations and expedients, from their own P. 432.

 irregularities

1790. Part II. irregularities. He believes when in health, the negroes are capable of doing all kinds of work they are called to.

If a man uses his slave ill to a degree, he is amenable to the magistrate; if he destroys him wantonly, he is tried for his life. He does not recollect any instances of conviction and punishment of white men for ill using their own, or other men's slaves. Chief protection of negroes from ill usage by other persons, consists in some degree in the interest their masters have in protecting them, but he hopes from humanity also.

P. 433. Understands the Spaniards treat their slaves better than we; we better than the French; and the French better than the Dutch.

Free negroes in Jamaica follow different trades, as carpenters, masons, &c. but wanting regulation are debauched, and a great nuisance; they raise and bring stock to market for sale.

There are, he believes, many more males than females, but of late he understands the planters would prefer a greater proportion of females. He never heard much about the comparative cheapness of breeding negroes, and working them out and recruiting by buying imported slaves: he holds the importation from Africa necessary, both for keeping up the present cultivation and extending it. A planter in easy circumstances he is persuaded would buy more negroes from humanity, to ease the work of those he already had.

For extending the cultivation of the island, and opening new grounds, a greater number of negroes would be requisite. He is pursuaded the loss in clearing new grounds, would be great in proportion to that in working of old settled plantations.

P. 434. Comparing the situation of field and domestic negroes, he repeats, the field negroes looks forward to something better, that is, to the cultivation of his own grounds and stock, which not only produce the necessaries

neceſſaries of life, but, with the overplus, give him what he underſtands to be the luxuries of it, yet in his opinion the lazy houſe ſlave would not change ſituations with him. 1790. Part II.

The number of domeſtic ſlaves may be trifling at firſt, but as their progeny are never turned into the field, they augment greatly in a few years.

Many Britiſh families carry over white domeſtics, but the maſters and ſervants ſoon tire of each other. More of them return to this country in proportion, than of thoſe whoſe duty requires them to be expoſed to the viciſſitudes of the climates.

He does not know whether the Spaniards uſe negroes for working their mines; he has heard, but does not know it, that Engliſh ſeamen taken on the coaſt of Spaniſh America, have been condemned to that employ. Has heard regulations exiſt in the Havannah, empowering domeſtic ſlaves to work out their own freedom, but does not know whether they exiſt among the plantation ſlaves. He has heard that the planters in Jamaica are frequently induced by the purchaſe of new negroes, to an unprofitable extenſion of their cultivation, but while the benefit remains to the ſucceſſor.

W. Indies.—Witneſs examined.—Sir R. PAYNE.

Sir R. Payne, very early in life viſited Weſt-Indies twice, to ſee his friends, and the property he was afterwards to poſſeſs. In the latter end of 1771 (which was a few years afterwards) he returned thither as Governor General of the Leeward Iſlands, continued there almoſt 4 years, viz. until June 1775, and occaſionally viſited the principal iſlands under his governments. P. 435.

The management of ſlaves in the iſlands he governed, ſeemed wiſe and humane. They moſt unqueſtionably appeared in general properly fed, cloathed and lodged. More labour never ſeemed required of them than they could properly bear. He truſts he may P. 436.

1790. Part II. may aver without being contradicted, there is no slave, (at least he never saw any one) whose labour is by any means comparable to that of a day-labourer in England. This opinion may be supported by slaves having better health and spirits in crop-time, than any other, and being best pleased with the labour attending it, tho' the severest they have.

General appearance of negroes does not indicate despondency, nor does he believe they are more dissatisfied with their state, than the bulk of mankind in their respective stations. It is very common for them to perform their labour singing, and with appearance of gaiety. Their necessities are supplied, and their situation has every appearance of comfort, but it will be more or less so in proportion to their industry, by which they may become comparatively affluent, as is proved by numbers being able to purchase their freedom. He manumitted a slave, who in slaves, houses, and boats, was worth between £500 or 600, and he is sure this sum was of the man's own acquiring He had been latterly a distiller on the St. Kitt's estate, seemed between 60 and 63 years old, and was not born in the West-Indies. This man shews the comfort to which a foreign negro, unassisted by the family, and other advantages attending natives, may arrive.

P. 437. He conceives it visionary to employ Europeans to cultivate plantations, and so impracticable, as that there cannot be two opinions among those acquainted with the subject

Has 2 West-India estates: one at St. Kitt's, the other, named Carlisle's, at Antigua. Having passed 2½ years on the Continent, he cannot specify with accuracy the numbers now on the 2 estates. On the latter he had 470 when he went abroad, and guesses the number must now be nearly 500; they are all Creoles. On the former, he thinks he may have about 140 or 150, partly Creoles, partly Africans. In 1771, when he came to this estate, he found on it about

about 170, and it was thought very liberally handed, so much that task-work had been occasionally performed by the former owner. But wishing that the slaves might play with the work, as on the Antigua estate, Sir R. P. by a purchase compleated the number to 200. On the Antigua estate, not a single slave has been added to the stock by purchase, but the number has greatly increased by births, and there are so many supernumerary hands on it, that had he not been unwilling to separate families and friends, he should have supplied his St. Kitt's estate from it. 1790. Part II. P. 438.

When Governor of the Leeward Islands, he found the management of his estates incompatible with his public duties. He therefore resided on neither of them, left them in the hands of his attornies, as before, giving no orders as to their management, tho' occasionally riding over them, and sometimes perhaps suggesting his ideas to his attornies. In doing the latter, he omitted nothing which would assimilate the mode of proceeding on the St. Kitt's, to that on the Antigua estate. P. 439.

Thinks he can confidently assert, equal care was taken of the slaves on his two estates. His attornies at St. Kitt's, were men of indisputable knowledge and humanity. Dr. Thomas was in this capacity when Sir R. P. was governor, and continued in it to his death, about 4 or 5 years since. He had the medical care of the slaves, not only under Sir R. P. but under his uncle. He had been regularly bred to surgery, under Mr. Warner of London, who expressed the greatest respect for his personal and professional merit, and Sir R. P. is satisfied, that the loss of slaves at St. Kitt's, was not occasioned by want of skill and attention on his part.

He cannot account for the encrease on the Antigua estate, and decrease on that of St. Kitt's, notwithstanding the purchases for the latter, and its being so circumstanced as to make it probable the slaves would encrease, at least, as fast as on the former. Tho' the situation

1790. situation of the Antigua eſtate is not unhealthy, yet it
Part II. is nearly a flat, and not comparable to that of the other, which is a tract of land gently riſing from the ſea to a mountain. The ſlaves at St. Kitt's have as much proviſion ground as they chuſe in the upper part of the eſtate, beſides two guts bounding it on the eaſt and weſt: the proviſion ground of thoſe at
P. 440. Antigua, is very ſmall. The allowance of food and cloathing at St. Kitt's, uſed to be more liberal under his predeceſſors, than at Antigua, where, tho' the eſtate has been in his family above 80 years, and the ſlaves always increaſing, little or no proviſions had been allowed. They have now the ſame as on other eſtates in this reſpect; and alſo as to cloathing, of which he had from the cuſtom of the eſtate, and almoſt without knowing it, not allowed a garb 'till a few years ſince, when on their requeſt they were ſupplied with cloathing, as on other eſtates, tho' experience had ſhewn it not abſolutely neceſſary. The St. Kitt's eſtate has ſuſtained that misfortune, as to population, which he fears inſeparable from almoſt all eſtates in the iſlands. The only reaſon he ever aſſigned for the uncommon encreaſe on his Antigua property is, his grandfather having always bought women inſtead of men, and thus made the eſtate for years a nurſery for young ſlaves. Mr. Blizzard his Attorney, and Chief Juſtice of Antigua, uſed to aſſign as a reaſon the high opinion theſe ſlaves had of themſelves, as of a ſuperior rank to all others in the iſland, becauſe they were all natives on the eſtate, and moſt of them the offspring of natives. Mr. Blizzard, tho' deſirous of getting ſome of their breed on his plantation, which was contiguous, could never induce any of the men to marry in it. Their marriages were among themſelves, tho' the women might have gallants from other eſtates.

P. 441. Thinks it infinitely more advantageous to breed than to buy ſlaves, and he never had a doubt of this being a general opinion among planters.

When

When visiting the islands as governor, no act of cruelty from masters to slaves came to his knowledge or hearing. The interest of the master is generally thought to be, and certainly is, a security for the good usage of the slave. 1790. Part II.

From his knowledge of the judges and magistrates, he is confident slaves and white persons would meet with equal redress for any cruelty sustained by them. This he fears is much more doubted in England, than in the colonies. He never heard a doubt expressed by any reasonable man, but that a master would be equally tried for his life for the murder of a slave, as for that of a white man.

The nine parishes of St. Kitt's, are served by five clergymen, the difficulty of procuring proper ministers making it usual to give 2 livings to a clergyman, both there, and in all the Leeward Islands. A parsonage house, glebe, surplice fees, and 16,000 pounds weight of sugar (or the current value of the latter, at the option of the clergyman) belong to each living. The income from 2 country livings is not, he believes, over-rated at between £5 or 600 sterling per annum. P. 442.

When he spoke of the lightness of a slave's labour, compared with that of an English labourer, he alluded to the former mostly out of crop-time, but he mentioned circumstances to shew that even in crop-time, it does not render the slave an object of commiseration. Tho' cautious of delivering an opinion on the interior œconomy of an estate, he can say without hesitation from casual observations, he thinks the field employments are not beyond the strength of women. Is convinced negroes only can cultivate West-Indies, and that they are as capable of labour there, as those of other countries are in climates congenial to them. P. 443.

He cannot say, what are the quantities of land in cultivation on his 2 estates. Should imagine from 150 to 170 acres at St. Kitt's, where he knows the

 cane-

1790. cane-land has been lessened from the diminution of
Part II. negroes; and if that diminution continues, and the
means of supplying it are taken away, the inevitable
(450) consequence must be a still farther reduction in the quantity of cane-land, and perhaps eventually the throwing of the whole of it out of cultivation.

P. 444. The state of the provision grounds on his 2 estates was, he believes, very different, owing to the different natures of the estates themselves; but speaks with
(445.) great diffidence as to all plantation matters. At St. Kitt's, these grounds are in the highest part of the estate, where the cane is not cultivated, but not much above a mile from the sea, and also in the 2 guts
P. 444. before-mentioned. The negro huts are, he imagines, rather nearer the sea than the mountain, in a spot, which, like the whole estate, is without exception one of the healthiest in the island. The provision ground is sub-divided, and the negroes have their separate properties in it. Besides this, negro-provisions are raised for general use on other parts of the estate, which at one time of the year bear canes, at others yams, potatoes and eddoes.

P. 445. He does not recollect the quantity of corn and rice allowed his own negroes; but is certain it was as great at St. Kitt's, as at Antigua.

Cannot tell the numbers of males and females on his estates, nor whether the loss on the St. Kitt's estate, since he augmented the slaves to 200 or thereabouts, before he left the islands, has taken place among grown slaves or infants, but believes it has been gradual and regular. He says he has not the least knowledge of the tetanus on his estates.

The manager who was on the St. Kitt's estate in 1771, had been appointed when Sir R. P. was abroad, and returned to England a few years after Sir R. P's return thither. A second was appointed, who died on the estate, and now there is a third.

P. 446. He cannot say, whether on his estates, lying-in women were delivered in their own huts, or in rooms for

for the purpose. There are hospitals on both of them, 1790.
as well as, he believes, on every other estate in the Part II.
islands, which he believes are attended with all possible care. A physician constantly attended on his, and he believes on all others, twice or thrice a week, who, besides his regular stipend, was, he believes, paid extraordinarily for cases of midwifry, inocculations, and on all extraordinary occasions.

The field negroes have certainly more or less property of their own.

As to their industry, that is matter of opinion, but those who are industrious are sure to be comfortable.

He apprehends the expence of maintaining negroes has considerably encreased since shutting up the American ports from the colonies.

Is unable to say what alterations have taken place in the treatment of slaves since he left the West-Indies.

In each island there are a chief justice, and, he P. 447.
believes, 4 puisne judges; and also magistrates chosen by the commander in chief, and vested with the powers of justices of peace, which latter he always appointed (448.)
when governor, out of the most respectable planters and merchants. Sometimes an island has been so P. 447.
fortunate as to have a professional man at the head of its law, but in general this is not the case, owing to the small emoluments of the office, which arise entirely from certain fees established by the law of the island. He has however heard that since he quitted his government, Mr. Robinson has been appointed judge of the Virgin islands, (which form a part of the government of the Leeward Islands) with a salary of £ 200 per ann. sterling. When no proper person of the law will accept the office of judge, the most scrupulous care is taken to select a planter of the fairest character for it.

The present chief justice of Antigua, practiced P. 449.
many years at the bar there with great reputation.

1790. At a diſtance of 15 years, ſome allowance muſt
Part II. be made for an inaccuracy of recollection, but he
does not remember any white being puniſhed for ill-
P. 448. treating a black, nor does he remember ever hearing
of any enormity of this ſort that deſerved puniſhment.

(449.) He cannot ſay whether the number of ſlaves employed in working the Antigua plantation, was
greater, compared with the quantity of cane-land, or
P. 448. of produce, than at St. Kitt's; but the whole number
of ſlaves at the former, was infinitely greater than at
the latter eſtate, even when the number at this was
200; for at Antigua there was a taſk-gang, at St.
(449.) Kitt's he never meant to eſtabliſh one. No particular
gang was appropriated to taſk-work at Antigua, but
all were by turns employed in it as occaſion offered,
and on certain exigencies the whole gang is employed
on the eſtate.

Witneſs examined—Sir Archibald Campbell.

P. 450. Sir Archibald Campbell reſided 3 years in the war
before laſt in the French iſlands of Martinique, Gauda-
loupe and Dominique, after the conqueſt of thoſe
iſlands, in a military capacity. He reſided alſo in
Jamaica 5 years during the laſt war, 2 of theſe he
was governor.

The conduct of maſters towards their ſlaves ſeemed mild, and marked with great kindneſs. Slaves appeared properly fed, clothed and lodged. He had no opportunity of aſcertaining, whether more labour was required of them than they could properly perform, but underſtands it to be the maſters intereſt not to give them more than they can bear.

P. 451. They appeared comfortable and ſatisfied with their
ſtate; heard no complaints to the contrary: cannot
compare their condition with that of the labouring
poor of England, not being able to judge of the
labour here.

Does

Does not conceive it poſſible that Europeans could cultivate Weſt Indies to advantage. 1790. Part II.

Should imagine a ſtop to the ſupply of African negroes, would prove an immediate ſtop to all improvement, and occaſion a general decreaſe in all ſugar eſtates.

The Spaniſh treatment of their ſlaves he thinks like ours, very humane. Does not remember any white man's being brought to legal puniſhment in Jamaica, for ill-uſage of his own or any other's ſlave or free negroes; his time was occupied in defence of the iſland, being ſhut up in the garriſon. Nor does he know any inſtance of the ſort in the French iſlands. P. 452.

Remembers many inſtances when in Jamaica, of runaway ſlaves brought in by Maroon negroes, according to their treaty with governor Trelawny. Underſtands the cauſe of their flight to have been in ſome the fear of returning home, after having ſtaid out too long with women they were attached to; in others a diſpoſition to idleneſs, and hopes of living undiſcovered with the Maroons; he cannot ſpecify any other cauſes. When brought back they were always returned to their maſters, if known, or elſe to head quarters.

Advertiſements for runaways often deſcribe the negroes by marks of brands, but theſe he underſtood to be marks of their own country, and his reaſon for thinking ſo is, that all new negroes imported while he was in Jamaica had their particular country marks; theſe he does not mean to ſay were received in the interior country, from which they originally came, but made in Africa previous to their exportation thence: he never ſaw them appear freſh; underſtood all ſuch marks to have been made in Africa before they came to the iſland, but where he never heard. He underſtood that the tribes in Africa diſtinguiſh themſelves by tattooing, or impreſſing marks on their faces and bodies. P. 453.

When

1790. Part II. When the Maroon negroes made their treaty with Governor Trelawny in 1739, he has heard they amounted to about 3000 men, fit for arms. During his government, he endeavoured to get all the fighting men in their towns, to turn out when Jamaica was threatened by the French and Spaniards, and was surprized to find they did not amount to 300.

He never knew the Maroons hire themselves to field labour.

There are great numbers of free negroes in the towns, and different parishes in the island; in general they are idle, and dissipated. Does not know, but thinks they had matrimonial connections with negro women on the plantations: He thinks it very probable that these connections were formed, in order to derive subsistence from the wives, and so live in idleness themselves.

He ascribes the decrease of the Maroon negroes chiefly to a free access to spirits. They have women among them, and have wives; another cause of their decrease, he has heard, is their cohabitation with the women of the neighbouring plantations. He understands they are daily decreasing; cannot say in what proportion. The decrease from 3000 men in 1739, to 300 in 1782, extends only to fighting men.

Witness examined——J. ORDE, Esq;

P. 455. John Orde, Esq; had been at Jamaica 3 years as midshipman and lieutenant; a few months at the Leeward islands as lieutenant in the navy, and near 6 years at Dominique as governor; it is 7 months since his return to England. In islands where he has been, has observed the treatment of slaves in general humane and good. Severe masters occur in all parts of the world; one or two he has known at Dominique. A knowledge of these, occasioned the legislature

legiſlature to paſs a law to give farther protection to negroes, and promote religion and morality among them; it obliges maſters, under heavy penalties, to give them a certain quantity of food, clothing, and medical aid; limits powers of puniſhing; ſecures them a trial by jury in all capital caſes; makes it felony in white men to kill them; enjoins maſters to chriſten their children within a certain time, and to have divine ſervice performed by a white perſon, on the eſtate, once a week. This law, but lately paſt, he believes is attended to: The negroes are, as in general before the law, well taken care of. He confines his anſwers here to Dominique; ſerving in the navy, when at Jamaica, though he was there 3 years, had but little opportunity to remark, ſo particularly, the treatment of maſters towards their ſlaves. 1790. Part II. P. 456.

More labour was not ſeemingly required of negroes than they could properly bear; 10 hours in the 24 was all the time required; they do not turn the negroes, at Dominique, into the field till after ſun-riſe, ½ an hour is given them for breakfaſt, which they eat in the field, and from 12 to 2 o'clock for their dinner, and they ceaſe labour at ſun-ſet, except bringing home a bundle of graſs. Believes they are generally thought moſt healthy at crop time, both at making ſugar and coffee. Their labour he thinks not greater than that of a common labourer in England; that of the hedger and ditcher, he thinks full as great.

When ſick they are well taken care of; many eſtates have hoſpitals for them; ſome have medical people living on them, and almoſt all are attended by the faculty once or twice a week, or oftener, if neceſſary. The old people, he believes, are well taken care of; he never ſaw a beggar in the ſtreet. P. 457.

They appear very well ſatisfied with their condition in general; ſome, he has heard, have been offered to return to Africa, but refuſed it: Old negroes conſider their ſituation as vaſtly preferable to that of the new, and go to the Beach to ſee them when imported. To prove

1790. Part. II. prove the attachment of ſlaves to their maſters, he relates that a number of foreign runaways had come over; that a number of the negroes of Dominique, perhaps tempted by the French, had left their maſters, and that others, perhaps through diſcontent, had deſerted alſo; that theſe altogether inhabited the woods of Dominique, and were armed, and there committed many acts of violence againſt the inhabitants, ſo as to determine the legiſlature, after an ineffectual trial of every lenient method, to endeavour to reduce them by force. Slaves from the different eſtates were on this ſervice, and through the whole courſe of it manifeſted the greateſt zeal and deſire to bring them back to their duty.

He conceives it impoſſible to cultivate Weſt-India plantations to advantage by Europeans; many white artificers work in all the iſlands for very great wages, and are thus enabled to live well; yet theſe work moderately, and almoſt always under cover; notwithſtanding, he believes more than ½ of thoſe who were at Dominique when he went there, were dead when he came away. The loſs of European troops in St. Lucia, he has heard, was due to their rolling proviſions, for a few hours only in the day, up to Morne Fortuné.

P. 458. He has his doubts, whether in Dominique, where the negroes have certainly not decreaſed for 6 or 7 years paſt, the numbers might not be kept up, if not attacked by epidemical diſeaſes, or other cauſes of extraordinary mortality, incident to that climate; but Dominique has advantages, perhaps not poſſeſſed by any other iſland; a great quantity of uncultivated lands allows them to raiſe as much proviſions as they pleaſe, and a ſurplus to buy a thouſand neceſſaries and conveniencies. The proximity of the foreign iſlands, and our frequent communication with them, affords them an advantageous market; and the good water, may alſo contribute to their health; but he only ſays, that the preſent number could be kept up without importation. There could be no poſſibility of extending the cultivation

vation, nor does he believe the quantity of land now in cultivation could be kept so; for as land grows old, it requires more labour. — Dominique contain about 186,000 acres, of these about 54,000 are in occupation, and 26,000 in cultivation. The merely keeping up the stock, therefore, would be very insufficient for the wants of the Dominique proprietors, and should the trade be abolished, they would certainly be great sufferers. If some such encouragements for breeding, were held out to Dominique, as are to the French islands in the Code Noir; and if the practice of separating children from their parents were more precisely dropt than it is, he thinks it would still more contribute to insure keeping up the present stock, without farther importation. 1790. Part II.

In explanation of the apparent difference between his own answers to the queries transmitted to him by the Secretary of state, and the returns sent home from the custom-house: he says, that in some of his answers, he stated the negroes of Dominique to have encreased in the last 5 or 6 years; whereas the custom-house returns declare, that the negroes imported, from 1784 to 1788, amounted to 27,553; that the numbers exported in the same period, amounted to only 15,781, and of course, that the number remaining in Dominique was 11,772. As a reason for the difference in these accounts, (as at the time explained by him to the Secretary of state) says, that previous to the free-port act of 1787, no slaves could be legally exported in foreign vessels, and in the French islands, so heavy a duty was laid on those imported in foreign bottoms, as to make that mode of sending them disadvantageous to the merchant, and the vigilance of the French cruisers rendered it dangerous to attempt running them illicitly; they were therefore smuggled out of Dominique, of which the custom-house had no returns, nor since the free-port act, can any returns be relied on. The French have, in fact, taken about 4-5ths of the whole number imported, and the Spaniards, and other P. 459.

 foreigners

1790. Part II. foreigners ſo many more, as not to leave, in his opinion, above 1000 in Dominique, and many of theſe, refuſe negroes, part of which died, perhaps, before they got on the eſtates. The encreaſe by births, was ſtated from documents received from Mr. Conſtable, deputy treaſurer of the iſland, a perſon very capable of giving true account. The returns of the French inhabitants, in the pariſh of St. Patrick, and his own obſervations, confirm them.

P. 460. The perſons to anſwer the queries of the privy council, were ſelected by Mr. Orde; finding the aſſembly backward to anſwer them, and deſirous of collecting the ſentiments of proprietors in the iſland, he ſent different copies of the queries to 4 or 5 of the principal ſettlers in each pariſh, to be communicated by them to the whole; he ſent alſo to the merchants for the ſame purpoſe, and requeſted anſwers. He conceives the anſwers he received, may be ſuppoſed the reſult of the experience, and knowledge of the moſt intelligent men in the iſland: Being firſt communicated to him, he ſent them to Great-Britain.

Where there is but little proviſion-ground on an eſtate, (a rare caſe in Dominique) the negroes are almoſt altogether fed by the owner; he believes they receive 2 lb. of ſalt fiſh, ſalt beef, or pork, or 7 or 8 herrings, and about 7 or 8 quarts of farine each ℔ week; the children in proportion: The ſame proportion of fiſh, or meat, and nothing more, is given where there is proviſion-ground, but not quite ſufficient for full ſubſiſtence; but where proviſion-ground is plenty, (generally the caſe in Dominique) the negroes are allowed to cultivate as much as they pleaſe, and have a day in the week, beſides Sunday, for it; this is the uſual method with the French inhabitants, and the moſt ſatisfactory to the negroes.

P. 461. The number of ſlaves loſt in opening new lands in Dominique was aſcertained, but being before his time, he cannot ſtate it; they were, he believes, very conſiderable, and partly owing to miſmanagement: A

cuſtom

custom then prevailed of working new negroes; which contributed to the loss, but this is not now followed. 1790. Part II.

Does not know that the difference of profit to the resident and to the absentee proprietor of estates in the West-Indies is so great as he stated to the privy-council, he believes it however to be in general very material.

Believes attention to moral and religious instructions of slaves would contribute to their comfort, and their masters interest; the French are more attentive to these points than we are, and benefit accordingly.

Understands that lately in Tobago the French have established a regulation, excusing female slaves from labour, in proportion to the number of children they bear and bring up, and liberating then after having 6 or 7.——Being asked if a slaves's security from ill usage does not depend on the temper of the owner, he answered, the laws in the Colonies are not so well executed as in England; in general, he dares hope the honor and humanity of the owners lead them to attend to the protection of slaves. The treatment of slaves in the French islands he believes more severe than in the English. In Dominique the French follow the custom of the English. The laws provide security for free negroes against ill usage of white men; their evidence is not good, in capital cases, against white. Thinks the Tobago law stated above, rewarding a woman who has brought up many children might be advantageously adopted; at present, negro women are certainly averse to bearing children, and careless in bringing them up; as he thinks bearing children interrupts their libidinous pursuits, and makes them less desirable to the men.

Were the planters to see the benefit of the Tobago regulation, as before stated, they would, no doubt, adopt it. P. 463.

Believes, if the slave trade is abolished, the consequence will be disadvantageous to the empire in general, and in particular to Dominique, the pro-

 prietors

1790. Part II. prietors of which bought their lands of government at a very high rate, trusting for their cultivation in an uninterrupted importation of slaves; no more than one-third of the island is now in occupation, and only 26,000 acres is in real cultivation: A stop to the importation of slaves would therefore make it impossible to clear more, and very difficult, perhaps, to keep what is now planted in the same state of improvement.

He does not recollect the refusal of a free negroe's evidence against a white man, except in one instance, which was a case of murder.

Witness examined.—DAVID PARRY, Esq;

David Parry, Esq; resided at Barbadoes near 7 years, as governor of the island, and left it July 6, 1789. Masters behave to their slaves with every possible kindness and attention Negroes seem properly fed, clothed,
P. 464. and lodged; had it not been so, he would, as it was his business, have enforced the law to that end. Not half so much labour was required of them, as their owners had a right to demand; the common labour of a negro would be play to any English peasant. Never saw the least degree of despondency among them; has every reason to suppose them perfectly satisfied, as no complaints ever reached his ear. Banishment is the severest punishment to a negro at Barbadoes; there is no corporal punishment they would not prefer; has known them even hesitate between banishment and death: In general, he thinks their state infinitely more comfortable than that of the labouring poor in England, or any other part of the world that he knows. He thinks it impossible that the West-Indies could be cultivated by Europeans, without such a destruction of the human race as would harrow up the feelings of the hardest breast, and would be (to the imaginary distresses of the negroes) inhumanity in the extreme.

He

He has not the smallest doubt, that a supply of negroes 1790.
from Africa is necessary to the cultivation of sugar Part II.
estates, particularly if they mean to improve more
land. The abolition of the slave trade, would, in his P. 465.
opinion, prove detrimental both to the colonies, and the empire at large; it would raise the productions of that country, beyond the power of the consumers here to purchase, and consequently lessen the revenue, in proportion as the consumption is diminished, and would injure the individual in his property, by encreasing his private expences; it would occasion the immediate declension, and final ruin of the sugar colonies, unless they were at liberty to seek for, and carry their sugar and other produce, to other markets; and this, in his opinion, would be bad policy.

If supplies of negroes be totally stopped, the gradual diminution of their produce, and finally the extinction of the sugar colonies, he thinks, would take place, and he thinks it a dangerous and unnecessary experiment to make; the planters of Barbadoes he knows, and the planters in general, he believes to be men of sense, discernment, and humanity; and he thinks, that good policy, ought to leave them in the quiet management of their own affairs, and so render them, as beneficial as possible to this country, to whose laws, constitution, and king, they are warmly and zealously attached.

One man will annually cultivate 3 acres of cotton, P. 466.
but only one of sugar; the substitution of cotton for sugar in many plantations in Barbadoes, arose more from the loss of negroes in the hurricane 1780, than from the depredations of vermin, or other causes. This substitution is going on, though in a less degree, because new negroes have been imported. The greater part of the lands, where cotton was substituted, is now again allotted to sugar. The substitution of cotton for sugar, might have been made immediately, but did not take place to any extent for 3 or 4 years afterwards. The difficulty of obtaining African negroes, was the cause of that substitution, aided by the blowing down

1790. down of the ſugar-works and buildings. That
Part II. difficulty aroſe from their not being brought to the iſland, and from their high prices. The anſwers ſent
P. 467. by him, to the queries of the Privy Council, were framed by himſelf; the anſwers of the council, and aſſembly, by thoſe bodies reſpectively; thoſe returned by individuals, were tranſmitted by him, for the purpoſe of returning thoſe anſwers: He ſelected men, on whoſe diſcernment, experience, and integrity, he could rely, and perſons alſo differing in ſentiments, in order to give the Secretaries of State, the fulleſt information.

Witneſs examined—Lord Rodney.

Lord Rodney went firſt to the Weſt-Indies in 1761, he reſided firſt at Barbadoes, then Martinique, Antigua, St. Kitt's, and a ſmall time at Guadaloupe, when thoſe iſlands belonged to Great-Britain; he was alſo in Jamaica $3\frac{1}{2}$ years.

P. 468. Maſters, in the ſeveral iſlands, ſeemed very attentive to their ſlaves; it is their intereſt to be ſo; he never ſaw one inſtance of cruelty, but many of forbearance, on an impertinent anſwer being given to the maſters. Slaves ſeemed properly clothed for the climate, in all the iſlands; in Jamaica, ſeemed better fed than the common labouring people here; the other iſlands have not grounds to give them ſuch food as Jamaica can afford; they appeared alſo extremely well lodged for the climate, and their houſes calculated for it. No more labour was required of them than they could properly bear: A hundred times he has noticed, that he thought a labouring man in England did more work in one day than any 3 negroes. He has often noticed in the many plantations he has viſited, that there is an hoſpital, called the ſick-houſe, with negro
P. 469. women attending as nurſes; there is ſcarce a plantation without a ſurgeon; it is their intereſt to be attentive.

The

The negroes appeared to him to be in a ſtate the reverſe of deſponding; after the day's work, they were generally dancing, and making merry. Thinks it impoſſible to cultivate Weſt-India plantations to advantage by Europeans. Believes the preſent ſtock in the iſlands could not be kept up, without freſh importations; for he believes, breeding is encouraged as much as poſſible; for one Creole is, in value, worth two new ones from Guinea.

Conſiders the ſhips in the French Weſt-India trade as the greateſt ſource of their power, for the Weſt-India commerce enabled France laſt war to diſpute with Great-Britain the empire of the ſea; their Weſt-Indiamen are generally much larger than the Britiſh, and appeared more than doubly manned. Thinks the Britiſh Weſt-India trade a conſiderable nurſery for ſeamen, and the Weſt-India fleet very advantageous in time of war in furniſhing men for the ſervice, who are ſeaſoned to the Weſt-Indian climate. P. 470. Thinks it extremely important to keep up a trade, which he conſiders one of our principal branches of commerce; without the African trade the Weſt-Indies he thinks could not be ſupported. In 1787, the French paid 200 livres a head premium for every ſlave imported into St. Domingo and St. Lucia, and 100 for each imported into Martinique and Guadaloupe, beſides a premium on ſhips that traded from the ports of France to the coaſt of Guinea, payable immediately on their ſailing, at ſo much per ton.—The abolition of the ſlave trade would tend to reduce the Britiſh Weſt-India trade, and leſſen the number of ſhips and ſeamen, it would tend to encreaſe the French marine in general; if the Britiſh ſlave trade were aboliſhed, and engroſſed by foreign nations, it would add to the naval power of France, who has already much more than half the Weſt-India trade in her hands, and diminiſh that of Britain in proportion.

Never

1790. Part II. P. 471. Never made a comparative estimate of the expence of breeding a negro till fit for the field, and that of buying an able African: declares that wherever he went, it appeared they encouraged breeding and took great care of the children. Does not recollect any regulation for the encouragement for breeding sanctioned by the legislature of the islands, but always understood they gave every encouragement for the negroes to breed, and for the settlement of the white people; it appeared so to him.

They were domestic slaves that gave impertinent answers.

The negroes seemed very bad labourers, compared with Europeans. Their inclination to labour was not equal to a labouring man's in England, not 3 of them could do so much work as one white man in Europe. In the West Indies they do more than the climate would permit a white man to do there.

P. 472. They are left to chuse their own wives; if there be any regulations concerning their marriages, he does not know them.

Being asked the grounds on which he concludes that the stock of negroes could not be kept up by breeding without importations from Africa, if proper regulations were adopted and adhered to, he answers, that he is not a judge of that. It is a long time before the children come to maturity. This opinion he draws from his own observations on what he has seen and heard; he knows no gentleman that does not attempt to keep up the stock, at least it appeared so to him.

He never heard what proportion of negro infants die within the month, or what grows up to maturity. He has been told they are apt to die very young of the locked jaw.

When we first took Martinique, 1761 or 1762, the French slaves appeared better clothed than the English; he desired the Barbadoes planters to observe that there was no naked slaves there, while in

in Barbadoes there were many naked. In conse- 1790.
quence, the Barbadoes people put their laws in Part II.
force and clothed their ſlaves. He thinks Engliſh negroes better lodged than French. Food in a great meaſure depends on having proper proviſion ground; ſuch as have not this, give ſalt fiſh, and Guinea and Indian corn to their ſlaves. Slaves ſeem better off in the Engliſh than in the French iſlands; the puniſhments in the French, greater than in the Engliſh iſlands. He never knew cruel treatment to any ſlave in the Engliſh iſlands, but the reverſe. He never knew or heard of any thing in the public adminiſtration of juſtice between a white man and a negro, but ſtrict juſtice to both. He was at the trial of a white man (about 1772 or 1773) for wantonly murdering a ſlave. The court condemned the man, and he believes he was executed. He ſpoke to the governor that he hoped he would not pardon him. The man he believes was not the owner of the ſlave.

P. 474.

The property of ſlaves in the produce of their gardens, their poultry and pigs, as far as he has obſerved, is held ſacred, and never taken from them without a juſt compenſation, and at the market price.

If it were poſſible for a ſlave to be happy, they ſeemed to be ſo. They never knew what liberty was. So far as regards only their food, clothing, lodging and care taken of them in ſickneſs and in health, he thinks their lives as happy as thoſe of the peaſants in this country.

As to ſeamen in the ſtreets of Jamaica dying in an ulcerated ſtate; falling without pity; without friends, without a look but of contempt from the hardened multitude that paſſes by, &c. He does not believe any thing of the ſort ever happened in any of the iſlands. (See page 475 3d. anſwer.) There may have been drunken ſeamen.

1790. Part II. If the crews of ſlave ſhips are ill uſed by the maſters, they have always a remedy at hand, by entering into any of his Majeſty's ſhips in that port. The ſhip cannot ſail till the maſter has paid the men their juſt wages. The ſeamen of Guinea ſhips too cuſtomarily leave them to navigate the loaded ſhips to Great Britain, as their wages for the men exceed the wages due from their own ſhips; he believes there have been many inſtances of harſh treatment in captains of thoſe ſhips, to get rid of their men. Regulations to this end are very neceſſary.

P. 475. He ſtates, that in 1747, he ſaw 180 ſail of French Weſt India ſhips in one convoy, bound from St. Domingo to France. That we took 40 of them, the value of which was £500,000, and refers it to the committee to judge how much that commerce muſt have increaſed the laſt 40 years. He is convinced that France could not have diſputed the empire of the ocean with us laſt war, but for their Weſt-India commerce.

He never ſuffered preſſing in the Weſt-Indies, without recourſe to the governor and council, who always allowed the impreſs, and gave every aſſiſtance in their power towards manning the fleet in every iſland.

P. 476. The officers of the navy always oblige the captains of Guineamen to pay the wages due to ſuch of their ſeamen as enter the King's ſervice: If theſe have been ill-uſed, by captains of Guineamen, the officer of the navy, if it come to his ears, applies to the attorney-general of the iſland to proſecute ſuch captains.

The African ſlave trade certainly ſupplies ſeamen to His Majeſty's navy, becauſe when they come to the Weſt Indies we get ſome of them. It is not a nurſery for ſeamen, that is certain; but it ſeaſons them to a hot climate.

W. INDIES—Witneſs examined—Sir PETER PARKER.

Admiral Sir Peter Parker was captain of a man of war on the leeward iſland ſtation the war before laſt about 3 years. He was at the taking of Guadaloupe, and occaſionally viſited Barbadoes and all the leeward iſlands except Nevis. In 1777 he was appointed admiral and commander in chief of all the King's ſhips at Jamaica, where he arrived Feb. 1778, and remained till 1782. 1790. Part II. P. 477.

The treatment of ſlaves in the ſeveral iſlands was lenient, mild and humane. He never heard of even one inſtance of ſeverity during his ſtay at Jamaica. The ſlaves not only ſeemed properly fed, lodged and clothed, but in a more comfortable ſtate than the lower claſs of people in any part of Europe, Great Britain not excepted. No more labour was required of them than they could properly bear. Our peaſantry ſcarce earn a livelihood by labour much harder than theſe are put to; and in age and infirmities, drag on a miſerable life on a pitiful allowance of 1s. 6d. or 2s per Week from their pariſhes; whereas the negro, when old and infirm, has particular attention paid to make him eaſy and comfortable; and if he has acquired money, which all induſtrious negroes may do, he may live in affluence the reſt of his days; he knows that his family and friends will be ſure of protection, and good treatment after his deceaſe, and that he may bequeath his property how and to whom he pleaſes. They are far from being in a ſtate of deſpondency, and generally chearful and merry.—It is abſolutely P. 478.
impoſſible to cultivate the Weſt Indies by Europeans; to ſhew how inimical the climate is to European conſtitutions, he ſays he need only refer to the military returns there of 1779, 1780, and 1781. The very exiſtence of the ſoldiers depends

 on

1790. Part II. on their being allowed negroes to carry their ſtores and proviſions, and do other acts of drudgery. Our ſeamen work under awnings, to keep off the ſun. The manning veſſels in our dock yards with negroes, to water and ſtore the King's ſhips, he is ſatisfied has ſaved the lives of thouſands. The captains under his command had all leave to enter a few negros. The ſhips when once watered, keep up the quantity with their own long boats. In proof that negroes are neceſſary for this ſervice, he relates that a frigate, about to ſail from Port Royal, ſent her long-boat to Rock Fort for water, with a midſhipman, cockſwain, and ſix ſeamen, and that on her return next morning, the midſhipman and ſix ſeamen were taken ill and died.

He thinks the preſent ſtock of negroes cannot be kept up without freſh importations from Africa; experience proves it otherwiſe.

He conſiders the ſhips in the French Weſt India trade, as a principal ſource of their naval power. Their ſhips in general are larger than ours, and carry double the number of men. Their Weſt India trade is immenſe, and, in his opinion, two thirds of their whole commerce; ſhould they obſtruct their African trade, which he thinks they are too wiſe to do, they would loſe their conſequence among the nations of Europe, and not be able to fit out fleets ſufficient to alarm their neighbours. He hears, and thinks it probable, that they are endeavouring to improve their Weſt India trade, and their African, as connected with it.

P. 479. The Britiſh Weſt-India trade is a great nurſery for ſeamen; we ſhould find it difficult to man a great fleet without it. There can be no doubt, that that trade, and alſo the African, are extremely ſerviceable in manning King's ſhips in the Weſt-Indies in time of war. He received upwards of 2000 into the fleet, under his command, and manned ſeveral ſhips that he bought for the King from Weſt-India merchantmen,

and

and African ſhips: Thoſe traders furniſh ſeamen pe- 1790.
culiarly adapted to Weſt-India ſervice, and more able Part II.
to manage the King's ſhips in that ſtation than ſeamen uſually employed in Europe. It is important to the kingdom to keep up Britiſh Weſt-India trade; but more important to keep up the African.

The abolition of the African trade would, in his opinion, cauſe a general deſpondency among the negroes, and gradually decreaſe population, and conſequently the produce of our iſlands, and muſt in time deſtroy near ½ our commerce, and take from Great-Britain all pretenſions to the rank ſhe now holds of being the firſt maritime power in the world.

In the ſame ratio that our power decreaſes, that of the French will encreaſe.

He has never ſeen nor heard of ſailors dying in the ſtreets of Jamaica in an ulcerated ſtate, objects both of commiſeration and horror, as ſtated in the report of the Privy Council, except in the committee room.

Witneſs examined.—STEPHEN FULLER, Eſq; Agent for the iſland of Jamaica.

Produced extracts from the minutes of the joint com- P. 481.
mittee of aſſembly and council of Jamaica, 3d December, 1789, which are inſerted from page 485 to page 496 of the minutes at large*.

He alſo produced a paper intituled, "Jamaica "export and import of negroes, and negroes retained "in

* Extracts from the minutes of the joint committee of aſſembly and council of Jamaica, 3d December 1789. Mr. Murray reported as follows:

Mr. Speaker,

Your committee appointed to meet a committee of the council P. 485.
in a free conference, to enquire into and to report to the houſe their opinion, what ſteps are neceſſary to be taken with regard to the ſlave trade, in conſequence of the information received from the agent of this iſland of the proceedings had in the Houſe of Commons in the laſt ſeſſion of parliament in reſpect of the ſaid trade,

1790. Part II. "in the island for 49 years, viz. from 1739, to "to 1787, both inclusive, distinguishing the years "of war from those of peace." This paper is to shew that the importation of negroes into Jamaica was

trade, have accordingly met, and have taken the examinations of several persons, and have agreed to the following resolutions:

I Resolved, It is the opinion of the joint committee, that the suppression, either direct or virtual, of the slave trade, by the British nation only, (other nations continuing the trade as usual) would not promote the purposes of humanity, either in respect of the negroes which are annually brought to the African markets for sale, or in regard to the negroes at present in a state of slavery in this and the rest of the British islands in the West-Indies. The effects in Africa of a partial abolition would be this, that the purchasers from Europe, being fewer in number, would have a greater choice of slaves, equal to the whole demand of the British merchants at present which is stated at 38,000 annually; whereby prime slaves only would be saleable; and the aged and infirm (many of whom are now purchased of necessity) being rejected in greater numbers than formerly, the horrid practice which has long existed among the slave-merchants on the coast, of putting to death such of their captives as are brought to market and rejected by the Europeans, would be more prevalent than ever. In the British West-Indies the effect (however lightly felt at first) must necessarily, in the course of a few years, from an unavoidable decrease consequent on the present inequality of the sexes, have this operation; that the labour which is now performed by a given number of negroes, must either be performed by a less number, or the planter must contract the limits of his plantation, and diminish his produce. Thus immediate interest, and in many cases urgent distress from the importunity of creditors, will be set in opposition to the principles of justice, and the dictates of humanity.

II. Resolved, It is the opinion of the joint committee, that to condemn the slave trade as peculiarly destructive to British seamen (the contrary whereof is proved by the evidence of Vice-Admiral Edwards before the privy council) and to adduce in proof thereof the losses sustained on certain unhealthy parts of the coast, without taking into the account the losses sustained in other branches of the African commerce, such as the wood and ivory trades, where the mortality principally occurs, and the encrease of seamen from such other parts of the British navigation as are principally dependant on the African commerce, is partial and unjust. Among these branches may be reckoned the West India and lumber trades, and above all, those great nurseries for seamen, the Irish, British, British-American and Newfoundland fisheries; the consumption of herrings and salted fish by the negroes, being immense. We have

was very considerable in war time. He formed the calculation from 1739 to 1772, from an original account found among Mr. Rose Fuller's papers, after 1790. Part II.

have likewise reason to believe, that since the late regulating act, the mortality of British seamen in the slave trade has decreased nearly one half.

III. Resolved, It is the opinion of the joint Committee, that the loss of Negroes which is sometimes sustained in the voyages from Africa, as well as in the harbours of this island, between the days of arrival and sale, and which is stated to happen from the mode of transporting them from the Coast, being *a remediable grievance*, affords no argument for a total suppression of the Slave Trade.

IV. It is the opinion of the joint Committee, that no just estimate can be formed of the effects which the Regulating Act of the British Parliament, passed in 1788, will ultimately produce in respect of the loss of the slaves in the middle passage, inasmuch as it appears, from a return of negroes purchased on the coast of Africa by ships that have entered in the port of Kingston since the first of January last, that, out of 2099 slaves purchased on the Gold Coast, 2042 have been sold in this island, a loss of only two and three-fourths per cent. but that, out of 2550 slaves purchased in the Bite of Benin, only 1642 have been sold; a loss amounting to thirty-five and three eighths per cent. and unknown before any regulation took place. Two vessels have since arrived from the same coast, the Ann and the Vulture: these vessels purchased 785, slaves of whom only 14 have died; a loss not exceeding *one and three-sevenths* per cent. This amazing difference, as appears by the evidence taken on oath, is partly to be attributed to the small-pox, which raged in some of the ships, and the measles and flux, which broke out in others. The loss by the flux was chiefly occasioned by the use of unripe yams, for want of other provisions.

V. Resolved, It is the opinion of the joint Committee, that the number of slaves at present in this island is about 250,000; of which, according to the best enquiries that can be made concerning the proportion of the sexes, there are 140,000 males, and 110,000 females: it follows therefore, that if future importations from Africa be discontinued, there will unavoidably ensue, from the disproportion of the sexes alone, a very great reduction from the present number of our slaves, before any augmentation can be expected from natural increase by generation; a diminution which must not only preclude all attempts at the further improvements of our unsettled lands, but likewise occasion a proportionable decrease in the present cultivation; it being an undoubted fact, that almost all the plantations already settled are much under-handed.

VI.

1790. after his death, printed part III. of the Privy-
Part II. Councils report; thence to 1787, from the Inspector-General's account, printed part IV. of that report. He

VI. Resolved, It is the opinion of the joint Committee, that it is absolutely impossible to cultivate the West India islands, so as to produce any commodities that would enrich the mother-country, by white labourers. Fatal experience demonstrates the fallacy of such an expectation. In the year 1749, the legislature of this island passed a law holding out great encouragement for the introduction of white families into this colony, which proved ineffectual; very few families having come in consequence thereof, and of those that came not a vestige is left. The French ministry in 1763, attempted to settle a colony by means of white labourers at Cayenne, on the coast of America; twelve thousand miserable people were the victims of this impolitic scheme. If further instances are wanting to prove, that Europeans cannot withstand the climate when exposed to the sun and the rains, recourse may be had to the accounts of the siege of Carthagena; the expedition to Cumberland Harbour; the siege of the Havannah; the returns of the regiments that came out under the command of General Garth in 1779 and 1780; and the expedition to Fort Saint Juan, on the Spanish Main.

VII. Resolved, It is the opinion of the joint Committee, that according to the best estimate which can be formed, this island may be stated to contain four millions and eighty thousand acres of land, of which not more than one-fourth part, or about one million of acres, is at present in actual cultivation; and although a considerable part of the country, consisting of high mountains and rugged precipices, is incapable of improvement, yet it may be presumed, that no part of the lands, which are actually patented, falls within that description; inasmuch as the owners thereof pay a quit-rent to the Crown for holding the same; which quit-rent, and the arrears thereof, collected since Christmas last, amount to the sum of 27,000l. or thereabouts, exclusive of 13,000 now in a train of settlement.

VIII. Resolved, It is the opinion of the joint Committee, that it appears, from the offices of the Clerk of the Patents and Receiver-General, that there are at this time patented in this island, or taken up by grants from the Crown, 1,907,589 acres of land; from which, the quantity in actual Cultivation being deducted, there will remain, with every allowance for unproductive territory, 900,000 acres of cultivatable land yet unsettled; the whole of which, if the Slave Trade be abolished, must become an absolute burthen and incumbrance on its present proprietors; who will, in such case, be entitled as of right, and on the principles of natural justice, to the liberty of surrendering the same back to the Crown, and receiving full compensation for the capitals therein vested,

He looked on this last account as more perfect than his own, which was that of a private gentleman (of Jamaica) only, and the other that of a publick officer.

vested, and all quit-rents paid on account thereof. The said land, valued only at 3l. currency per acre, is worth 2,700,000l. currency, equal to 1,928,500l. sterling.

IX. Resolved, It is the opinion of the joint committee, that the planters and proprietors of negroes in this island will in like manner, be entituled to compensation for the diminution which must necessarily ensue in the number of our slaves, should all further importations be discontinued by authority of parliament; the present disproportion between the sexes having arisen from causes which are not imputable to us. With the reduction of our slaves will likewise unavoidably happen a proportionate decrease in the value of our lands, buildings, and produce; for which and all other losses consequent on a change in the present system, it is the opinion of the joint committe, that the inhabitants of this, and the rest of his Majesty's sugar colonies, arc fairly and justly entitled to compensation; the said colonies having been originally settled under the most sacred compacts with the mother country, sanctioned by royal charters and proclamations, as well as by a succession of acts of parliament, authorising and encouraging the slave trade; particularly by the charters granted in 1662 and 1674, by King Charles II. which established a Royal African company, the last of which was granted in consequence of an address from both houses of parliament, and by the acts of the 9th and 10th of William the III. a period when the principles of civil liberty were minutely investigated, well understood, and freely asserted; and more recently, by the act of 23 George II. which recites the usefulness and absolute necessity of the African trade. Our claim of compensation is founded in, and supported by, not only the rules of natural as well as moral justice, but by the expectations we are warranted to entertain from the examples of compensation made by parliament to the Royal African company, for the resumption of their lands, forts, &c. &c. (see stat. 25 Geo. II. c. xl. in 1752, and to the British merchants and owners of ships engaged in the African trade, for losses sustained by them in consequence of the act for regulating the shipping aud carrying slaves in British vessels from the coast of Africa, passed in the last session of the British parliament: and it is our opinion that, before any further measures towards the abolition of the slave trade be taken by the parliament of Great Britain, commissioners ought to be appointed for ascertaining the losses to arise therefrom.

X. Resolved, It is the opinion of the joint committee, that the charges which have been brought against the planters of this island, of improper and inhuman treatment of our Slaves, may

1790. Part II. cer. Hence he has taken the last part of his calculation from the Inspector-General's account, which reaches from 1772 to 1787. The said account was delivered

be fully refuted and disproved; first by an appeal to our laws, and, secondly, by the evidence of respectable men who have resided among us, and have been witnesses to our manners. Whatever may be said of our ancient Colonial Slave-laws, the Acts which have been passed, within the last ten years, are written in characters of justice, mercy, and liberality. Concerning the general treatment of our slaves, we refer to the evidence already personally given to the Lords of the Council, by the Right Hon. Lord Rodney, Sir Peter Parker, Adm. Barrington, Sir Joshua Rowley, Admiral Hotham, Vice Admiral Edwards, and Sir George Young: and to the further evidence that may be produced from gentlemen of character in England who have resided many years in this island, and are intimately acquainted with our conduct and manners. We conceive that the testimony of such persons is unanswerable and conclusive; and shall therefore only remark, that it is notorious our Slaves, in general, are not only treated with kindness and humanity, but that they are also protected by law from immoderate chastisement or cruel treatment, and enjoy more easy, comfortable, and happy lives, than multitudes of the labourers in Great Britain.

XI. Resolved, it is the opinion of the joint committee, that, in confidence of the validity of plantation security, and the support and encouragement the sugar-colonies, and the African trade, have hitherto experienced from government, the merchants in Great-Britain have been induced to enter in very large advances, and engage in extensive loans to the West-India planters; and, on the faith of an act of parliament, passed on purpose to make the receiving of six per cent. on colonial securities lawful in Great-Britain, great numbers of private persons at home as well as the subjects of foreign states, have likewise embarked considerable sums on mortgages, and have purchased annuities to a very large amount on West-India estates: now the slave trade being the great source of every West-India improvement, its abolition must inevitably diminish the value of all such securities, and drive the creditors to use every means in their power to extricate their property from such a precarious situation; to the immediate distress of the planters and their families, and the ultimate ruin of many of the mortgagees and annuitants themselves.

XII. Resolved, It is the opinion of the joint Committee, that the present value of property in this island may be fairly and reasonably estimated as follows; viz. 250,000 negroes, at 50l. sterling per head, is 12,500,000l. The patented lands, with their erections, and the personal property appertaining thereunto, at double the value of the negroes (being the most general rule of valuation) delivered in and read, and is inserted from page 497 to 499 of the minutes at large. By this account it appears that, in 1790. Part II. (499.)

				Years	Total slaves retained	Average per Ann.
War from	1739	to	1749	10	55230	5523
Peace from	1749	to	1755	7	43645	6235
War from	1756	to	1763	8	49368	6171
Peace from	1764	to	1775	12	88443	7370
War from	1776	to	1782	7	41536	5791
Peace from	1783	to	1787	5	32218	6444
				49	310440	

AVERAGES.

War 25 years.	Peace 24 years.
5523	6235
6171	7370
5791	6444
3)17485	3)20049
5828	6683
	5828

Peace annual average exceeds war 855
Annual average retained for 49 years 6335

Cc 2 Witness

valuation) amount to 25,000,000l. and the article of houses in the towns, the coasting and trading vessels, &c. may be estimated at one million and a half at the least; it appearing, by the Report of the Committee of the Lords of the Privy Council, that the houses in Kingston and Spanish Town are alone worth 1,428,521l. sterling. The total is thirty-nine millions of pounds Sterling; the whole profits and produce of which capital, as also of the various branches of commerce to which it gives rise, center in Great Britain, and add to the national wealth, while the navigation necessary to all its branches, establishes a strength which wealth can neither purchase nor balance.

Witneſs examined.—ROBERT NORRIS, Eſq;

Produced a paper, intitled, "An account of the
1790. Part II. "veſſels and amount of their cargoes, now employed "by the merchants of Liverpool in the African
(483.) "ſlave trade, 3d March 1790." It was ſent him by the ſecretary of the committee of African merchants at Liverpool. He believes it to be a true ſtatement of facts It was delivered in and read, and is inſerted from page 500 to 509, of the printed minutes. By this account it appears that there were then 139 ſhips, 24907 tons, 3853 ſeamen, employed by the Liverpool merchants in the ſlave trade; that the value of ſhips and outfit was £ 361,608 : 0*s.* : 8*d.* and the total amount £ 1,092,546 : 0*s.* : 9*d.*

The witneſs alſo produced the following account and liſts.

An account of the number of men diſcharged by the maſter tradeſmen of Liverpool employed in the ſlave trade, and who are now out of work, or gone to other places, from the reſtrictions laid on that trade by parliament, with their occupations, and wages in a year. This account is dated 15th March 1790, and is inſerted page 510 of the minutes at large. The perſons ſpecified in it, are 1007 tradeſmen and labourers, 22 maſters of ſlave ſhips, 47 mates, 356 ſeamen: total 1432 perſons, in the ſituations deſcribed.—N. B. In 1787, there were only 719 perſons in the poor-houſe of Liverpool; but from the ſaid reſtrictions, there are now in the poor-houſe 1227: increaſe 508. Added to theſe, the poor relieved out of the houſe, are now 1060; and in 1787, were 700: increaſe 340.

A liſt of African ſhips laid up in Liverpool, from the reſtrictions on the trade, inſerted page 512 of minutes at large: total 22 ſhips of 5366 tons.

P. 484. A liſt of African ſhips ſold out of the trade, or ſent on other voyages from the ſaid reſtrictions, inſerted ibid. Total 16 ſhips of 3061 tons.

W. INDIES—Witneſs exd.—Capt. JOHN ASHLEY HALL

Now in the Weſt-India trade from London, was in the African trade from 1772 to 1776 incluſive. Made two voyages to Africa in the Neptune, as third, ſecond and chief mate; touched at C. Mount, and ſailed along ſhore, ſometimes trading for rice to C. Palmas; ſailed thence the firſt voyage to the river Del Rey, in the bight of Biaffra, where they ſlaved. Second voyage, ſailed from C. Palmas to Del Rey; but the trade being dull, went to the R. Old Calabar. 1790. Part II. (513.) P. 514.

The ſlaves were brought on board by the black traders pinioned, and ſometimes 4 or 5 with collars chained together.

Theſe traders always went for the ſlaves, after the arrival of the ſhip, with goods they got, and in war canoes. He ſaw from 3 to 10 canoes in a fleet, each with 40 to 60 paddlers, and 20 to 30 traders, and other people, with muſkets, ſuppoſe one to each man, with a 3 or 4 pounder laſhed on the bow; they were generally abſent from 10 days to 3 weeks.

Often aſked the mode of buying ſlaves inland; was told by the traders they were priſoners of war, and ſold by the captors. He never ſaw a ſlave brought on board with a freſh wound, and a few with old ſcars.

Often aſked them how they became ſlaves: they conſtantly ſaid, either ſurprized in their towns, at work in the fields, or taken in fixed battle.

Often ſaw ſlaves brought on board from 8 to 13 years old, always without relations; never knew but one inſtance to the contrary, which was a woman with a ſucking child about 6 weeks old. P. 515.

The trade in the rivers Calabar and Del Rey is carried on by means of pawns, who very often are children of the traders. They were always particularly

1790. cularly anxious as to the fate of the pawns, and
Part II. ſeemed much diſtreſſed when ſuſpicious of the ſhip's
ſailing away with them.

Never ſaw more guns in the king's and principal trader's houſes than appeared for uſe; never any trade guns but of a better ſort. On the ſea coaſt they were afraid to fire a trade gun.

In Old Calabar river are two towns, Old Town and
New Town. A rivalſhip in trade produced a jealouſy between the towns; ſo that through fear of
each other, for a conſiderable time, no canoe would
leave their towns to go up the river for ſlaves;
(537.) which happened in 1767. He corrects an error of its
being in 1768, when examined before the Privy
Council, from a copy he has ſince ſeen of the de-
poſition of William Floyd, mate of the Indian
(516.) Queen. In 1767 ſeven ſhips lay off the point
which ſeparates the towns; ſix of the captains invited the people of both towns on board on a
certain day, as if to reconcile them: at the ſame
time agreed with the people of New Town to cut
off all the Old Town people who ſhould remain on
board the next morning. The Old Town people
perſuaded of the ſincerity of the captains' propoſal,
went on board in great numbers. Next morning at
8 o'clock one of the ſhips fired a gun, as a ſignal
to commence hoſtilities. Some of the traders were
ſecured on board, ſome were killed in reſiſting, and
ſome got overboard and were fired upon. When
the firing began, the New Town people who were
in ambuſh behind the point, came forward and
picked up the people of Old Town, who were
ſwimming, and had eſcaped the firing. After the
firing was over, the captains of 5 of the ſhips delivered their priſoners (perſons of conſequence) to
the New Town canoes, two of whom were beheaded
along ſide the ſhips; the inferior priſoners were
carried to the Weſt-Indies. One of the captains,
who had ſecured three of the king's brothers, delivered

vered one of them to the chief man of New Town, 1790.
who was one of the two beheaded along side; the Part II.
other brothers he kept on board, promising, when the ship was slaved, to deliver them to the chief man of New Town. His ship was soon slaved from this promise, and the number of prisoners made that day; but he refused to deliver the king's two brothers, and carried them to the West-Indies and sold them. Thence they escaped to Virginia, and thence, after 3 years, to Bristol; where the captain who brought them, fearing he had done wrong, meditated carrying or sending them back to Virginia. Jones, of Bristol, who had ships trading to Old Calabar, had them taken from the ship (where they were in irons) by Habeas Corpus. After enquiry how they were brought from Africa, they P. 517.
were liberated, and put in one of Jones's ships, for Old Calabar, where the witness was, when they arrived in the ship Cato, Langdon. They said they were treated very ill in the West-Indies, but much better in Virginia.

So satisfied were the people of Old Town, in 1767, of the sincerity of the captains who invited them, and of the New Town people towards a reconciliation, that, the night before the massacre, the chief man of Old Town gave to the chief man of New Town one of his favorite women as a wife. It was said, that from 3 to 400 persons were killed that day, in the ships, in the water, or carried off the coast.

The king escaped from the ship he was in, by killing two of the crew who attempted to seize him: he then got into a one-man canoe, and paddled to the shore; a 6-pounder from one of the ship's struck the canoe to pieces, he then swam on shore to the woods near the ship, and reached his own town tho' closely pursued; it was said he received 11 wounds from musket-shot.

Captain

1790. Part II. Captain Hall in his first voyage on board the Neptune, had this account from the boatswain, Thomas Rutter, who, in 1767, had been boatswain to the Canterbury, captain Sparkes, of London, and concerned in the said massacre; Rutter told him the story exactly as related, and never varied in it; and also from the king's two brothers, who agreed exactly with Rutter.

When sailing along the windward coast, he often saw canoes hovering about the ship for a considerable time, after much intreaty they came on board, but were so suspicious that they kept constantly near the P. 518. ship's side, to jump overboard; they said they were fearful of being taken off the coast, as some of their countrymen had been.

The slaves when brought on board to be sold always appear dejected. It soon wore off with the young slaves, and some women; but not with the men, which he ascribed to their being forced from their dearest connections, and native country.

The men were immediately put in irons, two together, and kept in irons, hands and feet, 'till their arrival in the West Indies, unless taken ill, when the irons were taken off. Never saw a female in irons.

They often disagree in the night about their sleeping places; the men linked together often fight, when one wants perhaps to obey the calls of nature, and the other is unwilling to go with him.

Their usual food on board was horse-beans, rice P. 519. and yams, with a little palm oil and pepper. They often refused to eat, especially beans, when they were corrected with a cat o'nine tails. He has known their refusal to eat attributed to sullenness, when owing to sickness, particularly one man who was corrected moderately for not eating, and was found dead next morning.

They were made after meals to jump on beating a drum. This is called dancing. When they refused, they were compelled by the cat.

Often

Often heard them cry out below for want of air. 1790.
Between decks is ſo hot, that often after being below Part II.
a few minutes, his ſhirt was ſo wetted by perſpiration, that he could have wrung it.

Their veſſel was about 180 tons by regiſter. They purchaſed firſt voyage about 270 ſlaves: the ſecond voyage 280. In the firſt voyage they loſt he thinks 20; but having been ill, was obliged to give up his journal; in the 2d, exactly 90. In the Weſt-Indies he P. 520.
found the loſs of ſlaves to be very conſiderable on board many ſhips: Knew ſome bury half their cargo, ſome a quarter, and ſome a third; it was very uncommon to find ſhips without ſome loſs of their ſlaves. They loſt 10 ſeamen the firſt voyage out of 23; and the ſecond voyage 9 out of 30. He kept a journal, ſo that the facts were mentioned as they happened.

The Venus ſailed with them both voyages, belonging to the ſame owners; they kept company to the river Del Rey the firſt voyage, where they ſlaved; that ſhip buried in that voyage 18 ſeamen out of 30. The ſecond voyage they kept company to the river Calabar, where they both ſlaved, and in that voyage her loſs exceeded their's in proportion to her crew; but cannot ſpeak exactly.

In his 2d voyage they ſpoke to the York, Adams, on the windward coaſt; ſhe had been 10 months from Liverpool, had loſt 51 of her people including 6 mates, out of 75 men. He relates this, from a remark P. 521.
made in his journal on the day they ſpoke to the York.

In May 1788, two ſhips arrived in the Weſt-Indies from Africa, called the Hornet and Benſon; they anchored cloſe to his ſhip. He went on board the Hornet, and was told they had loſt 11 men out of 35; when the Benſon came to anchor, he was in his own ſhip, and could only ſee 2 whites handing the ſails, the reſt were black boys, ſlaves.

1790. Part II. The crews of the African ships when they arrived in the West-Indies, were generally (he did not know a single instance to the contrary) in a sickly, debilitated state; the seamen who were discharged or deserted from those ships in the West-Indies, were the most miserable objects he ever met with. He often saw them with their toes rotted off, their legs swelled to the size of their thighs, and ulcerated all over; such was their state, that however inclined to relieve them, by taking them into their ships, they were deterred by not having surgeons on board to give them the necessary assistance; he saw them on the wharfs in Antigua, Barbadoes and Jamaica (especially the two last) laying under the cranes and balconies expiring, and some dead. He saw last July a dead
P. 522. seamen laying on the wharf in Bridge Town, Barbadoes, who had been landed out of an African ship.

Never shipped an African seamen in any voyage he made to the West-Indies. He commanded a West-Indiaman 10 years, made 10 voyages, and never lost but one seaman, and that was through intemperance. Believes the African trade to be destructive to seamen, and beyond all comparison with any trade he knows; believes they are in general treated with great barbarity in the slave ships; and does not know of their being ill-treated in any other service.

On the windward coast he had seen rice, ivory, and Malaguetta pepper, plantanes, bananas, yams, and many tropical fruits; also on the leeward coast, palm oil, ivory, bar wood, and most tropical fruits, and has seen very fine sugar canes brought on board
P. 523. the ships. Has seen traders and canoe men smoaking tobacco of their own growth. The African rice was considered in the ship he sailed in much heartier food than the Caroline rice; they put two crues of water, to one crue of Caroline rice; and three crues of water, to one crue of the Afrcian rice. Has been at South Carolina, but never saw rice growing; but informed upon enquiry that it grew in swamps; had seen

ſeen rice grow in Africa, in a dry ſoil: has bought it 1790. on the windward coaſt from the natives, who brought Part II. it on board in ſmall canoes, (often with only one man) had been often on ſhore buying it in the ſhip's boats, and he does not recollect ever loſing any from the ſurf.

Has ſeen the ſurf at Dominique and St. Kitt's, full as high as he ever ſaw it on the windward coaſt. On the leeward coaſt, he was in the rivers were there was no ſurf.

The Europeans who trade for ſlaves in the bight of P. 524. Benin, buy great quantities of yams and eddoes from the people of Fernandipo, where he had often been from Del Rey and Calabar to buy yams, and always found them very ready to trade. The ſhips from Old Calabar, Del Rey and the Cameroons, he believes all ſend thither: has been 7 miles in the inland part of Fernandipo, and the yam and the eddoe plantations he always found in the higheſt order, and much more ſo than thoſe of Calabar. The yams were much better than any he ever ſaw in the Weſt-Indies.

There is no ſlave trade carried on by the natives P. 525. in Fernandipo, but ſome of them have been taken off by the ſhips and boats touching there.

At Calabar and Del Rey the only people that he heard called ſlaves, were the canoe boys: has always ſeen the ſlaves treated there with great kindneſs and familiarity; ſo much ſo as to be ſometimes difficult to diſtinguiſh maſter from ſlave.

He believes negroes to be as ingenious as Europeans, under the ſame diſadvantages, and as capable of all the virtues: he never ſaw them particularly indolent, when there was an opportunity of working to advantage.

He quitted the ſlave trade from conviction, that it was perfectly illegal, and founded in blood. He could often have had a ſhip in that ſervice, which was then very lucrative for the maſters: was ſecond mate P. 326. when aged 22.

1790. Part II. Was often on ſhore on the windward coaſt in the river Calabar, not often at Del Rey. Was very often on ſhore at Calabar, ſometimes 3 or 4 times a day to bring on board ſlaves, palm oil, and other articles. Quitted the trade from conſcientious principles, and not to receive a legacy in the Weſt Indies. Was firſt offered the command of an African ſhip in

P. 527. Antigua, by Mr. Taylor in 1782; and from Mr. Cox in 1781 and 1782.

P. 528. He ſaw at Calabar in the poſſeſſion of the king's two brothers, their depoſitions taken at Briſtol; and of William Floyd, who was mate of one of the ſhips when the tranſaction happened; he took no copy. The names of ſome of the ſhips there (i. e. 1767) at Calabar, were the Duke of York, Beaven, of Liverpool; the Edgar, Lace, of Liverpool; the Indian Queen, Lewis, of Briſtol; the Nancy, Maxwell, of Briſtol; the Canterbury, Sparks, of London. Was told above 400 people from the old town came on board

P. 530. the ſhips, and moſt of them remained all night. Has ſaid before the privy council that the Engliſh were as well received after the tranſaction, alluding to the time he went thither.

Believes it not general in Guineamen to put the firſt 8 or 10 negroes in irons; but after that, every man is put in irons when he comes on board, and ſo continued, unleſs in ſickneſs, till they reached the Weſt Indies. It was ſo in his ſhip.

Believes the boats he ſaw going from Calabar (in which many then were armed) went to trade.

Was told by Capt. Jeremiah Smith, that the voyage before, he (Capt. Hall) was with his brother, (which was in 1772) a Capt. Fox had taken off ſome people from the windward coaſt.

P. 532. Never knew a ſhip ſail away without giving notice.

Believes the calamity of the ſeamen, mentioned in page 521, proceeded in general from the ſcurvy, oftener to be found in African ſhips than in any others; having never ſeen a man, in any ſhip that he had

had ſailed in, with the ſcurvy in a great degree. As 1790.
to having ſeen people in Barbadoes, with that calamity, Part II.
that had not been in African ſhips, has ſeen people labouring under the black ſcurvy. Does not know whether the ſcurvy produces the effect mentioned on the toes and legs, but believes it does.

When on the windward coaſt they were two ſhips in company both voyages, and procured as much rice in addition to what they had, as they wanted. Has ſeen fields of rice. The moſt diſtant plantation from the ſea he has ſeen, was from 3 to 4 miles: the rice was carried to the ſhips in baſkets on perſons heads: does not know whether he could have got rice to load a ſhip of 200 tons. Saw but little ivory P. 534.
on the windward coaſt, which was brought on board in canoes; believes on the leeward coaſt they might have bought about 3 tons of ivory in each voyage. P. 535.

Has known a little bread given now and then to the ſick; procured at the iſland of Annabona ſome cocoa-nuts and caſſada flour, of which occaſionally gave the ſlaves a little,—and the ſick ſlaves ſometimes had a dram in the morning—confined his anſwers to his own ſhip.

Suppoſes the armed canoes, ſeen in Del Rey river, were equipped for the protection of thoſe on board them, and their goods; but believes they would take any opportunities that might offer of ſeizing and carrying off any perſons whom they might be able to ſurprize, page 558.

At Calabar and Del Rey the ſlaves were always bought by the captain's; on the windward coaſt, they P. 536
are in a great meaſure bought in boats by the mates.

Thinks many ſlaves are killed, and of courſe that it is a bloody trade, founded his opinion on having heard ſome traders ſay the ſlaves were taken in war; and from ſome of them in the W. Indies having told him they were kidnapt. Said before the privy council P. 537.
he did not believe wars were entered into on the ſea-coaſt, to make ſlaves.

Heard

1790. Part II. Heard that captains Fidler and Doyle, of Liverpool, in 1775, were poiſoned; but believes by the New Town people. His ſhip lay abreaſt of the Old Town, the people of which always behaved

P. 539. very well to his ſhip. Heard that the natives on the windward coaſt detained the officers of ſhips a-ſhore, and extorted goods for their releaſe, but never ſaw one inſtance. Heard that they attemptd to ſeize and boarded his majeſty's ſhip Cheſterfield, capt. Barton, off cape Palmas. Has heard, but does not know, that they attacked trading ſhallops and boats, murdered the crew, and plundered the goods on board them: and ſuch actions may in ſome inſtances be the probable cauſe of the caution ſtated, when they came on board our ſhips. Brings

P. 540. the journal of his ſecond voyage. The evidence of his firſt voyage was from memory, having loſt his journal.

Continued ſecond mate till the ſhip arrived at Dominique, and came home chief mate; the ſecond voyage he was ſecond mate, and came home chief

P. 541. mate from Jamaica. His duty, as ſecond mate, was in the hold, when proviſions and water were to be ſerved, or goods wanted for trade; on every other occaſion he deemed his duty on deck and in the boats neceſſary. In the middle paſſage to ſerve out proviſions and attend on the quarter deck and round-houſe when the ſlaves were meſſing. The neceſſary duty conſiſts in overhauling the rigging, going on ſhore according to the captain's directions, and any other requiſite duty. When ſent a-ſhore it was his duty to bring on board fire-wood, and any thing elſe that was wanted. Had been ſent to Fernandipo as officer of the boat to buy yams and eddoes. Never bought ſlaves, it not being the mate's duty, but the

P. 542. captain's, at Del Rey and Calabar. Never ſlept on ſhore in Africa. Was never abſent from the ſhip more than 8 or 9 days at a time, when he truſted himſelf

himſelf with the natives; and gained his information 1790.
relating to the ſlave trade from the traders, who all Part II.
ſpeak Engliſh.

On the different parts of the windward coaſt, P. 543.
whe he had been, he landed with equal ſafety as at
St. Kitt's and Dominique. The ſurf does ſometimes
run very high on the windward coaſt, and the ſea, in
ſome places, breaks at ſome diſtance from the ſhore;
but he always went on ſhore without meeting with
any accident to the people or boat; and was there,
he thinks, from 16 days to 3 weeks each voyage;
not in the rainy ſeaſon. He anchored at a diſtance,
and went on ſhore in a ſmall boat on account of the
ſurf. Had they had any bulky articles to take into
the large boat they could have effected it in the ſame
manner as at Dominique and St. Kitt's, which is by
anchoring near the ſhore, and having 2 ſkids from P. 544.
the boats ſtern to the ſhore, which is the way of
taking off ſugars where there is a ſurf. Where they
were on the windward coaſt they could not have
landed always, but believes they could have landed
as often as not; and they obſerve the ſame precautions in landing at St. Kitt's and Dominique as upon
the windward coaſt. At Dominique he has been in
Roſeau bay; and at St. Kitt's Baſſeterre. Theſe
ports are at the leeward of the iſland, but he had
frequently known the ſea breeze blow very ſtrong
in both theſe ports, ſo as to do miſchief, and make
landing difficult. The trade wind generally blows P. 545.
from E.N.E to E.S.E. and continues from April to
July, at times in each of thoſe months. When
goods were to be ſhipped on the windward coaſt he
never anchored in the large boat above 50 fathoms
off ſhore; and uſed the ſame precautions at Dominique, about 30 feet diſtance, becauſe he had bulky
articles to take in. Saw the ſame precautions uſed P. 546.
at St. Kitt's, and could have gone as near between
cape Meſurado and cape Three Points.

The

1790. The ivory bought on the windward coaſt, was all
Part II. ſmall; he bought each voyage about 5 tons of
rice on the windward coaſt, which was got in from
16 days to about 3 weeks. Another ſhip, in
company both voyages, bought about as much.

The rice is ſometimes wet with ſalt water, when
brought in the little canoe. Believes oftner dry.
P. 547. It is reddiſh, and is a very hearty food.

Thinks exerciſe neceſſary for the ſlaves health, in the middle paſſage.

He never knew the ſlaves complain of being cold in the ſhip he belonged to, which had grating, but no air-ports. Has often met with African ſhips without air-ports, but ſince he left the trade has ſeen more with air-ports coming to the Weſt-Indies than without.

Moſt of thoſe who died on board the Neptune
were able ſeamen, had no landſmen on board in
one voyage, but the cooper, armourer, and carpenter's mate; and never an apprentice, but 2
P. 549. boys each voyage. Thinks the Venus loſt all her
officers the firſt voyage, except the chief mate and captain. At Annabona ſome cocoa nuts and caſſada flour were all the refreſhments they got. He ſaw ſome live ſtock, plantains and bananas brought along-ſide his ſhip; the captain bought ſome of them for the cabin, but the ſick ſlaves had no refreſhments of that ſort. In that voyage they had a dyſentery, ſo that the captain was afraid to give them plantaines and bananas; and they had no room on deck for fowl-coops, nor any where, except in one of the ſmall boats, coops might have been laſhed on the ſhip's quarters, but were not.

P. 550. It is very high land at Fernandipo, and much
rain falls there in the rainy ſea. The yams are much better than at Calabar, he thinks from the difference of the ſoil, and the people of Fernandipo, not having any ſlave trade, give all their attention to cultivation. At

At Fernandipo in his 2d voyage, a boat of the 1790.
Venus, Smith, which had been sent there for yams Part II.
from Calabar, enticed a canoe to come along-side with about 10 men in her; as soon as she got very near, the men fired into her from the ship's boat. on which they jumped over-board; some of them were wounded, one was taken out of the water, and died in less than an hour in the boat; 2 others were taken up unhurt, and carried to Calabar to the ship. Captain Smith was angry at the officer, and sent another officer in the boat to land the two men in the bay. whence they were taken. Immediately after the boat had brought off these two persons, the witness went into the bay in their own long-boat, and sending on shore two men to fill water, they were surrounded by the natives, who drove three spears into one of the men, and wounded the other with a large stick, in consequence of taking away the two men just mentioned. Knows of no other instance. It was said P. 551.
they had disputed with the people on shore when trading with them for yams, but they had not done any of the boat's crew any injury.

Never was more than 2 miles from the ship; except in the long boat to Farnandipo. When he spoke of 15 leagues up the river, said the ship lay at anchor thereabouts.

He never saw any slaves in the country of Del Rey and Calabar, except the women and canoemen. First entered into the West-India trade, as P. 552.
commander of a vessel from London in 1780; between 1777 and 1780, was on board the Tartar privateer. As to the property acquired on board a private ship of war being a traffic founded in blood, does not think himself competent to speak to it. The Tartar carried 34 guns, 230 men; he was first lieutenant.

Knows the surf to be less at Woodbridge's bay, P. 544.
than at Roseau, and has heard that to be the general

1790. place where all Guineamen in particular bring up
Part II. on their arrival, and where they take on board their homeward-bound cargo. The large boats come to anchor at ſome diſtance from the ſhore at Baſſeterre,
P. 555. St. Kitt's, which is open to the ſouth. Has not ſeen much ſugar taken off from St. Kitt's. Does not know Half-moon bay.

Is not competent to ſpeak of the treatment of the ſlaves in Weſt-Indies: wiſhes to decline it: has often heard that the ſurf at Baſſeterre is often ſo high as to prevent the boats from taking off ſugar for days together.

When he ſaw the Benſon in the Weſt-Indies, he heard that ſhe had loſt 31 perſons.

Has ſeen the ſlaves in Africa eating with their maſters.

Diſputes were the cauſes he generally heard aſſigned for the natives of Africa detaining the officers and crews of ſhips' boats, and requiring a ranſom and retaliation.

Rutter told him, that the king of the Old Town gave his daughter for a wife to the chief trader of the New Town, but the two king's brothers ſaid ſhe was a favorite woman.

P. 558. Capt. Smith was particularly attentive to the ſick ſailors and ſlaves. He remembered an inſtance of a woman being bought, with her child about ſix weeks old; the child was very croſs from ſickneſs, and made much noiſe at night. The boatſwain wiſhed much to throw it overboard, and ſolicited the captain for permiſſion to do it, alledging it would not live, and, if it did, would fetch nothing; which requeſts the captain received with horror and deteſtation.

P. 559. It was always neceſſary for the perſon to have a cat who attended the ſlaves, in meſſing, and taking their exerciſe; they ſometimes received a few ſtrokes when they refuſed: he attended by the captain's order, but uſed the cat at his diſcretion.

Remembers

Remembers at Dominique they could not land with either of the ſhip's boats for 48 hours. 1790. Part II.

One of the captains at Calabar did not combine with the people of New Calabar, to ſurprize the Old Town people; but knows not the captain's or ſhip's name.

Knew a ſlave jump overboard in the river Del Rey, and another in Antigua.

Witneſs examined —— ISAAC WILSON,

Surgeon in his Majeſty's navy, made 1 voyage to Africa, in the Elizabeth of 370 tons, John Smith, from London, ſailed 10th May, 1788, and returned 6th Dec. 1789, the crew and ſlaves were as well treated as in any other ſhip; took on board 602 ſlaves, who were P. 562.
all confined, and crowded between decks at night, during the voyage; (a few women excepted) when brought on board, a gloomy penſiveneſs ſeemed to over caſt their countenance, and continued in a great many. They loſt in the voyage 155 ſlaves, of whom there were, in his opinion, two-thirds; the primary cauſe of whoſe death might be deemed melancholy; the ſymptons of their diſorders generally the ſame, and he does not recollect ever to have cured any of them: Another reaſon for believing that their deaths might be aſcribed to melancholy from their ſituation was, that ſome taken ill, who had not the melancholy, took medicines with very good effect. He heard them
ſay, in their language, that they wiſhed to die, and was P. 563.
told by captain Smith, the mortality of the ſlaves, was owing to their thinking ſo much of their ſituation. The flux prevailed in their ſhip, which he conceived in a great meaſure owing to the ſame cauſe, and to their refuſing ſuſtenance, by which they became debilitated, but the ſlaves had no other very fatal diſorder. Has heard the ſlaves complain of heat; the ill effects which

 reſulted

1790. reſulted from this, and their confinement, was weak-
Part II. neſs, and fainting; which he believed had been the
cauſe of the death of ſlaves, having ſeen ſome die a
few minutes after being brought up, which proceeded
from corrupted air, and heat, jointly. Has ſeen them
go down apparently quite well at night, and found
P. 564. dead in the morning They had an hoſpital, but
the ſick ſlaves lay on the bare planks, which by the
motion of the veſſel, often cauſed excoriations from
the prominent parts of the body. The loſs of men
was greater than that of women. The men were
generally kept in irons, the ſickly excepted. Thinks
this trade could not be purſued ſafely, if the men were
not in general in irons. They attempted to riſe on
them at Bonny; a few of them jumped over-board,
and were picked up. The ſlaves on being brought
P. 565. on deck, are placed cloſe to each other, and on each
of their irons there is a ring, through which a chain is
rolled, and faſtened with ring-bolts to the deck, by a
hook, in which ſituation they are compelled to dance
by the cat often. It is very common for the ſlaves to
refuſe ſuſtenance; with ſuch, gentle means are uſed,
but if without ſucceſs, the cat is generally applied:
Slaves appeared much crowded below. He generally
took off his ſhoes before going down, and was very
cautious how he walked, leſt he ſhould tread on them.
Three veſſels belonging to the ſame houſe as their's,
ſailed to the coaſt for ſlaves —Elizabeth, Wallis, and
the Favourite, Bamfield, both of London; and the
Elizabeth, Marſhall. The Elizabeth, Wallis, the firſt
P. 566. voyage bought about 450 ſlaves, and buried above 200
before her arrival in the river Plate, as he was told by
the Commiſſioner of the Royal Phillippine Company
of Spain. The Favourite bought 466 in Africa; her
mortality 73, and delivery 393 in the river Plate, as
he was told by her chief mate and ſurgeon. The
Elizabeth, Marſhall, bought 546; mortality 158;
delivery 388, as told by Mr. Duffin. There were 2
or 3 in captain Marſhall's ſhip in the ſmall pox, when
ſhe

ſhe arrived in the river Plate; and after delivery of the 1790.
cargoes of the 3 ſhips, 220 ſlaves died by this diſorder, Part II.
which he knows, by being appointed, with the Spaniſh ſurgeon, to take care of the negroes on ſhore. His ſhip's company were 55 in all; of which they loſt 18, P. 567.
viz. 16 by ſickneſs, and 2 drowned. Of the crew of the Elizabeth, Marſhall, he was told by the ſurgeon, the mortality was 27, (a woman found means to get rope-yarn, the night preceding, which ſhe tied to the head of the armourer's vice, then in the woman's room; ſhe faſtened it round her neck, and in the morning was found dead, whence it appeared, ſhe muſt have uſed great exertions to accompliſh her end. A young woman alſo hanged herſelf, by tying rope-yarn to a batten, near her uſual ſleeping place, and ſlipping off the platform; the next morning ſhe was found warm, and he uſed the proper means for her recovery, but in vain. Among many caſes where force was neceſſary to oblige the ſlaves to take food, he would relate that of a young man, who, he conceived, ſtarved himſelf; he had not been very long on board before he perceived him get thin; they found he had not taken his food, and refuſed taking any; mild means were uſed to divert him from his reſolution; they endeavoured to make him underſtand that he ſhould have any thing he wiſhed for; but he ſtill refuſed to eat; they then uſed the cat with as little ſucceſs; he always kept his teeth ſo faſt, that it was impoſſible to get any thing down; they endeavoured to introduce a *ſpeculum oris*; but the points were too obtuſe to enter; and next tried a bolus knife without effect. In this ſtate he was 4 or 5 days, when he was brought up as dead, to be thrown overboard; but he, agreeable to his general expreſs directions, was called and uſed endeavours to recover him, tho' in vain; two days afterwards he was brought up in the ſame ſtate as before; he then ſeemed to wiſh to get up, they aſſiſted him and brought him aft to the fire place, when in a feeble voice, in his own tongue

1790. tongue, he aſked for water, which was given him,
Part II. and he drank; they began to have hopes of diſſuading
him. but he again ſhut his teeth as faſt as ever, and
reſolved to die, which on the 9th day from his per-
P. 569. ceivable refuſal, he did: has known ſlaves jump
overboard, he believes to drown themſeves; could
relate two inſtances in their own ſhip; the firſt, when
off Annabona, a ſlave on the ſick liſt, jumped overboard, and was picked up by the natives; the
ſecond, when at ſea; the captain and officers, at
dinner, heard the alarm of a ſlave being overboard,
and perceived him making every exertion to drown
himſelf, by putting his head under water, and lifting
his hands up, and thus went down, as if exulting
that he got away; the perſon picked up in the
former inſtance, died ſoon after: the ſhip is fitted
up in a way to prevent ſuch attempts, by high
nettings round the quarter deck, main deck and
poop. A man who came on board apparently well,
ſhortly after looked melancholy; a certain wildneſs
appeared in his countenance; he began to eat his
food voraciouſly, and ſometimes as if inſenſible what
it was, at other times refuſed it entirely; at length
he became noiſy, and called out, "armourer," who
generally took the ſlaves out of irons when neceſſary:
he at length died inſane.

An inſtance on board, induced him to believe
they were as affectionate as moſt other people. At
P. 670. Bonny, one of the people called Breeches, of the
higher claſs, was brought on board. He ſeemed to
take his ſituation to heart, and got ill; but from
indulgencies, which none of the reſt had, he partly
recovered. When he was convaleſcent, a young
woman, was alſo brought on board, who proved to
be his ſiſter. On their firſt meeting, they ſtood in
ſilence, and looked at each other apparently with
the greateſt affection;—they ruſhed into each others
arms—embraced—ſeparated themſelves again—and

agai

again embraced. The witneſs perceived the tears to run down the females cheeks. The man had a return of his former complaint, and his ſiſter attended him with the greateſt care: the firſt thing ſhe did of a morning, was to come to the witneſs, and aſk how her brother did.—He at length died—on the news of which, the ſiſter wept bitterly, tore her hair, and ſhewed other ſigns of diſtraction. They carried her ſafe to South America, and there delivered her.

1790. Part II.

They generally found more females than males for ſale on the coaſt, and the males he believed ſold at the higheſt price. There were 80 ſlaves ſick and on recovery, when they arrived in the river Plate.

He quitted the trade becauſe it did not perfectly coincide with his ideas, and being obliged to uſe means for the preſervation of the cargo contrary to his feelings, which was the frequent uſe of the cat P. 571. to oblige them to take their food; and even in the act of chaſtiſement he has ſeen the ſlaves look up at him with a ſmile, and, in their own language, ſay, " preſently we ſhall be no more." There never was a man of greater feelings, of more humanity, or who paid more attention to the preſervation of the ſlaves for the ſake of his employers, &c. than the capt. of their ſhip. He never allowed any one to chaſtiſe the ſlaves except himſelf and the ſurgeon. Has been told by the ſurgeon of the Elizabeth, Marſhall, that while they lay at the iſland of St. Thomas, the Hero, Withers, was there, and had loſt 159 ſlaves of the ſmall pox. In the river Bonny he was on board a Spaniſh veſſel, under American colours, the St. Antonio. The captain had buried the ſurgeon, and all the officers (the boatſwain excepted) and moſt of the crew, he himſelf was taken ill, and begged the witneſs might attend him. He did ſo, but he died going over the bar; by which means a Spaniſh gentleman (ſupercargo of their ſhip) went down to this veſſel: finding Spaniſh papers on board, he put officers in her from their veſſel, and the two others which were there

1790. Part II. there in the ſame employ. Before the death of capt. Daniel, of the St. Antonio, he told the witneſs he came from Carthagena in North America, went into ſome port in Holland with the cargo, got goods there to buy ſlaves in Africa, and carry them to Carthagena or ſome other Spaniſh ſettlement. This information he deſired him to give the Spaniſh gentleman. Believes, for her ſize, the ſaid Spaniſh veſſel ſuffered more loſs than any Engliſh veſſel he ever knew.

They bought the ſlaves at Bonny, which being an iſland, he believes they were brought from the inland country. Had three in the Elizabeth in the

P. 574. medical line. He was head ſurgeon; is 25 years of age.

Never took any on board, but what were apparently in good health; and believes two or more males died to one female. The ſlaves oft complained of heat, and he was induced to believe they were diſſatisfied with their ſituation, from their refuſing food and endeavouring to kill themſelves.

P. 575. Recollects ſomething of the ſhip being very near on ſhore in going out of harbour; believes they were one day in that ſituation, and the men ſlaves were kept below, but the women were on deck at intervals he believes, and that their health was viſibly affected, while they were kept below by the diſtreſs of the ſhip. Believes fixed melancholy to be one cauſe of the loſs of ſlaves; the ſymptoms, lowneſs of ſpirits and deſpondency: refuſing nouriſhment encreaſes them, the ſtomach gets weak, fluxes enſue, and, from debilitated ſtate, ſoon carry them off.

The ſhip hoiſted Spaniſh colours after they left Africa, and were ſomeway to the ſouth of the line. He underſtood Meſſrs. Firmin de Taſtet and Co. were the owners, and believes they were Britiſh ſubjects. The ſhip came home under Engliſh colours, which he believes were hoiſted ſhortly after they left

P. 577. the river Plate. Believes the two ſhips in company with them were bound to Cadiz. After it was ſet-

tled

tled that he ſhould go with capt. Smith, he under- 1790.
ſtood they were to ſail to Africa to take in ſlaves, Part II.
and deliver them to commiſſioners of the Philippine Company of Spain at Montevided on the river Plate. They had a Spaniſh ſupercargo, ſurgeon, boatſwain, and mate in their ſhip. The ſlaves attempting to riſe, was a reaſon for keeping a ſtricter guard over them than they otherwiſe ſhould have done. Their ſhip had proper gratings and air-ports, though the negroes complained of heat. He alſo heard the negroes complain of cold, and deſire the air-ports to be ſhut, when they got near the mouth of the river Plate. They ſometimes ſtationed a white man at
night in the men's room. Has not heard melan- P. 579.
cholic habit aſcribed by medical men as a cauſe of dyſentery. Believes the melancholy of the ſlaves was the reaſon of their not eating, they became weak, and incapable of digeſting their food; the conſequences were belly-ach, and a dyſentery generally enſued. Debility is often the cauſe of indigeſtion. This is his opinion. Melancholy or grief has been held by phyſicians to produce a coſtive habit. The dyſentery in their ſhip, he believes, was in ſome meaſure contagious. Debility of ſtomach increaſes the melancholy: are obliged to give medicines, which their weak ſtate is ſcarcely able to bear. Melancholy, therefore, the remote cauſe of dyſentery.

AFRICA. - Witneſs ex^d. ALEX FALCONBRIDGE

Is a Surgeon, has been four voyages to Africa, in P. 581.
3 of them to Weſt Indies, from 1780 or 1781 to 1787, firſt in the Tartar, Frazer, ſecond and fourth Emilia, Frazer, third Alexander, Mc Taggart, was taken in firſt voyage at C Mount, in the
2d went to windward and Grain Coaſt, in 3d and P. 582.
4th to Bight of Benin, ſuppoſes Slave Trade chiefly

 ſupplied

1790. Part II. supplied by kidnapping and crimes; believes so because on second voyage at C. Mount, a man was brought on board well known to Frazer and his officers, by name of Cape Mount-Jack, then spoke a little English, was very tractable and learned more. He said he was invited one evening to drink with his neighbours. When about to depart, two of them got up to seize him; would have escaped, but was stopped by a large dog; said this was a common practice in his country; told his story often, (607) never varied. From his behaviour thinks his veracity might be relied on; was entrusted by witness with various articles, of which he lost none, also by the sailors. Has seen several dogs, large enough to hold a man at Cape Mount, on Windward Coast. Tucker has 1 or 2 mastiffs. Africans there will always give a good price for such dogs; (606) has seen many small ones at Bonny not large enough to hold a man: (ibid) was told by Cape-Mount-Jack this was a common practice. (607)

P. 583. In 3d voyage at Bonny, a woman was brought on board big with child; asked her by the interpreter how she came to be sold; said that returning from a visit was seized, passed through several hands before brought on board. Same voyage an elderly man brought on board said, (thro' interpreter) that he and his son planting yams were seized by professed kidnappers, by which he means persons who make kidnapping their constant practice. (604) (605)

On last voyage at Bonny, saw a canoe came along side belonging to Blundell Foubre, a trader; saw no slaves in the canoe; two traders on board handed up a fine stout fellow, desired he might be put in irons, which was directly done, and he was paid for: witness enquiring why he was sold, he said that he came to Bonny to the Trader's house, who asked if he had ever seen a ship? replying no;

no; the Trader ſaid he would treat him with the 1790.
ſight, and he was ſold; was induced to be the more Part II.
curious about this man, from his appearing amazed when brought on deck. Cannot tell whether Frazer knew the man was thus trepanned, but he was paid for on board the ſhip. (625)

Capt. Gould of the Alert, told witneſs he had taken a man from little C. Mount. He was turned out of the brig Alert, perhaps for this.

On laſt voyage landing ſome ſlaves at Grenada, one, when on ſhore, converſed with a Black called Liverpool, captain of a ſloop. Witneſs aſking the P. 584.
ſubject of converſation, he ſaid the ſlave knew his parents in Africa, and told him that being concerned in kidnapping ſome neighbours, their friends had kidnapped him, or cauſed it to be done, ſaid this was a common practice in his country: thinks he can depend on the authenticity of theſe inſtances. Neither the ſlaves nor himſelf had any intereſt in miſrepreſentation. Does not immediately recollect any others within his own knowledge; has heard an hundred other accounts.

In the ſecond voyage, two black traders came in a canoe, and informed the Captain there was trade a little lower down. The Captain went there and finding no trade, ſaid he would not be made a fool, and detained one of the canoe-men. In about two hours a very fine man was brought on board and ſold, and the canoe-man was releaſed. Was informed by a Black pilot that this man had committed no crime, but was ſurrounded and ſeized on the beech, and brought on board.

Is induced to think the people on the Grain Coaſt are ſometimes carried off by the Europeans. They ſhew great ſuſpicion when in ſhips, always ſtand as near the gangway as they can, and on the leaſt alarm jump overboard.

 Thinks

1790. Thinks crimes are falsely imputed for the sake
Part II. of selling the accused. On the 2d voyage at R.
Ambris, among the slaves brought on board was
P. 585. one who had the craw-craw, a kind of itch. Was
told by one of the sailors, that this man was fishing
in the river, a king's officer called Mambooka,
wanted brandy and other goods in the boat, but
having no slave to buy them with, accused this
man with extortion in the sale of his fish, and after
some kind of trial on the beach, condemned him
to be sold. Was told this by the boat's crew who
were ashore when it happened, who told it as of
their own knowledge, (618)

In last voyage was assured by the Rev. Mr.
Philip Quackoo, chaplain to C. Egaitcaute, the
greatest number of slaves were made by kidnapping.

Has heard that the great men dress up and employ
women to entice young men, that they may
be convicted of adultery and sold.

Children were brought to the vessel to be sold
almost every day. Never recollects their parents
coming with them, or relations known to be such.

Does not believe many slaves are prisoners of
war, as we understand the word *war*. In Africa
a piratical expedition for making slaves is termed
P. 586. *war*. Blundell Foubres before-mentioned, at
Bonny said white men went to war like fools when
they knew their enemies were prepared, *They*
went in the night, set fire to the town, and caught
the people as they fled from the flames. This
Trader said this practice was very common. 608

Does not recollect ever seeing a slave with a
fresh wound, has seen their wrists and arms excoriated
by the country ropes they were tied with.

Has never heard of slaves being bred in Africa
for sale.

Believes violent means are used by Europeans to
force trade for slaves. Heard the Captain of a

Briſtol ſhip ſay at Bonny when his traders were ſlack, he fired a gun into or over the town, to freſhen their way. Capt. Vickers told this to him and other people of the ſhip. Has ſeen no inſtance of it himſelf (609) 1790. Part II.

Few guns kept in Africa for ſhew; has ſeen great numbers lying in a heap with other goods; always underſtood they were for trade, particularly at Bonny. Many black people ſaid theſe ordinary trade guns kill more out of the butt than the muzzle.

Five to ten ſlaves, more or leſs generally bought every day, greateſt numbers come from fairs. Large canoes, ſome having a 3 or 4 pounder laſhed on their bows, go to the up-country, in 8 or 10 days return with great numbers of ſlaves; heard once to the amount of 1200. The ſhip that has been longeſt in the river has firſt choice, and generally ſails in a few days. People in theſe canoes have generally cutlaſſes; a quantity of muſquets is always in the canoes, cannot tell for what uſe. P. 587.

Slaves examined generally by the ſurgeon. All he has ſeen appear dejected when brought on board. Some are ſo the whole voyage, others till they die. Has known ſeveral refuſe ſuſtenance with a deſign to ſtarve themſelves; compulſion uſed in every ſhip he has been in to induce ſlaves to take their food. Has known many inſtances of their refuſing to take medicines when ſick, becauſe they wiſh to die. A woman on board the Alexander, was dejected, taken ill of a dyſentery, and refuſed both food and medicine. Being aſked by the interpreter what ſhe wanted, ſhe replied, nothing but to die—and ſhe did die. Many other ſlaves expreſſed the ſame. P. 588.

A great miſtake in his evidence before the Privy Council reſpecting the tonnage of the ſhip he ſail'd in, being there ſtated twice the real ſize, were as near as he can gueſs, from 200 to 250 tons. On ſecond

1790. Part II. second voyage purchased about 300 slaves, and lost between 30 and 40. In the Alexander, purchased 380, lost 105: In last voyage, purchased
P. 589. about 420, and lost 51 or 52.

When employed in stowing slaves made the most of the room and wedged them in, they had not so much room as a man in his coffin either in length or breadth impossible for them to turn or shift with any degree of ease, had often occasion to go from one side of their rooms to the other always took off his shoes, but could not avoid pinching them; has the marks on his feet where they bit and scratched him. In every voyage when the ship was full they complained of heat and want of air. Confinement in this situation so injurious that has known them go down apparently in good health at night and found dead in the morning: On last voyage opened a stout man who so died, found the contents of the thorax and abdomen healthy, concludes he died for want of fresh air; thinks it possible he might have died of an apoplexy, but thinks that was not the case in this instance. (610) (626)

The surgeon goes below the first thing every morning, was never among them 10 minutes, but his shirt was wet as if dipt in water. The Alexander coming out of Bonny, got a-ground on the bar, was detained there 6 or 7 days, with a great swell and heavy rain; air ports obliged to be shut and part of gratings on weather-side covered; almost all the men slaves taken ill with the flux;
P. 590. last time he went down so hot, he took off his shirt, more than 20 had fainted or were fainting, got several hauled on deck, 2 or 3 died, and most of the rest, before they reached the W. Indies; was down about 15 minutes, and made so ill that could not get up without help, was taken of a dysentery and disabled from doing duty the rest of the passage.

A

A place in every ſhip for ſick ſlaves, no accommodations for them, lie on the bare planks, has ſeen frequently the prominent part of the bones of the emaciated about ſhoulder blade and knees, bare. If plaiſter or bandage applied they generally remove them. 1790. Part II.

Moſt prevalent diſorders in Negro-ſhips are fevers and dyſenteries; conſequences of numbers being ill of the latter extremely noxious; cannot conceive any ſituation ſo dreadful and diſguſting. In the Alexander, deck was covered with blood and mucus, reſembled a ſlaughter-houſe; the ſtench and foul air were intolerable, from being down a ſhort time in the Alexander is perſwaded a night's confinement in that ſituation would have deſtroyed him (630) thinks as the tradeſmen ſtand many of theſe inconveniencies cannot be prevented.

Never could recover a ſlave from a bad dyſentery, thinks it cannot be done while the cauſe remains, has known ſome few ſlaves recover who P. 591.
ſeemed not to reflect much on their ſituation. Applies this obſervation to ſhip-board (625) principal cauſes, a diſeaſed mind, ſudden tranſitions from heat to cold, a putrid atmoſphere, wallowing in their own excrement, and being ſhackled together; men die in twice the number of women, who are not ſhackled, believes no man would attempt to carry them without ſhackling. Slaves ſhackled together frequently quarrel; believes in all ſlave ſhips: In each appartment are 3 or 4 tubs, ſlaves at a diſtance find it difficult to get over other ſlaves to them; ſometimes if one wants, his companion refuſes to go; if relaxed, one exonerates, while diſputing over their neighbours, this cauſes great diſturbance. In the Alexander, has known 2 or 3 inſtances of a dead and living ſlave found in the morning ſhackled together.

On laſt voyage purchaſed 18 male negroes, who were part of a cargo which had roſe on the whites, killed

1790. killed all but 3 or 4, run the ſhip on ſhore; moſt
Part II. were taken again. Has heard of inſurrections on board the Vulture of Liverpool, and the Waſp of Briſtol.

Slave ſhips are fitted up with a view to prevent ſlaves jumping over-board, particularly at Bonny theſe precautions there neceſſary.

Has known inſtances of ſlaves jumping overboard. In the Alexander one forced his way thro' the netting when brought on board, and was drowned or devoured by the ſharks. Same voyage, near 20 jumped overboard out of the Enterprize, Wilſon, as did a number out of a large Frenchman; remembers miſſing a ſick man in the Alexander, whom he ſaw over-night, muſt have got over-board. On laſt voyage, a fine young woman brought on board, cried continually, refuſed her food, and waſted much in 3 or 4 days, was ſent on ſhore to Bonny for her recovery, ſoon became chearful, but hearing ſhe was to be ſent
P. 593. again on board ſhip, hung herſelf, as was informed by Billy Frazer. (She had not the venereal diſeaſe, would have known it if ſhe had, 611)

On firſt voyage, ſaw at Bonny, on board the Emilia, a woman chained on deck, who the chief mate ſaid was mad. On ſecond voyage, had a woman on board whom they were forced to chain at certain times, in a lucid interval, was ſold at Jamaica. Aſcribes this inſanity to their being torn from their connections and their country.

While on the coaſt, the irons of male ſlaves examined as they come up in the morning, a large chain is reeved through a ring on the ſhackles of each, thro' ringbolts on deck and locked.

They are made to jump in their irons; this called dancing by ſlave-dealers, has been often
P. 594. deſired in every ſhip to flog ſuch as would not jump; had generally a cat in his hand among the women;

women; the chief mate had alſo, he believes, a cat among the men.

Being aſked if in caſe of ſhips ſtriking or blowing up, ſlaves could be diſengaged from fetters ſo as to ſwim on ſhore; ſays every man looks firſt to his own ſafety. On ſecond voyage, a ſhip under imperial colours, Capt. Bell, was blown-up off river Galenas. Was informed by people of Galenas and cape Mount, moſt of men ſlaves were drowned; had one woman on board their ſhip who had ſaved herſelf by ſwimming, but much burnt; believes others were ſaved: Was informed the ſhip was Engliſh.

Horſe-beans and rice principal food of ſlaves on Windward and Gold Coaſt, at Bonny one meal of yams a day, ſometimes a little bread and beef.

In the firſt part of middle paſſage each ſlave is allowed a pint and ½ of water daily, on approaching the iſlands as much as they chuſe; has frequently known ſlaves call out for water in the night, owing to the heat of the rooms. P. 595.

Has heard ſlaves ſing on board, the ſubjects always lamentations for loſs of country and friends.

Had refuſed ſlaves in every voyage, moſt in the Alexander, 16 ſold by auction, 1 or 2 as low as 5 dollars each; was informed by ſome of the purchaſers that they all died before they ſailed.

The ſlaves in the Emilia and Alexander were ſold by ſcramble. The Emilia was darkened by ſails, and covered round; men ſlaves placed on main deck, women on quarter deck. Purchaſers on ſhore were informed by a gun when ſale was opened. A great number with cards or tallies in their hands, inſcribed with their names, came on board and ruſhed thro' the barricado door with the ferocity of brutes; ſome had 3 or 4 handkerchiefs tied together to encircle thoſe they thought fit for their purpoſe. At Grenada the women P. 596.

 were

1790. Part II. were ſo terrified that ſeveral got out of the yard and ran about the town as if mad.

In the ſecond voyage, ſaw a ſcramble on board the Trial, Macdonald, 40 or 50 ſlaves leaped into the ſea, believes were all taken up again.

Were not divided in lots, but placed promiſcuouſly; the purchaſers put cards or tallies about the necks of thoſe they chuſe. The ſeparation of parents from children, &c. very little attended to.—Frazer, however always adviſed the planters never to part relations or friends. No precautions uſed in the ſcramble to prevent it: ſlaves uſed to beg that ſuch a friend or relation might be bought and ſent with them.

Has heard of a perſon's refuſing to purchaſe a man's wife, and was next day informed the man had hanged himſelf.

P. 597. Did not always meet with a ready market for ſlaves, particularly laſt voyage; ſtopt ſome time at Barbadoes, went thence to Tobago; no demand there; thence to Grenada, and ſold them on the Merchant's own terms for bills at very long dates. Bill for his own privilege (the ſlaves allowed the officers by the owners) was at 12 months.

Was on ſhore on all the W. India iſlands he was at, except Tobago; uſed to think the general treatment of ſlaves very cruel. Saw a man in a goal at Jamaica, who had been ſo ſeverely flogged as to have a ſack of ſtraw between his back and the board he lay on; the lacerations were ſhocking; did not inquire whether it was in conſequence of a legal ſentence, or by his maſter's order Was told by the black gaol-keeper that the ſlaves he ſaw in priſon were runaways. (612) Saw great numbers of ſlaves at Grenada; hardly ever ſaw one whoſe back had not ſcars. They often complained to him (particularly the wharfingers) of being hard worked and poorly fed.

Seamen

Seamen in the African Slave Trade are treated with the greateſt barbarity. Have no lodging at all except, in frigate-built ſhips, in which they may creep under the forecaſtle or aft-deck. There is a tarpauling over the booms; always preferred being in the rain to getting under it, on account of the noxious effluvia which continually riſes thro' the gratings. 179?. Part II.

As ſoon as the ſlaves were ſold, the ſeamen received half that was due to them in currency. P. 598.

In Frazer's ſhip they were well treated, allowed a dram in the morning, and grog in the evening; had victuals from his table when ſick: he always inquired after them daily, allowed ſurgeon to give them wine when proper. Believes Frazer one of the beſt men in the trade. Saw very different treatment in another ſhip. Sailors were knocked with the firſt thing that came to hand, for trifling or imaginary faults; were tied up and flogged with the cat frequently. The boatſwain a quiet inoffenſive old man, having ſome words with the mate was ſeverely beat, had one or two teeth knocked out, ſaid he would jump overboard, was tied to the rail of quarter-deck, and a pump-bolt put in his mouth as a gag; being untied was put under the aft-deck and a centinel placed over him all night; releaſed next morning. Same voyage a black boy beat every day; once after being beaten jumped thro' a cabin gun-port into the river, was picked up by a canoe; witneſs gave him a ſhirt, aſked him if he did not expect to be devoured by the ſharks; ſaid he did, but that it was better to be killed at once than to be ſo cruelly treated daily. Same voyage a man beaten ſeverely, never heard the cauſe. Heard one Sullivan a ſeaman grumbling, aſked what he muttered about having been never ill uſed in the ſhip, Replied, "If I am not, I cannot bear to ſee my ſhip-mates ſo cruelly uſed." Same night the man who had been beaten

1790. Part II. P. 599. and 10 others ran away in a long-boat, and intended going to Old Calabar, got into the wrong river, were seized and stripped by the natives, and marched to Old Calabar; was informed that 2 or 3 died on the march, the remainder went on board the Lyon, Burrows: Had this information from one of them named Sermon, whom he saw in Bristol infirmary. The treatment was the same during the whole voyage, Captain did not go again in this ship or any other that he has heard of; does not know that he was dismissed. (612) Made another since with Frazer whose behaviour was as before described. Every man in the Alexander was beat except himself, the chief mate and Sullivan. Has mentioned the barbarous treatment of sailors on board that ship to Mr. Frazer, and many others in Bristol, and to Mr. Norris of Liverpool.

On last voyage to Bonny, was told by the King and black men on shore, that the steward of the Vulture then in the river, had been cruelly treated, chained in a boat along side the ship, and found dead in the morning; has had this account confirmed by two sailors named Ormond and Murray, at Liverpool, both belonging to the Vulture.

P. 600. In the second voyage had 42 or 43 persons altogether on board; buried 3. In the Alexander had 50 and buried 9. In the last, had 44 or 45, and buried 3. Is an inaccuracy in his evidence in the Privy Council Report relative to the loss of seamen.

In last voyage stopt at Mesurado, and assail'd, came on board, and said most of their crew were dead. Does not recollect the ship's name; was told she belonged to Mr. Barber.

Was a pupil 12 months in the Bristol Infirmary, a great many seamen were brought there; greatest number of the diseased were Guinea seamen, the others were generally for accidents. The Guinea seamen

feamen generally went out better than they came 1790.
in, but thinks their health fo far deftroyed as never Part II.
to be perfectly reftored.

The productions obferved on the coaft of Africa were cotton, wax, ivory, gold, a variety of woods, different kinds of fpices, wild cinnamon, all the Tropical fruits, the beft rice in the world, tobacco, and many other articles. The largeft quantity of unmanufactured cotton he faw on the coaft was about 4 or 5 pounds. (614)

Rice is cultivated all over the country, has feen P. 601.
it with his glafs, plantations of rice on very high ground, particularly at Cape Mount.

In fecond voyage faw the people at work on a plantation belonging to a black man called Tucker, at Manna, between Cape Mount and the river Galenas. Never faw or heard of a driver there, they feemed to work with great willingnefs and feeming fatisfaction. Thefe were all men, (605) never faw women at work in Africa out of doors (ibid.) This the only plantation he was on in Africa. (606) Tucker was born at Sherbro', fpoke exceeding good Englifh. (606)

In fame voyage purchafed about 40 or 50 tons of rice at Junk. This the largeft quantity he faw; believes might have loaded the fhip at Junk and Cape Mefurado; the natives of thofe places faid they had plenty, does not fpeak with precifion as to the quantity, has no journal to produce of the fhip's tranfactions. (619) Never heard of any (614.)
being loft in the furf; believes it was not at a time when the furf was very high; it was the rainy feafon; has landed at Cape Coaft in a canoe belonging to the Caftle 3 puncheons of goods and a hogfhead of tobacco; loft no bulky articles in attempting to land them; thinks he has feen as great a furf (619.)
at St. Chriftopher's as he ever did on the coaft of Africa.

Has

1790. Part II. Has bought ſeveral pieces of cotton cloth made by the natives at river Galenas and Bonny, (608) the cotton grew in the country, has ſome dyed by the natives with a beautiful and permanent blue. Never ſaw the indigo or cotton grow in Africa, not having been far up the country. (608)

Has ſeen many trinkets made in metal by the Africans on the coaſt; has been ſurpriſed to ſee ſome of the work in iron, particularly ſpears and cutlaſſes. Is convinced their capacities are equal to thoſe of Europeans.

The natives of Windward and Gold Coaſt much better tempered than thoſe of Bonny; their diſpo-
P. 603. ſitions very good. Was landed ſick at St. Thomas's, and would have died, but for the care of a black man there, to whom when better he offered money —which he refuſed, ſaying, he had done no more than his duty.

The Africans in general attached to their native country; are as much attached to their near relations as the natives of other countries.

At Cape Coaſt Caſtle, on chuſing 18 ſlaves he objected to one who was meagre, obſerved him to weep, which he endeavoured to conceal, on inquiry found it was becauſe he was to be parted from his brother, this induced witneſs to take him.

Is perſuaded the natives would work if properly encouraged by Europeans (613) they have notions of performing contracts in a given time. The rice before mentioned was contracted for, and he thinks, part of the money paid, it was ready at the time, natives appear to have a turn for conducting trade. Believes, ſome of the natives now employed in the ſlave trade, if that were aboliſhed would cultivate the ſoil. Billy Frazer before mentioned, ſaid at Bonny when they had no trade they were forced to plant yams.

Thinks the females more prolific than thoſe of other countries; out of 4 or 5 deliveries on ſhipboard two had twins. Never

Never ſaw any perſon in Africa when by their treatment he knew to be ſlaves; has been told by the perſons themſelves they were ſlaves. 1790. PartII.

As to the cauſe of quitting his employment as ſurgeon of a Guinea-man, anſwered, that in his 1ſt and 2nd voyages reflected little on the juſtice of the trade. On the laſt reflected more, and the more he did the more he was convinced that it is an unnatural, iniquitous and villainous trade, and could not reconcile it to his conſcience.

Could have continued his employment he believes with Captain Frazer, was afterwards ſolicited repeatedly to go to the gold coaſt by Captain Thomſon. If Clarkſon applied for employment for him at Liverpool, it was without his knowledge (613)

Was on the ſhore many times at Augola, ſaw numbers of people at the river Ambris with beads and crucifixes about their necks, they appeared to be Roman Catholics; Mangova one of the King's Officers told him they were prieſts in the Country. P. 608.

Always underſtood ſhips cannot begin to trade without leave of the King, thinks if King refuſed, that firing a gun into or over the town would force a trade; daſhes are given to keep the King in temper, trade might be carried on by Engliſh and French without the King's conſent if they choſe at all times in their power to batter his town about his ears in Bonny River. P. 609.

Slaves at Bonny purchaſed with iron bars, brandy, india and mancheſter cotton, cloths, guns, gunpowder, braſs pans, beads, and other articles. Never ſaw or heard of gold duſt at Bonny.

If ſtated otherwiſe in report of Privy Council, their miſtake and not his. Gold an article of exchange on gold coaſt.

The care and cleanlineſs of negroes generally attended to by the mates. In Frazer's ſhips mates always cauſed the ſlaves rooms to be waſhed and P. 610.

dried

Part II. 1790. dried with fire pans. In many ſhips this not permitted; but they ſcrape the filth off the deck: uſed to attend to the cleanlineſs of the negroes, has often waſhed them with a ſponge and warm water from head to foot. Believes the mate is reſponſible for the cleanlineſs of the men. The ſurgeon and his mate for that of the women. The caſe thus divided in the ſhips he was in. In the Alexander having a flux himſelf during the whole middle paſſage, cannot ſay how the ſlaves were managed. From the number who had the flux on that voyage, the apartments very diſagreeable, the diſcharge being involuntary, impoſſible to keep them comfortable. Believes the apartments generally kept as clean as the nature of the diſorder permits, unleſs as often happens greateſt parts of the whites are ill.

P. 611. Conjectures ſome ſlaves come from a diſtance, all he has talked to by means of interpreters ſaid were ſtolen; does not recollect any confeſſed they were ſold for crimes, apprehends if criminals were not purchaſed by the ſhips they would be ſet to work in their own country.

P. 613. Europeans have always power to get what they pleaſe done by holding out their commodities. Blacks at Bonny always wooded and watered the ſhips on being paid. Thinks the manners of the Africans may be changed by means of trade with this country. Is going to try the experiment.

P. 614. Does not underſtand Portugueſe. Traders at St. Thomas's all ſpeak Engliſh enough to be underſtood, converſed with the men who took notice of him there in corrupt Engliſh. Has been on board a French African ſhip at Bonny, officers ſaid a good quantity of wine given to the ſlaves every day, when on board Engliſh ſhips, but not enough.

Offered voluntarily to give the Rev. Mr. Clarkſon, at Briſtol, all aſſiſtance and information in his power. Knows not that Mr. C. has any church preferment,

preferment, has employed himſelf in gaining in- 1790.
formation about the ſlave trade, went with him PartII.
from Briſtol to Liverpool in (1787) or (1788)
believes his travelling expences were paid by the P.616.
committe in London, is out of pocket, ſpent more than he received, was at Liverpool 8 or 9 weeks, returned from thence to Briſtol. Has ſince generally reſided with his father in Briſtol, to whom is conſiderably in debt. His emoluments when he quitted the trade nearly the ſame as when he entered into it, Captain Thompſon in 1787 offered him any thing in reaſon to go with him.

Cannot converſe in the African languages; the P.617.
knowledge he has obtained of their laws and cuſtoms, has been from perſons employed in the ſhip as interpreters, watermen, or pilots: At Bonny talked with the King, Blundel Foubre, a principal trader, down to the canoe boys. On windward coaſt has talked with ſome of the firſt men. As Tucker and Robin Gray, King of cape Mount, but not on the manner of making ſlaves, they not troubling themſelves on that head. Never profeſſed to know the hiſtory of the windward coaſt; believes the natives are little acquainted with any thing out of their own towns: Has been often on ſhore on the windward coaſt. Believes the King at Bonny never does any thing of conſequence
without conſulting the parliament men; knows P.619.
not how far their power extends; believes a book which was produced is Capt. Frazer's journal or trade book. Cannot ſpeak with certainty as to the quantity of the rice, or the time in which it was ſhipped; was always on board the ſhip while the rice was taking in. There was no apparent difficulty in getting this quantity (630) thinks the time agreed was 6 weeks, if wrong, not ſo intentionally. Rice was brought along-ſide in a canoe in baſkets; has ſeen ſmall quantities brought on board in boxes or old liquor-caſes: Never weigh-

1790. ed a baſket. When Frazer made the agreement
Part II. with Joſe Will, heard the word tons mentioned ſeveral times; knows not whether 20 hundred weight was meant, underſtood it ſo, but does not pretend to be accurate, ſpeaks from conjecture, (ſee 631)

Extract from Capt. Frazer's journal, by which it appears that from Sept. 19 to Oct. 15, 1783, Joſe Will, King Will and Joſ. Weſt had ſeveral articles, to pay 240 baſkets of rice in 40 days, and left a girl as ſecurity. Tom Wilſon had ſundries,
P. 622. to pay 120 baſkets rice, left one of his people as pawn. Joſe Campbell had ſundries, to pay 45 baſkets rice, left a boy in pawn. Robin Campbell had ſundries, to pay 140 crews rice, left a man in pawn. Robin Gray had ſundries, to pay 120 crews rice. Sold ſundries in barter for about 60 cwt. rice and other articles; total 405 baſkets,
P. 623. 260 crews, and 60 cwt. rice, and that from No. 5 to 10. Received all the rice, &c. and diſcharged the pawns; but Frazer, put down all the rice he bought at Junk-witneſs to purchaſe rice at different places on the grain coaſt, of which he believes no account was taken. (631)

Does not recollect that the rice was damaged in its paſſage from the ſhore to the ſhip, or by the ſurf. Believes it was often wetted by the rain, which is violent at times.

Believes Allan and Campbell were Guinea-factors, who ſold the ſlaves in Jamaica, in the voyage of 1783 and 4. An account of ſales exhibited ſigned by thoſe gentlemen, and inſerted page 637, 638, 639, and 640.

Never ſaw at any one time on the coaſt in Africa a ſufficient quantity of rice, cotton or indigo to load a veſſel of 200 tons; but does not know what there may be inland; was ſcarce a mile from the ſea. Remembers to have ſlept a-ſhore at Bonny once or twice.

Never

Never knew Frazer refuſe any likely good fe- 1790.
male ſlaves; knows little of the African laws; PartII.
underſtood from the natives that kidnapping was
an avowed practice, i. e. a very common practice. P. 625.
Believes all the captains on the trade would purchaſe ſlaves, knowing them to be kidnapped.

Has been at Grenada and Jamaica, and touched
at St. Chriſtopher's, but was not on ſhore, ſtanding P. 626.
off and on at St. Kitt's, ſaw as he thought a great
ſurf, boats ſeemed to have ſome difficulty in getting thro' it; thinks he has ſeen the ſurf on the P. 627.
windward coaſt of Africa as high as that in the road
of Baſſeterre.

Never a ſlave flogged in the Britiſh Iſlands; ſaw one who had been ſeverely flogged; did not enquire by whoſe authority it was done.

Never ſaw a ſoldier flogged, has ſeen a ſailor; P. 628.
never heard of a ſoldier dying in conſequence of flogging. Has been informed ſlaves are flogged on the back in Grenada.

Is going to induce the Africans to cultivate their country, and raiſe ſuch articles as will ſell in this country in exchange for our manufactures—the plan not yet entirely ſettled—has no fortune—expects to be paid by his employers. The Committee for the abolition of the Slave Trade not concerned; two or three members are ſubſcribers. P. 629.

Slaves ſo crouded in all his voyages as not to have more room to lie on than a man in his coffin, told the privy council that the ſhip on the ſecond voyage was not much crouded becauſe they had not the ſame number as in the laſt.

Has not heard that the Europeans go up the country to the places from whence the ſlaves are brought, their information on the manner in which
ſlaves are made is from the black traders and pur- P. 630.
chaſed negroes. Has every reaſon to believe from the concurrent teſtimony of others that the practice of firing villages for the purpoſe of making ſlaves does really exiſt.

1790. Part II. On board the Alexander the black cook having one day broken a plate had a fiſh-gig darted at him, which would have deſtroyed him if he had not
P. 631. ſtooped or dropped down. The carpenter's mate having let his pitch-pot catch fire, he and the cook were both tied up, ſhipp'd and flogg'd, the cook with greateſt ſeverity, and had ſalt water and Cayenne pepper rubbed on his back. A man who came on board in a convaleſcent ſtate, being ſeverely beaten for he knows not what cauſe, aſked the witneſs for ſomething to rub his back with, was ordered by the captain not to give him any thing; the man went and lay under the forecaſtle; viſited him often when he complained of his bruiſes; had a return of his flux, and died in 3 weeks from the time he was beaten; his laſt words
P. 632. were, "I cannot puniſh him (the captain) but God will"—The boiling over of the pitch pot attended with danger, was the fault of the carpenter's mate, not of the cook, who deſerved no puniſhment for it.

Attends by deſire of the committee for the abolition of ſlave trade, it is at their option to give him any thing or not, but having attended on their buſineſs expects to have his expences paid.

Witneſs examined—Captain AMBROSE LACE.

P. 633. Has been in the African trade; was at Old Calabar, in 1767, captain of the Edgar. Nine Engliſh ſhips were then there, all in the African Trade. To end a diſpute which had ſubſiſted ſome time between the people of the Old and New Town, both parties agreed to meet on ſhip-board.

When firſt there, in 1748, there were no inhabitants at Old Town. Some time after diſputes aroſe between thoſe now called Old Town people and New Town people.

Were

1790. Were not invited on board insidiously, to be made
PartII. slaves. The chief people of Old Town came on board the Edgar; the duke (chief man of Old Town) was to have met them. Came on board at
P. 634. half past 7 in the morning. About 8 witness was going to breakfast with a man calling himself king of Old Town, 4 of whose large canoes were along side; cannot tell where the others were; was just pouring out coffee when he heard a firing; king said Imo, a brother of his, was firing. Went on deck with the king, and was told his gunner was killed. King went into his canoe, left his son with witness on board. Firing lasted 10 or 15 minutes, but cannot be certain. The canoes were then most of them got a-stern of his ship, within 300 or 400 yards. Had not time to make observations of the two parties; wanted to defend himself; was no further molested; the canoes were gone. The small arms are always loaden; they were locked up; the chest was broke open; key afterwards found in the gunner's pocket. None of his people concerned in the affray; no guns, great or small, or even a pistol, fired
P. 635. from his ship; nor, that he knows, from any other.

The king killed no one on board his ship, nor was the king, that he knows, on board any other. No slaves were made on the occasion.

Went to Old Calabar the beginning of July, sailed first week in December; cannot exactly state when this happened.

Never heard the English entered into this business with an improper view; they reaped no benefit from it; it was against the trade. Knows of no consultation of the English captains about this difference.

Never stopt to windward but twice. Rice crews hold from 2 to 3 gallons; differ in different parts of the coast; largest he saw three gallons.

Breakfasted with the Rev. Mr. Clarkson and
P. 636. Mr. Rathbone at Mr. Chaffers's, Liverpool. Mr. Clarkson

Clarkſon aſked him ſome queſtions about the produce of Africa. The Calabar buſineſs was mentioned. Told Mr. Chaffers (who aſked him) he could not tell how many blacks were killed that day; that his ſhip was fired into, his gunner killed, and that he did not know whether they did not mean to ſacrifice him. Gave no advice to any of the captains at that time.

Knows not who killed his gunner; it muſt have been done from ſome of the canoes at a diſtance: thinks fom the New Town people, becauſe the Old Town people were along ſide his ſhip.

FINIS.

www.ingramcontent.com/pod-product-compliance
Lightning Source LLC
Chambersburg PA
CBHW021123270326
41929CB00009B/1014

* 9 7 8 3 7 4 4 7 8 6 9 5 9 *